The Child in His Family
Volume 10

The Yearbook of the
International Association for Child
and Adolescent Psychiatry and
Allied Professions

Why Children Reject School

Views from Seven Countries

EDITED BY

COLETTE CHILAND, M.D., Ph.D.

J. GERALD YOUNG, M.D.

With the editorial assistance of Diana Kaplan, Ph.D.

Translation of the French chapters by Maev-Ann de la Guardia

Yale University Press   New Haven & London

This work was supported by a grant from the Medical Fellows Program of the Office of Mental Retardation and Developmental Disabilities, State of New York.

Set in Primer type by The Composing Room of Michigan, Inc.
Printed in the United States of America by Vail-Ballon Press, Binghamton NY.

Library of Congress Cataloging-in-Publication Data
Why children reject school : views from seven countries / Colette Chiland, J. Gerald Young.
    p.   cm. — (The Child and his family ; v. 10) (Yearbook of the International Association for Child and Adolescent Psychiatry for Allied Professions ; v. 10)
    Includes bibliographical references.
    ISBN 0–300–04438–0
    1. School phobia—Cross-cultural studies.   I. Chiland, Colette.
II. Young, J. Gerald.   III. Series.   IV. Series: Yearbook of the International Association for Child and Adolescent Psychiatry and Allied Professions ; v. 10.
RJ506.S33W48 1990   89–49522
618.92′85225—dc20   CIP

10 9 8 7 6 5 4 3 2 1

CONTRIBUTORS

James R. Brasic, M.D., M.P.H., Instructor in Psychiatry, Developmental Neurobiology Unit, Division of Child and Adolescent Psychiatry, New York University School of Medicine and Bellevue Hospital Center, 550 First Avenue, New York, N.Y. 10016, USA

Salvador Celia, M.D., Ph.D., Leo Kanner Institute, Rua Dario Pederneiras 513, CEP 90610 Porto Alegre, RS, Brazil

Colette Chiland, M.D., Ph.D., Professor of Clinical Psychology, René Descartes University (Sorbonne–Human Sciences); Psychiatrist, Alfred–Binet Center (Association for Mental Health of the 13th District of Paris), 76 Avenue Edison, 75013 Paris, France

René Diatkine, M.D., Ex-Professor of Psychiatry, School of Medicine of Geneva University; Deputy Director, Association for Mental Health of the 13th District of Paris, 76 Avenue Edison, 75013 Paris, France

Lionel Hersov, M.D., F.R.C.P., F.R.C.Psych., D.P.M., Professor of Psychiatry and Pediatrics, University of Massachusetts Medical School, 55 Lake Avenue North, Worcester, Mass. 01605, USA

Teruhisa Horio, Ph.D., Dean of the Faculty of Education, Tokyo University, Hongho 7–3–1, Bunkyo-Ku, Tokyo 113, Japan

Diana Kaplan, Ph.D., Clinical Instructor, Developmental Neurobiology Unit, Division of Child and Adolescent Psychiatry, New York University School of Medicine and Bellevue Hospital Center, 550 First Avenue, New York, N.Y. 10016, USA

Reimer Jensen, Ph.D., fil.dr.h.c., Professor of Clinical Psychology, Borups Alle 179, 2400 Copenhagen NV, Denmark

Hiten Kisnadwala, M.D., Instructor in Psychiatry, Developmental Neurobiology Unit, Division of Child and Adolescent Psychiatry, New York University School of Medicine and Bellevue Hospital Center, 550 First Avenue, New York, N.Y. 10016, USA

Eiji Koizumi, Ph.D., Professor of School Counseling, Department of Health Sciences, School of Human Sciences, Waseda University 2–579–15 Mikazima, Tokorozawa-Shi, Saitama 359, Japan

Richard Lansdown, Ph.D., Chief Psychologist, Department of Psychological Medicine, The Hospital for Sick Children, Great Ormond Street, London WC1N 3JH, U.K.

Serge Lebovici, M.D., Emeritus Professor of Child Psychiatry, Paris-North University, 74 Rue Marcel Cachin, 93012 Bobigny, France

Len Leven, M.D., Research Assistant Professor of Psychiatry, Developmental Neurobiology Unit, Division of Child and Adolescent Psychiatry, New York University School of Medicine and Bellevue Hospital Center, 550 First Avenue, New York, N.Y. 10016, USA

Fritz Mattejat, Ph.D., Clinical Research Psychologist, Department of Child and Adolescent Psychiatry, Philipps-Universität, Hans-Sachs Strasse 6, D–3550 Marburg, FRG

Kayoko Murase, Ph.D., Professor at Taisho University, 3–20–1 Nishi-Sugamo, Toshima-Ku, Tokyo, Japan

Akira Nakane, M.D., Director, Tokyo Metropolitan Umegaoka Hospital, 6–37–10 Matsubara, Setagaya-Ku, Tokyo, Japan

Helmut Remschmidt, M.D., Ph.D., Chairman, Department of Child and Adolescent Psychiatry, Philipps-Universität, Hans-Sachs Strasse 6, D–3550 Marburg, FRG

Jean-François Sabouret, Ph.D., Research Director, CNRS, Member of the Research Center on Contemporary Japan, Ecole des Hautes Etudes en Sciences Sociales, Paris, France

Koji Suzuki, Ph.D., Director of the Division of Socioenvironmental Research, National Center for Neuropsychiatry, National Institute of Mental Health, 1–7–3 Konodai, Ichikawa, Chiba 272, Japan

J. Gerald Young, M.D., Professor of Psychiatry and Director, Developmental Neurobiology Unit, Division of Child and Adolescent Psychiatry, New York University School of Medicine and Bellevue Hospital Center, 550 First Avenue, New York, N.Y. 10016, USA

CONTENTS

Introduction / ix
   Colette Chiland and J. Gerald Young

Part I: Overview

1. Children Rejecting School and Society Rejecting Children / 3
   J. Gerald Young, Colette Chiland, and Diana Kaplan
2. School Refusal: An Overview / 16
   Lionel Hersov

Part II: School Refusal: A Japanese Analysis

3. Education in Japan: The Issues at Stake at the Dawn of the
   Twenty-First Century / 45
   Teruhisa Horio and Jean-François Sabouret
4. School Refusal: Psychopathology and Natural History
   Akira Nakane / 62
5. School Refusal and Family Pathology: A Multifaceted
   Approach / 73
   Kayoko Murase
6. School Nonattendance and Psychological and Counseling
   Services / 88
   Eiji Koizumi
7. School Refusal Viewed through Family Therapy / 98
   Koji Suzuki

**Part III: School Refusal and School Problems
in Other Countries**

8. Nonattendance at School and School Refusal in Britain / 109
   Richard Lansdown

9. Treatment of School Phobia in Children and Adolescents
        in Germany / 123
        Helmut Remschmidt and Fritz Mattejat
10. How Children Respond to School in Denmark / 145
        Reimer Jensen
11. School Refusal and School Problems in Brazil / 152
        Salvador Celia
12. School Failure in France / 160
        Colette Chiland
13. Rejection of School in France / 172
        René Diatkine

Part IV: Clinical and Research Strategies

14. School Phobia: A Psychoanalytic View / 187
        Serge Lebovici
15. Strategies for Research on School Refusal and Related
        Nonattendance at School /199
        *J. Gerald Young, James R. Brasic, Hiten Kisnadwala,
        and Len Leven*

Index / 225

INTRODUCTION

This book was designed to prepare for and accompany the Twelfth International Congress of the International Association for Child and Adolescent Psychiatry and Allied Professions, to be held in Kyoto, Japan, in July 1990, on the subject of child rearing, education, and psychopathology.

The book focuses on the subject of school refusal, whether as refusal to attend school or as refusal to take advantage of what school has to offer (school failure and dropout). This subject was selected because school refusal is a source of acute concern to our Japanese colleagues, in view of its high incidence in their country and the great difficulty encountered in dealing with it.

School refusal in Japan is here described in the context of cultural changes in society and within the family, inadequate paternal involvement in children's education, the extraordinarily competitive educational system, and the frequency of bullying in schools.

The authors discuss whether school refusal is a phobic manifestation (school phobia) or an anxiety disorder (separation anxiety disorder). They offer an overview of the problem in several other countries (Federal Republic of Germany, Brazil, Denmark, United States, France, and United Kingdom).

In France the problem of school phobia and school refusal is relatively less alarming than that of school failure in a large number of children with normal intellectual capacities. School failure and dropout are the cause of greatest concern in the United States, whereas in Brazil, where differences between social classes are extreme, attention is concentrated on the problem of educating the most disadvantaged children.

Rather than proposing an exhaustive review of the world literature and clinical activities in relation to school refusal, this book presents a transcultural approach in preparation for international exchanges on the subject.

Colette Chiland
J. Gerald Young

I

Overview

1

Children Rejecting School and Society Rejecting Children

J. GERALD YOUNG

COLETTE CHILAND

DIANA KAPLAN

*There is nothing on earth intended for innocent people so
horrible as a school. To begin with, it is a prison. But it is
in some respects more cruel than a prison. In a prison, for
instance, you are not forced to read books written by the
warders and the governor.*
—G. B. Shaw, Parents and Children

If you want to gather honey, don't kick over the beehive.
—*Anonymous*

An uneasy, indecisive attitude toward school begins in childhood (Jensen, this volume) and lingers in adulthood. Nonattendance at
school, in one form or another, is accepted for a statistical segment of
the school-age population. This tolerance toward a common educational and public health problem begins to erode when its socioeconomic consequences are recognized: the decline of an adequate pool of
skilled laborers, billions of dollars of lost earnings and tax revenues each
year, the genesis of a distressing reappraisal of cultural values, and the
suffering of individuals who find themselves not fitting into their own
societies.

Nonattendance at school is not a distinct disorder, but rather it is
comprised of multiple syndromes; prominent examples are truancy,
childhood phobias, and separation anxiety disorder. The provisional
classification and relationships of these disorders is the subject of con-

tinuing research. An intriguing aspect of school nonattendance syndromes is that their form and features are molded by the varying contributions of causative factors, including genetic endowment, brain dysfunction, family psychopathology, and individual symptoms and character pathology. This makes school nonattendance an especially useful model for the study of the development of psychopathology in childhood.

Another aspect of school nonattendance that makes it of special interest is that social and cultural influences affect the prevalence and form of these disorders. This suggests that the study of this group of disorders from socioeconomic and cultural viewpoints would provide a new understanding of the disorders and their causes, and how cultural influences on the development and psychopathology of children are mediated. The transcultural approach of this book is a first step in this direction; it will likely stimulate further studies.

This volume reviews psychopathological features of school refusal and the current understanding of causes for children's rejection of school in seven countries. The patterns of psychopathology in school refusal vary according to the similarities or differences of the cultures compared. This mirrors a fact that is obvious, but easily forgotten: children reject school in the context of the meaning of education for them within their own society. How a society cares for its children and designs its schools becomes an essential consideration for those attempting to understand school nonattendance.

In order to initiate a consideration of transcultural influences on school nonattendance, this chapter examines the effects of cultural influences, mediated through social policy, on the lives of children. They are reviewed in relation to a single country, the United States; contrasts to social conditions in France and Japan are presented and subsequent chapters add to the understanding of these influences.

OPPORTUNITIES FOR CREATIVE SOCIAL POLICIES FOR CHILDREN

As the U.S. plans for the twenty-first century, presuppositions about child rearing and education have given way to alarming reports on the front pages of newspapers and in the prime time of television networks. This was unthinkable ten years ago. More than 20 percent of American children live in poverty. A mix of indulgence and neglect leads the U.S. to submit to a devastating drug abuse problem among youth. The academic skills of children are sufficiently disappointing to push Americans to rethink their strategies and commitment to education. The highest level of federal and state governments, as well as leading business executives, have responded with tentative steps to make children and education fundamental priorities for the U.S. in the next decade. In this climate the problems faced by youth have captured an unusual degree of interest that presents welcome opportunities. Yet, this quest for new strategies is blunted from two directions. First, from the perspective of the individual child, if childhood psychopathology results from multiple causes, there may be little practical value in examining socioeconomic influences alone. Second, the impact of socioeconomic conditions is so broad that it is difficult to measure its effects on individual children.

One strategy for estimating the effects of society's policies toward its children is to concentrate on a single problem (such as school-age pregnancy, adolescent suicide, or school dropouts), and examine its form, frequency, and severity in countries with similar and different cultures. This difficult task could best be accomplished with the structure and guidance of an international organization. The chapters in this volume reflect this approach by the International Association for Child and Adolescent Psychiatry and Allied Professions (IACAPAP), as it attempts to identify causes of a common psychopathological disorder through comparisons of its features across countries. New scientific knowledge of this type is essential to the development of successful public policy (Pizzo 1983).

School nonattendance occurs in all socioeconomic classes. The causes and characteristics of the syndrome vary across these groups, however, so it is necessary to focus on a specific class. This chapter describes possible causative factors for school nonattendance in economically deprived children. A first reason for this choice is that there is evidence that the prevalence of nonattendance is higher in this group (Rutter et al. 1975). The types of nonattendance characterizing this class of children are much more common than the specific school refusal disorders in countries such as Britain (Landsdown, this volume), France (Chiland, this volume), and Brazil (Celia, this volume). A second advantage is that more "childhood social indicators" are available to characterize these children, an essential means for measuring changes in the conditions of children's lives (Zill, Sigal, and Brim 1983). This provides a direct means for assessing socioeconomic influences on a childhood disorder.

SOCIAL POLICY FOR CHILDREN IN THE U.S.

Malignant problems infiltrating the lives of children are widespread across the world, but the depth of their penetration in developed countries is remarkable. Statistics available in the U.S. make it a useful example of the plight of children in developed countries. In order to understand the problems of youth in the U.S., the sociopolitical and economic background in which their welfare is embedded should be surveyed. Before we inquire into the nature and severity of their difficulties, what should we anticipate from the resources given to them?

The number of children in the U.S. below the age of fifteen years declined by 7 percent during the period from 1960 to 1982. This suggests that individual children would benefit from a larger share of allocated resources, even if there was no increase in overall funding. In contrast, an increase of 54 percent in the number of elderly (65 years or older) between 1960 and 1980 placed them at risk for a serious loss in per capita resources. Surprisingly, the reverse occurred.

Many statistics document the deteriorating conditions of children and the improving living standards of the elderly. Among those younger than fourteen years of age in 1970, 16 percent were living in poverty, while 24 percent of those over 65 years were below the poverty line in the same year.

This situation was turned upside down by 1982, when 15 percent of the elderly and 23 percent of children lived in poverty. When non-cash transfer payments from the government (such as food stamps) are added to these comparisons, the disparity is greater: the proportion of elderly living in poverty in 1982 drops from 15 to 4 percent, while the reduction for children is less, from 24 to 17 percent (Preston 1984). These trends reflect the minimal political and economic influence exerted by children. Advocates for children in the U.S. have failed to create the stable government mechanisms required to initiate necessary changes and enforce them. Political advocates must utilize creatively the same political structures and processes for children that other political policy lobbyists do for their interest groups (Marmor 1983).

Children have now been relegated to a position as the poorest sector of the U.S. population, and are seven times as likely to be poor as the elderly. In recent years there has been a stable statistic indicating that more than one-fifth of children under eighteen live in families below the poverty line. The fact that 25 percent of children under six live in poverty suggests that these problems may become worse. Almost two-thirds of these children in poverty are white, but black and Hispanic children are proportionately much more vulnerable to poverty: 43 percent of black and 40 percent of Hispanic children are below the poverty level (Committee for Economic Development 1987).

The diverse problems of families and youth are inevitably intertwined with one another. For example, the feminization of poverty is well established. Almost 80 percent of those living in poverty are women and children, and half of those in poverty live in families headed by single-parent women (Thurow 1987). Thus the chain of social deterioration begins: children of single parents perform more poorly in school than those with both parents at home. Their dropout rate is nearly twice as high and they constitute a large segment of children identified as school failures, school refusers, and school dropouts. Children born into poor, single-parent households are more likely than other children to be the children of teenage parents and are more prone to become teenage parents themselves. These children, by the time they are five years old, have a greater risk that they will later be unemployable, and will be unable to pass on adequate living skills to their own children in the future (Committee for Economic Development 1987). New generations of school refusing children emerge.

When "more than one-fifth of our children live in poverty and a third grow up in ignorance" (Committee for Economic Development 1987), it can be assumed that the statistics concerning the education of our children will be alarming. Approximately one million youth in the U.S. leave high school without graduating, leaving them practically unemployable and barely literate. Nearly that many (about 700,000) are estimated to attend school without real participation.

Overall, fewer than 50 percent of high school seniors are thought to read at levels adequate for developing the capacity to accomplish moderately complex tasks; 80 percent are said to have inadequate writing skills. The U.S. is confronted by the specter of the 30 percent of its children who have become the educationally disadvantaged facing failure and lifelong dependency (Committee for Economic Development 1985, 1987).

When new malignant disorders of families and society invade children's lives, socioeconomic influences on the appearance of psychopathology are visible. For example, the rate of admission of newborn infants to neonatal intensive care units in New York City because of drug abuse by their mothers has increased dramatically in the past ten years (French 1989). Public health officials attempt to awaken policy makers to the inevitable outcome when these babies become adolescents. They recognize the physical impairments likely to afflict these children in later years. In addition, there is the likelihood that a subgroup with mental retardation will emerge and virtual certainty that a substantial number of these children will have developmental disabilities. Finally, many children damaged during the neonatal period, and subsequently neglected by a drug-abusing single parent, will have more subtle problems. Some will have low-normal intelligence, rudimentary social skills, and minimal impulse control. As they struggle with continuous stress, they will be unable to adapt to the formal requirements of school and jobs. They will be an addition to a new generation of school refusing children.

There is a long history of abuse and neglect of children stemming from a misunderstanding of children and their needs. This ignorance is best understood in the context of evidence that seven centuries ago children were not conceptually differentiated from adults other than in their physical size. It is only in recent centuries (the thirteenth through the seventeenth) that prevailing views of children were gradually modulated into the basic understanding that we have of them today (Aries 1962).

This does not excuse current neglectful policies toward children as an expected and unavoidable social and economic outcome. Detailed knowledge of the developmental needs of children and the families nurturing them begets responsibility. Actions reflecting recognition of this responsibility are visible in (1) the decisions enacted as social policy and (2) in the day-to-day reality of the lives of children.

A SOCIAL POLICY CONTRAST:
DAY-CARE PROGRAMS IN FRANCE AND THE U.S.

American social policies toward children can be shortsighted. Bullied by fears of excessive cost, policy makers back into long-term expenditures that dwarf the original expenses that were "avoided." Day-care programs are not affordable for lower- and middle-class families and require substantial government investment (Ruopp and Travers 1982). The U.S. has not been willing to undertake this commitment. Its distance from this goal is evident in the fact that even regulations for infant day care are inadequate (Young and Zigler 1986), a step considerably easier than attempting actual funding of the programs. The U.S. cannot assume that these programs are not feasible economically. Other Western countries have designed successful national day-care programs and the U.S. continues to spend heavily for programs for teenagers who could have been aided in the earliest years of life.

There is a stable and successful national system of day-care programs in France. If we again begin with an analysis of the simple provision of resources before examining the actual circumstances of children, France provides an instructive example. While the U.S. spends 5.5 percent of its gross national product on public education, including preschool programs, France spends 7.1 percent. What does this increment purchase?

The French system consists of a blend of child care, education, and health services integrated into free full-day preschool programs, subsidized day-care centers, and licensed infant and toddler family day care in private homes. Almost 80 percent of the cost of child-care services in France are underwritten by public funds, with the remainder paid for by parents. This provides services for children from all strata of society in France, encompassing 90 percent of French children three to five years of age. In the U.S., the focus of programs is conventionally on special groups, such as those at risk in some way, or the poor. The quality of staff personnel is higher in France than in the U.S. Their educational levels are higher and they are paid at higher rates than in the U.S., according them greater professional status. In contrast, the American wages for such staff are notoriously low and there is a 40 percent turnover annually (Ruopp and Travers 1982; New York Times 1989). These differences reflect the commitment of the French nation to its children. Their preschool programs are the pride of the French educational system (see Chiland, this volume). They reflect their recognition of the importance of the preschool years for the development of essential psychic structures. These allow the productive and unconflicted use of mental images to help children manage their emotions, interact comfortably with others, and use a playful imagination as they leave the safety of the family and enter the larger social world (Diatkine, this volume).

NEW BENEFICIAL FORCES

Is there room for optimism as we confront the neglect of children and education in many countries? Fortunately, the destructive effects of this neglect begin to be obvious and society becomes aware of its choices and their results. This may be happening in the U.S. The Commission on Industrial Productivity at the Massachusetts Institute of Technology has examined industrial performance in the U.S. in order to determine if there are fundamental problems in an economy characterized by a mix of strengths and weaknesses. They identified six problems within U.S. industry that impede its capacity to compete optimally in the changing international business climate. One was neglect of human resources and another was operating with short time horizons. They recognize that the neglect of human resources begins long before the often inadequate training received at the job site. Children in school systems are abandoning their education without acquiring basic skills. Other remedies for deficiencies in industrial performance will be insufficient unless solutions for these educational deficiencies are forged (Berger et al. 1989).

The Research and Policy Committee of the Committee for Economic Development (a group of national business leaders) has come to a similar conclusion. They state it bluntly: it is estimated that school dropouts each year will cost the U.S. more than $240 billion in lost earnings and forgone taxes over their lifetimes. This does not take into account the additional billions lost through payments for health care, welfare, crime control, and other social services for this group. Their initial report, *Investing in Our Children: Business and the Public Schools,* led to the recognition that attention to educational systems was inadequate, and it resulted in a second report. *Children in Need: Investment Strategies for the Educationally Disadvantaged* recommends three strategies for reform that will give children a better start and the chance to learn when they are in school: prevention through early intervention, restructuring the foundations of education, and retention and reentry (Committee for Economic Development 1987).

CULTURAL INFLUENCES ON CHILDHOOD PSYCHOPATHOLOGY: MEDIATING FACTORS IN SCHOOL REFUSAL

Discouraged by the apparent inevitability of continuing social problems, responsible adults often dismiss them as insurmountable. As a result, the chance to observe the effects of discrete vectors of developmental pathology in specific groups of children is missed. However, a practical strategy is available. This is to confine research attention to a single disorder in different cultural settings in order to elucidate mediating influences. The objective is to identify pathways between broad destructive influences, such as poverty, and the later loss to society of groups of children as they approach adulthood (school-age mothers, delinquents, drug addicts, and others, including those who fail to attend school).

School refusal is well adapted for use as a model for investigating these mediators. It is a "measurable" disorder. A child is or is not present in school, and schools and their funding are clear instruments of the vagaries of governmental social policy. School refusal is responsive to cultural changes, is sufficiently inclusively defined to allow clinical variation in its expression, and has specific diagnostic subcategories whose prevalence can be altered by cultural change.

Psychiatrists traditionally sought the pathogenic effects of more subtle influences on the development of childhood psychopathology, such as communication patterns within the family or the impact of brief mother-infant separation. Transcultural research on developmental psychopathology examines sources and routes of pathogenic social influences, particularly the effects of broad cultural trends. For example, a culture such as Japan with strict social norms would be expected to generate conflicts within an individual deciding whether or not to conform to written and unwritten rules. This culture will have a high prevalence of disorders consisting of conflict resolution through symptom genesis, including internalizing types of school nonattendance disorders. In a culturally heterogeneous country with less agreement about acceptable social conventions, such as the U.S., more individuals will resolve internal conflicts by discarding the external regulations; this trend will spawn a higher prevalence of externalizing types of school nonattendance disorders. Transcultural comparison of available data and clinical experience of this type is a logical preparatory step before any attempt at rigorous but expensive research protocols with subject groups in several countries.

CONCLUSION: TRANSCULTURAL PERSPECTIVES
ON SCHOOL REFUSAL

This volume of the *Yearbook* surveys the varieties of school refusal and probable causes across countries in Asia, Europe, and North and South America. The next chapter (Hersov) offers a comprehensive review of the psychopathology and causes of school refusal. It surveys phenomenology, diagnostic subgroups (school phobia, separation anxiety disorder, and others), current classification systems, emerging data from genetic research, treatment, and historical trends in research.

Five chapters address the subject of school refusal from psychiatric, educational, and family perspectives in Japan. Throughout these chapters there are recurrent questions about the contribution of sociocultural influences to the increasing incidence of school refusal in Japan. Several theories concerning the nature of these influences are presented. For example, a highly structured and refined educational system, in which academic expectations are clearly defined and rigorously tracked, has been criticized from within Japan as excessive and destructive to some children (Horio and Sabouret, this volume). School refusal and bullying are increasing problems, and it is suggested that they directly mirror the student discontent with current academic structures (Nakane, this volume; Koizumi, this volume). Some Japanese professionals suggest that school refusal is partially rooted in these and other features of their society, which are then mirrored in the phenomena observed in the families of school refusing children (Murase, this volume; Suzuki, this volume).

The third section of the book contains contrasting data from other countries. For example, in spite of the Japanese view of school refusal as an increasingly serious problem in their country, its prevalence is lower than that of school nonattendance in Britain. School *refusal* affects 1 percent of British schoolchildren, while school *nonattendance* affects 10 percent. The characteristics of British schools are suggested to be powerful influences on the rates of nonattendance in specific districts; this effect will stimulate new attention to social influences mediated through the educational system (Lansdown, this volume).

Educational problems take on varying forms in other countries. In Brazil the education of the vast socioeconomically deprived sector of children is faltering in response to sociocultural influences. By the second year of elementary school, 40 percent of the children who entered in the first year remain in class; by the eleventh year (third year of secondary school), the proportion of the initial first-year class still remaining has fallen to only 6.4 percent. The major factors identified as causes for these problems are social stratification, inadequate educational resources and teaching methods, absence of relevant incentives, malnutrition, and cognitive deficiencies from insufficient environmental stimulation (Celia, this volume).

Failure while attending school is a more pervasive problem in France. One source of this type of school "nonattendance" is educational policy: school programs are set at a level beyond the abilities of most of the children, so that half repeat at least one year of primary school and few reach the final grade of the lycée (Chiland, this volume). During the preschool years the child has the opportunity to develop the language of society, a mediating capacity allowing the child to participate in the world beyond the family. However, this transition from a personal to a universal language may not be achieved by socioeconomically deprived children. They lose a gratifying freedom of imagination and an essential bridge to the reality of life outside the family (Diatkine, this volume). This can contribute to a restricted emotional life and subsequent academic problems. For example, there is evidence that those children who are falling behind in reading skills by age six are later less likely to receive their *baccalauréat* (Chiland, this volume). The impoverished language makes the child less able to utilize others to help him or her cope with the predictable developmentally related anxieties, such as those encountered at first entry into school (Jensen, this volume). Left vulnerable, the child is more likely to retain primitive psychic structures and defenses. On the one hand, this might be reflected in minimal development of the superego and diluted identifications with parents (eliminating these bulwarks against his or her drives), leading to character or symptom disorders centered on poor impulse control. Such children may later be truant or drop out of school. On the other hand, better development may be achieved, but a reliance on relatively primitive defenses may still handicap the child. This may include displacement and projection, as the child develops phobic personality patterns, such as a school phobia. In this case the symptom structure is specifically that of a phobia; it lacks the greater disorganization that may characterize some truant children. Nevertheless, school phobia can be seriously disabling (Lebovici, this volume).

While the difficulties of treatment of truancy and other school nonattendance disorders are frustrating to clinicians and educators, solid success has been achieved for many school refusing children. Treatment is more effective when the patient is young and the disorder is diagnosed and treated early. The elements of treatment are becoming increasingly specific. The importance of a specific treatment contract in the context of family therapy has been emphasized, as well as the necessity for the therapist to take over some control within the family in the initial stages of treatment (Remschmidt and Mattejat, this volume).

School failure includes many children with a typical conflict-driven internalizing disorder, such as separation anxiety disorder or school phobia. The psychoanalytic understanding of symptom genesis in these disorders has been the basis for the largest sector of clinical research and care during the past fifty years and is reviewed in the final section (Lebovici, this volume).

The final chapter reviews research strategies that will guide the next era of investigation. The success of new research will depend on improved classification of this broad group of disorders. Clinical and neurobiological measures may become more sensitive in the discrimination of subgroups of school nonattendance disorders, and methods for differentiating genetic subtypes may be developed. Cultural influences on these disorders can be examined by determining comparative differences in the prevalence of school refusal and its subtypes across cultures. The work accomplished in the past decades has generated a large range of research questions that can now be tested (Young et al., this volume).

This volume illuminates many commonalities of clinical practice and conceptualization of this group of disorders, a result not expected from such a diverse range of cultures. Further research taking advantage of a unified investigative approach in several countries would make a novel contribution to the understanding of school refusal and the development of psychopathology in childhood.

REFERENCES

Aries, P. (1962) *Centuries of Childhood: A Social History of Family Life.* Trans. R. Baldick. New York, Alfred A. Knopf.

Berger, S., Dertouzos, M. L., Lester, R. K., Solow, R. M., and Thurow, L. C. (1989) Toward a new industrial America. *Scientific American* 260:39–47.

Celia, S. (in this volume) School refusal and school problems in Brazil.

Chiland, C. (in this volume) School failure in France.

Committee for Economic Development. Research and Policy Committee. (1985) *Children in Need. Investing in Our Children: Business and the Public Schools.* New York, Committee for Economic Development.

———— (1987) *Children in Need. Investment Strategies for the Educationally Disadvantaged.* New York, Committee for Economic Development.

Diatkine, R. (in this volume) Rejection of school in France.

French, H. W. (1989) Rise in babies hurt by drugs is predicted. *New York Times,* 18 October.

Hersov, L. (in this volume) School refusal: An overview.

Horio, T., and Sabouret, J.-F. (in this volume) Education in Japan: The issues at stake.

Jensen, R. (in this volume) How children respond to school in Denmark.

Koizumi, E. (in this volume) School nonattendance and psychological and counseling services.

Lansdown, R. (in this volume) Nonattendance at school and school refusal in Britain.

Lawson, C. (1989) When it comes to child care, French have a lesson for U.S. *New York Times,* 9 November.

Lebovici, S. (in this volume) School phobia: A psychoanalytic view.

Marmor, T. R. (1983) Competing perspectives on social policy. In *Children, Families, and Government: Perspectives on American Social Policy,* ed. E. Zigler, S. L. Kagan, and E. Klugman. Cambridge, Cambridge University Press.

Murase, K. (in this volume) School refusal and family pathology: A multifaceted approach.

Nakane, A. (in this volume) School refusal: Psychopathology and natural history.

Pizzo, P. (1983) Slouching toward Bethlehem: American federal policy perspectives on children and their families. In *Children, Families, and Government: Perspectives on American Social Policy,* ed. E. Zigler, S. L. Kagan, and E. Klugman. Cambridge, Cambridge University Press.

Preston, S. H. (1984) Children and the elderly in the U.S. *Scientific American* 251:44–49.

Remschmidt, H., and Mattejat, F. (in this volume) Treatment of school phobia in children and adolescents in Germany.

Ruopp, R. R., and Travers, J. (1982) Janus faces day care: Perspectives on quality and cost. In *Day Care: Scientific and Social Policy Issues,* E. F. Zigler and E. W. Gordon. Boston, Auburn House.

Rutter, M., Yule, B., Quinton, D., Rowlands, O., Yule, W., and Berger, M. (1975) Attainment and adjustment in two geographical areas. (III) Some factors accounting for area differences. *British Journal of Psychiatry* 126:520–533.

Suzuki, K. (in this volume) School refusal viewed through family therapy.

Thurow, L. C. 1987. A surge in inequality. *Scientific American* 256:30–37.

Young, J. G., Brasic, J. R., Kisnadwala, H., Leven, L. (in this volume) Strategies for research on school refusal and related nonattendance at school.

Young, K. T., and Zigler, E. 1986. Infant and toddler day care: Regulations and policy implications. *American Journal of Orthopsychiatry* 56:43–55.

Zill, N. II, Sigal, H., and Brim, O. G., Jr. (1983) Development of childhood social indicators. In *Children, Families, and Government: Perspectives on American Social Policy,* ed. E. Zigler, S. L. Kagan, and E. Klugman. Cambridge, Cambridge University Press.

2

School Refusal: An Overview

LIONEL HERSOV

SUMMARY

School refusal has continued to interest clinicians and re-searchers in all the disciplines concerned with children and adolescents since it was first described in the 1930s. Separation anxiety disorder is found predominantly in young children. In older children and adolescents school refusal is often a manifestation of a phobic disorder or a depressive disorder. Modern treatments include such different methods as psychotherapy, behavior therapy, family therapy, pharmacotherapy, and milieu therapy. Genetic-familial studies have shown important links between affective and depressive disorders in first-degree relatives of children with school refusal and anxiety disorders.

Prolonged or recurrent absence of some children from school is a continuing problem for educational authorities in societies in which school attendance is compulsory. Mandatory schooling was introduced in the modern industrial states of the West at the end of the nineteenth century (Debiesse 1951; Lester-Smith 1951). In the United States attendance laws were first instituted in the early 1800s, with a common requirement of twelve weeks attendance per year, although actual enforcement did not occur for decades. In the United Kingdom compulsory school attendance was introduced only in 1880. Nowadays we regard regular school attendance as necessary and important in the education and socialization of children. Prolonged absence for any reason may have serious consequences for learning and social development and is a cause for concern.

About one-tenth of all pupils in Britain are absent at any given time (Fogelman and Richardson 1974), and absence is without legitimate cause in 22 percent of these cases (Hansard 1974). Illness is much the most common reason for school absence (Tyerman 1974; Weitzman et al. 1982), and up to four-fifths of children are kept away on these grounds. Other children are unlawfully withheld from school by parents, often on the pretext of illness, to keep a healthy family member or ill parent company, or sometimes to do the shopping and carrying for a phobic housebound mother. Withholding or withdrawing a child from school for these reasons is more common than is realized. In socially disadvantaged areas some children stay at home with parental connivance, but this is more commonly a social than a psychiatric problem. Eventually some such children are brought to psychiatric notice for a number of reasons. Most referrals to children's mental health services for persistent nonattendance, however, are either truants or children who refuse to go to school. These two groups have been distinguished in a number of empirical studies (Warren 1948; Hersov 1960a,b), and the distinction has both theoretical and practical implications.

Until about sixty years ago all forms of persistent nonattendance at school were labeled truancy. In the second half of the nineteenth century, the "truant" schoolboy was also regarded as lazy, idle, neglectful of his duties, and prone to antisocial acts. Truancy was considered a precursor of delinquency, and steps were taken to identify the children and keep them at school. Correctional institutions were also built to try to rehabilitate the more incorrigible among them.

THE ORIGIN OF THE CONCEPT OF SCHOOL REFUSAL

In 1932, Broadwin, an American psychoanalyst, first described what he considered to be a variant of truancy, a form of persistent nonattendance at school that was later labeled school phobia by some (Johnson et al. 1941; Suttenfield 1954; Bowlby 1973) and school refusal by others (Millar 1961). From his study of a small number of children, Broadwin considered difficulties in school attendance to be symptoms of a personality problem occurring in children who suffered from a deep-seated obsessional neurosis or who displayed a neurotic character of the obsessional type. Broadwin's original observation that these children feared something terrible happening to their mother, which made them run home for reassurance and relief of anxiety, was repeated in many later clinical studies and is the basis of the often repeated statement that apparent fear of school is really a fear of leaving home. This form of neurotic refusal to go to school had been remarked upon in passing by Jung in 1913 and Melanie Klein in 1932 in descriptions of analytic treatment of anxious children with other manifestations of neurosis.

Some years later Johnson et al. (1941) emphasized the fairly sharp differentiation between absence from school stemming from deep-seated psychoneurotic disorder and the more frequent variety of non-attendance called truancy. The descriptive term *school phobia* was first used by these authors and taken up in later publications (van Houten 1948; Goldberg 1953; Suttenfield 1954; Coolidge et al. 1957; Talbot 1957). Johnson and her colleagues viewed the syndrome of school phobia not as a clear-cut clinical entity but rather as phobic tendencies overlapping with other hysterical or neurotic obsessional patterns. Early abortive forms of school phobia that cleared rapidly were mentioned. Johnson and her colleagues discuss for the first time a thirty-one-year-old female with severe untreated school phobia that later developed into a crippling widespread chronic phobic state and resisted all forms of analytic treatment. E. Klein (1945) broke down the child's fear of school into fear of the teacher, of other pupils, and of schoolwork with expectation of failure, distinctions that still need to be made today to define the focus of treatment in those cases where the child's fears are predominantly of school situations. However, E. Klein (1945) then discounted the possibility of real stresses in the school and explained the child's fears in terms of fixation at the Oedipal or pre-Oedipal level of psychosexual development.

Both Johnson et al. (1941) and Warren (1948) observed that fear of school and refusal to attend occurred in family settings where maternal anxiety, marital disharmony, and parental inconsistency were often significant factors. Warren (1948) also showed that both acute anxiety and depression were often present. Clinical observations of that time and more current observations support the notion that school phobia or refusal is not a true clinical entity with uniform etiology, psychopathology, course, prognosis, and treatment but rather a collection of symptoms or a syndrome occurring during the course of a variety of psychiatric disorders (Davidson 1960; Hersov 1960a,b; Millar 1961; Kolvin et al. 1984; Bernstein and Garfinkel 1986). Precipitating and etiological factors vary with age, sex, school setting, family structure and function, level of psychosexual and psychosocial development, and temperamental and personality factors in the child.

THE PREVALENCE OF SCHOOL REFUSAL

The prevalence of school refusal has proven difficult to establish, since most early estimates were based on clinical populations that covered a wide age range and had been referred to child psychiatric or child guidance clinics. The reported rate in these settings varied from 1 percent of a complete sample of clinic attenders over ten years (Chazan 1962) to 8 percent (Kahn and Nursten 1962). Smith (1970) found a rate of 3.8 percent among children with emotional disorders attending the Maudsley Hospital Children's Department. A recent study in Sweden found a frequency of 7 percent (Flakierska et al. 1988). The prevalence in a total population of ten- and eleven-year-old children on the Isle of Wight, however, was less than 3 percent of all children with psychiatric disorders (Rutter et al. 1970). It is possible, even likely, that family doctors, primary health care practitioners, and pediatricians deal effectively with early or incipient cases of school refusal if they are perceptive enough to recognize them so that these children never reach the mental health services. Shepherd et al. (1966) found in a study of a British sample of general practitioners that four-fifths indicated they would themselves manage a straightforward case of persistent nonattendance, whereas one-fifth would refer such children to a clinic.

Rutter et al. (1976), in a study of the same Isle of Wight schoolchildren then aged fourteen, found fifteen cases of school refusal, in association with either an affective disorder or other psychiatric symptoms. This was in marked contrast to the negligible prevalence at age ten or eleven. On the basis of these and other figures given above, a reasonable overall estimate of the clinical prevalence of school refusal would be about 5 percent of all children referred for psychiatric disorder, with a higher rate in early adolescence and in secondary schools than in infant or primary schools.

These studies show a pattern of incidence that appears highest at three periods of school-going age. The first peak is at school entry or soon after, between the ages of five and seven (probably a feature of the separation anxiety often seen at this age); a second peak occurs at eleven years, associated with change to a more senior school and accompanying a variety of emotional or neurotic disorders; a third peak occurs at fourteen years and older. The last group may differ from the younger cases in the type and severity of psychiatric disorder, generally with more frequent occurrence of major depressive disorder and inferior treatment outcome and long-term prognosis.

THE DISTINCTION BETWEEN TRUANCY AND SCHOOL REFUSAL

The clinical distinction between children who are truant from school and those who are unable to go to school has been clarified in several studies (Hersov 1960a,b; Cooper 1966; Torma and Halsti 1975a,b; Blagg 1979; Heath 1983). In general, significant associations have been found between truancy and excessive parental control (particularly by corporal punishment), dirty homes, uninterested parents, keeping the child at home in the past without good cause, and homes in a working-class area (Tyerman 1968; Sommer 1985). Truancy also occurs frequently in association with poor school attainment in children from families where marital discord, criminality, and adverse social circumstances are common (Farrington 1980). School characteristics are potent factors (Reynolds et al. 1980), as are peer group influences (Fogelman et al. 1980). Children with mixed features of school refusal and truancy have been described, although they are less often seen in clinic populations (Cooper 1960; Tennent 1969; Berg et al. 1985). A recent study by Berg et al. (1985) showed that as many as 20 percent of children taken to juvenile court in Britain for school nonattendance are school refusers, not truants. Some truants may evidence a psychiatric disorder, more often conduct than emotional disorder, and a smaller number will show anxiety symptoms and social isolation (Berg et al. 1978) of the same order as those nonattendees diagnosed as school refusal. School refusers, however, are highly unlikely to display antisocial behavior and most show clear evidence of an emotional disorder. Their pattern of nonattendance has a form and quality distinct from that of truants. The family structure and pattern of relationships and parental management of the children also differs greatly in the two forms of nonattendance.

THE CLINICAL PICTURE IN SCHOOL REFUSAL

The earliest symptoms of school refusal are vague complaints about school or a reluctance to attend, progressing to refusal either to go to school or to remain at school in the face of entreaty, persuasion, recrimination, threats and punishment by parents, and pressure from teachers, family doctors, and educational welfare officers. There may be overt signs of anxiety or frank panic when the time comes to go to school, and most school refusers cannot even leave home to set out for school. Many who manage to leave home get only halfway to school and return, and some, once at school, may rush home in a state of anxiety. Many insist they want to go to school and make appropriate preparations but fail to go when the time comes. Characteristically they remain at home, with their parents' knowledge, when they should be at school.

An acute onset is more often seen in younger children, whereas a more insidious development is exhibited in older children and adolescents. Precipitating factors such as a minor accident, illness or operation, leaving home to go on a school holiday or to camp, moving to a new house, changing class or school, the departure or loss of a school friend, or the illness or death of a relative to whom the child was attached may be found at all ages. Such events appear to represent a threat to the child's security, arousing anxiety that cannot be controlled away from home.

In older children and adolescents there is often no abrupt or definite change in personality but a gradual withdrawal from peer group activities formerly enjoyed, such as scouts, guides, or youth clubs. The youngster ceases to go out, clings to and tries to control a parent, usually the mother, and may express a general fear or dislike of the world outside the home. A stubborn, argumentative, critical style may replace formerly compliant behavior. Often anger is directed against the mother. In Japan family violence, most frequently directed against the mother, has been reported in association with simultaneous refusal to go to school (Honjo and Wakabayashi 1988).

Precipitating factors are even less clear-cut in adolescence and may only appear to be a change to a senior school (Blyth and Simmons 1983), which may have occurred as long as a semester earlier. Complex, long-standing family psychopathology is common, and frequently the earlier personality development of the child has been deviant in regard to social relationships, anxiety when entering new situations, and developing independence and sexual identity. School refusal is often only one indication of the young adolescent's general inability to cope with increasing demands for an existence independent of the family and entry into normal peer group relationships.

When the clinical picture resembles the above description, the diagnosis is hardly in doubt. When it assumes a somatic disguise (Eisenberg 1958; Waller and Eisenberg 1980), careful assessment by the family doctor or pediatrician will clarify the problem. Here the predominant complaint will be not of an inability to go to school but of nausea, loss of appetite, vomiting, syncope, headache, abdominal pain, vague malaise, diarrhea, limb pains, or tachycardia (Schmitt 1971). These complaints occur in the mornings before school or even at school, without any overt expression of fear about school, which may only be elicited on careful inquiry. At times, the somatic symptoms are not experienced but fearfully anticipated; the child may avoid school in case he or she might faint or vomit in such situations as school assembly or morning prayers.

Boys and girls are equally affected by school refusal, but the younger age groups have a preponderance of girls. Most school refusers are of average intelligence, with educational attainments up to grade level and sometimes beyond expectations (Hersov 1960a; Berg et al. 1975; Heath 1983), although some studies have reported educational retardation or the need for remedial help (Chazan 1962; Blagg 1979). Families tend to be of average size, but findings vary about the child's position in the family. Berg et al. (1972) found that school refusers tended to come late in the birth order, whereas Blagg (1979) and Heath (1983) found them more often to be eldest or younger children, in line with earlier findings by Hersov (1960a) and Smith (1970). One-fifth of mothers of school refusers suffer from a psychiatric disorder, usually an affective disorder (Hersov 1960b; Berg et al. 1974; Last et al. 1987), and there are higher rates of anxiety and depressive disorders in first-degree relatives of children with school refusal (Bernstein and Garfinkel 1988).

DIFFERENTIAL DIAGNOSIS

In his classic paper, Broadwin (1932) viewed both everyday truancy and the atypical group of nonattenders he described not as clinical entities but as different manifestations of total personality adjustment to difficult or threatening situations at home and at school. Subsequent clinical studies have confirmed the validity of his description of school refusal, and there is also broad agreement about parental personality, behavior, and symptomatology (Waldfogel et al. 1957; Eisenberg 1958; Malmquist 1965; Berg et al. 1969; Johnson et al. 1941) although different patterns of parent-child interaction have been noted (Hersov 1960a,b; Bowlby 1973).

Agreement on the broad clinical phenomena has not been paralleled by agreement on the diagnostic labels *school phobia* or *school refusal,* although the latter appears to be increasingly used. Views also differ about the psychological mechanisms responsible for the behavior. The term *school phobia* is used by those who explain the behavior in terms of individual psychopathology, based on the classical psychoanalytic theory of phobic symptom formation: externalization of frightening impulses and their displacement on to a previously neutral object or situation that is then avoided, for example, the teacher or school (Suttenfield 1954; Waldfogel et al. 1957; Sperling 1961, 1967). Explanations based on learning theory also emphasize individual psychopathology, in which the learning of maladaptive responses through respondent or operant conditioning, or a mixture of both, leads to avoidance behavior maintained by fear reduction and resultant school phobia (Ross 1972a,b).

School refusal is considered a more appropriate description of the child's behavior by many experienced clinicians and family therapists, because it neither implies a commitment to any particular theory of psychopathology such as the origin of phobias nor assumes that we are dealing with a unitary homogeneous disorder. Family therapists locate the origins of the child's anxiety within the family system. From the systemic point of view, refusal rather than phobia points to the interpersonal rather than the purely intrapsychic sources of fear of school, whether it be separation or anticipatory anxiety. Using the concept of family homeostasis, symptomatic behavior has a stabilizing family function and attempts to resolve underlying conflict and stress, albeit in a dysfunctional way (Hsia 1984).

Other contributors offer simpler explanations: that such children overvalue themselves and their achievements and try to maintain an unrealistic self-image. If threatened in school by failure in work or peer group relationships, the student can begin to exhibit anxiety, avoidance of school, and attempts to maintain a narcissistic picture of the self, aided by a permissive mother (Leventhal and Sills 1964; Leventhal et al. 1967). These assumptions were not supported by Nichols and Berg (1970) and Cooper (1984), who used objective tests of self-evaluation, or by Heath (1983), who found that school refusers did not have a higher academic self-image or higher general self-image than did their peers. Heath (1983) also found that school refusers fell into two distinct groups of "high" and "low" anxiety, although the mean levels were similar to their peers. Curiously, separation anxiety was not prominent in Heath's sample. School refusers tended to have a higher "L" score on the Junior Eysenck Personality Questionnaire (Eysenck and Eysenck 1975) and may therefore tend to be more socially conforming than their peers (Aldridge-Smith 1974; Blagg 1979).

In early descriptions of school refusal (Broadwin 1932) school factors were seldom mentioned as playing a part in the genesis of the behavior. Although E. Klein (1945) mentioned fear of teacher, schoolmates, and school work, he did not accord these factors as much weight as the child's individual psychopathology. Interestingly, recent papers about school refusal in Japan (Hishiyama and Furukawa 1982; Lock 1986, 1987; Honjo et al. 1987) have recorded a rise in cases of school refusal (according to Ministry of Education figures) from 31.1 percent to 52.7 percent especially among children in middle school. The percentage of school refusal cases, however, is still small, comprising only 0.36 percent of all middle-school students in 1982. The reasons given for this increase by educators and mental health professionals are multifactorial, including changing physical and social environments, especially modernization and urbanization. It is generally agreed that the modern Japanese school environment is not ideal for children and that those who are different in any way are likely to feel unhappy. The Japanese school system is intensely competitive, and the pressure to get places in prestigious universities requires students to achieve well in frequent and demanding examinations. Competition is especially fierce to enter a good high school, but the pressure to achieve begins as early as in kindergarten. Refusal to go to school, not surprisingly, causes great concern about future academic success and employment, and the causes of school refusal are seen as stemming from the family as well as from school and society. Lock (1986) sees it as a form of resistance to social pressures and expectations.

The earliest report of school phobia (Johnson et al. 1941) stressed a particular quality in the mother-child relationship. The children were described as unduly dependent and therefore likely to be caught up in maternal anxieties and preoccupations. Later papers (Estes et al. 1956; Johnson 1957; Davidson 1960) viewed school phobia as a symptom (Reger 1962; Radin 1967) of an underlying anxiety about leaving mother rather than as a fear of being at school. Estes et al. (1956) used the term *separation anxiety* to describe the child's response to attempts to alter this pathological emotional state. Later empirical studies supported observations that the source of anxiety about school was the child's fear of being separated from the mother (Coolidge et al. 1957; Waldfogel et al. 1957; Eisenberg 1958; Hersov 1960a,b; Smith 1970).

Waldron et al. (1975) listed three overlapping syndromes encompassed within school phobia: (1) the family interaction type, with a predominance of separation anxiety, was found in two-thirds of cases; (2) the typically phobic, according to the presence of usual psychodynamic mechanisms, accounted for only three out of thirty-five children and (3) the situational-characterological type, with school avoidance resulting from fear of real situations in school that threatened self-esteem or even bodily harm, accounted for more than half the cases.

Gittelman-Klein and Klein (1980) suggested that separation anxiety was the major psychological determinant in school phobia, finding it in over four-fifths of their cases with no significant differences between seven- to twelve-year-olds and thirteen- to fifteen-year-olds. It has been argued that dependency and anxiety about separation are more likely to be found at the earlier ages (Leventhal and Sills 1964), even though the literature does not support this conclusion. Smith (1970) found that separation anxiety was not found exclusively in school refusal and that it occurred more often in younger patients but was still an important feature of the psychopathology that may be precipitated by a real or threatened loss of an important figure in the child's life. In some, anxiety is related primarily to some aspect of the school situation; in others, the main anxiety is about leaving home and separating from parents. Some studies (Waldron 1976) find both forms of anxiety in many cases. Eysenck and Rachman (1965) use the term *school phobia* for the first group and *separation anxiety in the school situation* for the latter. Others (Yates 1970) have put forward an interactional theory based on learning principles. In some children anxiety may have become attached to separation situations, generated and reinforced by maternal anxiety. When a young child goes to school, he or she may or may not develop varying degrees of intensity of fear of school depending on the experiences there and the mother's reaction to this anxiety.

In a recent study, Last et al. (1987) commented that in the past and even today the term *school phobia* has been applied to children who show separation anxiety as well as to those who show a phobic reaction to school. The aim of their study was to examine and compare the clinical and associated features of children who exhibit separation anxiety and those who show phobic avoidance of school, through a semi-structured diagnostic interview and several other self-report anxiety measures. They found that more children with separation anxiety disorder were female, prepubertal, and from families with lower socioeconomic backgrounds and more were likely to have a DSM III diagnosis other than separation anxiety disorder. Children with school phobia tended to be male, postpubertal, and from higher socioeconomic backgrounds. Mothers of the children with separation anxiety disorder showed a rate of affective disorder (mostly major depression) four times greater than that found in the mothers of the school phobia group. Most children (73 percent) with separation anxiety disorder displayed school refusal.

The advent of multiaxial classifications (Rutter et al. 1975) with the application of uniform diagnostic criteria, as well as the use of structured and semistructured diagnostic interviews, has led to more valid comparisons among different studies of the same disorder and among different treatment methods and outcomes. DSM III (American Psychiatric Association 1980) introduced the category of separation anxiety disorder, with school refusal as one of the items required to make the diagnosis. In DSM III R (American Psychiatric Association 1987) "persistent reluctance or refusal to go to school in order to stay with major attachment figures or at home" (pp. 60–61) is one of nine diagnostic criteria for separation anxiety disorder. The disorder is considered to represent a form of phobia but is not included among the phobic disorders because it has unique features and is characteristically associated with childhood. This tends to relegate school refusal to the status of a symptom rather than the complex disorder about which so many have written. It is probably true that in young children the diagnosis of separation anxiety disorder appropriately describes the psychopathology and points the way to treatment. As children grow older, however, there is a progression from such "involuntary" symptoms as separation anxiety, phobic avoidance, and the somatic disguise to willful "refusal" (Hsia 1984). What was a simple fear response in a young child appears to become a more complex disorder involving the whole family in the older child or adolescent. Straightforward fear reduction approaches (either through medication or behavioral techniques) may be useful in the acute presentation of the disorder, but the older child and adolescent may require a different approach, including a family systems model as a basis for treatment.

TREATMENT OF SCHOOL REFUSAL

Since school refusal was first described, treatment methods have been of a broadly psychotherapeutic kind, reflecting the dominant influence of psychodynamic theory. Johnson and her colleagues (1941) emphasized mother-child relationships in treatment while paying attention to the child's individual problems. Estes et al. (1956) considered that treatment of the child alone was inadequate because the neurosis originated with the mother. Talbot (1957) proposed treatment plans involving child, parents, and school personnel, with the proviso that the older the child, the more direct the treatment of the child should be. Relieving pressure on school attendance was an initial step toward relieving tension in parents and school personnel and anxiety in the therapist. Talbot (1957) warned that these would reappear and prescribed gradual reintroduction into the feared situation in an effort to bring the conflict into the open. Other (Eysenck and Rachman 1965b) regarded this approach as akin to behavior therapy in terms of the familiar anxiety hierarchy used to treat separation anxiety in school situations. Most modern treatments combine elements of a behavioral approach to the problem of reintroduction to the school itself, together with work with the parents (Yule, Hersov, and Treseder 1980; Mansdorf and Lukens 1987).

Contrasting approaches concern the issue of timing the return to school and the amount of pressure that should be applied to ensure attendance. E. Klein (1945) was the first proponent of early return to school, using pressure up to the point of harshness to get the child back into the school building. Others have also put forward the advantages of early return (Talbot 1957; Eisenberg 1958; Berryman 1959; Glaser, 1959; Rodriguez et al. 1959; Kennedy 1965; Lassers et al. 1973) on the grounds that continuous and lengthy absence creates secondary problems due to missing schoolwork, losing friendships, having a secondary gain of being at home, and missing a healthy environment for emotional growth.

Learning theory and behavior therapy now have a definite place in the treatment of school refusal. Ross (1972b) described school phobia as a maladaptive avoidance response maintained by fear reduction that requires modification or elimination. There may be either fear of school or fear of leaving home. Only fear of school, strictly speaking, is a school phobia, whereas fear of leaving home is a symptom of separation anxiety disorder. The distinction is akin to that made by Eysenck and Rachman (1965a,b) on the grounds that the two situations require different treatment plans. They give more attention and weight to factors in the school situation history as possible sources of anxiety at school. They would focus on possible traumatic experiences in the school situation and would carry out a desensitization program, added to a program of graded reentry to school with little or no attention to contributing factors in the family system.

Ross (1972b) points out that the complex behavior shown in school refusal has components of both a respondent and an operant nature—though the avoidance response may originally serve a fear-reducing function, it is likely to be maintained by reinforcements available in the home to the child who is not going to school, and since there is usually a long history of such reinforcement, it becomes difficult to treat. Yates (1970) suggested a possible interaction between these two sorts of behavior based on the developmental and family factors that influence the growing child. Parents (mainly mothers) are strongly reinforcing stimuli in the preschool period, acting as a refuge for frightened and uncertain children. Separation experiences in children may be associated with increased fear and return to mother, which reduces fear. Mothers may also induce fear by their own undue anxiety about letting the child go. If intense fear at school develops, it will depend both on school experiences and parents' (mothers') reactions. The average child masters the anxiety and finds school rewarding because of success, among other things, in schoolwork, games, and peer relationships. The vulnerable child's school experiences are insufficiently rewarding to counteract any arousal of anxiety by such traumatic experiences as a critical or unsympathetic teacher. If the child has already developed a response of separation anxiety leading to overdependence on home as a refuge, this response will be evoked by any particularly stressful school situation, including change to senior school, so causing a predictable parental response. Yates (1970) has sought common ground between psychodynamic and learning theory explanations of school refusal. Clinical experiences support his ideas to some extent: many children with school refusal do have a history of separation difficulties in nursery school or kindergarten that precedes the later onset of frank school refusal, and their mothers, particularly if elderly, show an anxious, stereotypical way of dealing with these problems that tends to reinforce and perpetuate school avoidance. Treatment must take these interactions into account.

A fair number of case reports in the literature, usually single-case studies illustrating various behavioral approaches to school refusal (see Yule, Hersov, and Treseder 1980; Hersov 1985), show how early intervention, together with help from school authorities, given good parental cooperation and a defined treatment program, can produce good results if the criterion of success is simply return to school (Kennedy 1965). More complex types of school refusal require much more attention to parent-child interaction and family relationships in general (Mansdorf and Lukens 1985).

Until recently the only accounts of the use of medication to treat school refusal were anecdotal (Frommer 1967, 1972; Skynner 1974); there were few, if any, empirical controlled studies. Gittelman-Klein and Klein (1971, 1973, 1980) reported a study of forty-five children aged seven to sixteen who were randomly assigned to placebo or imipramine in a double-blind trial for six weeks to treat school phobia of at least two weeks' duration. A multidisciplinary team made "vigorous" efforts to return the children to regular school for two weeks without success before the children entered the study. The dose of imipramine was raised gradually from 25 mg/day to a maximum of 220 mg/day, and child and parent were seen weekly. A social worker based with the school supported the parents in a combination of treatments, including persuasive desensitization methods coupled with the active drug or placebo. After six weeks of treatment 70 percent of those on imipramine were back at school, compared with 44 percent of placebo-treated children, a significant difference, although two-fifths of those on continuing psychosocial treatment alone also returned. Significantly more children on the active medication reported feeling better than did those on placebo, many of whom continued to feel uncomfortable. Those on imipramine were free of secondary somatic symptoms to a much greater extent. It was suggested that imipramine lowers the child's level of separation anxiety, thus easing return to the classroom, but that strong anticipatory anxiety may also inhibit attempts to return.

A later study by Berney et al. (1981) involved a double-blind therapeutic trial using clomipramine and placebo with psychotherapy for six weeks on forty-six patients aged nine to fourteen with school phobia. It showed that clomipramine in doses from 40 mg/day in the youngest to 75 mg/day in fourteen-year-olds neither reduced separation anxiety or other neurotic symptoms nor had a specific effect on depression. The medication appeared to add little to the effects of psychotherapy, and Berney et al. remarked on the persistence of emotional symptoms even after return to school, in line with earlier findings (Hersov 1960a,b; Waldron 1976; Berg and Fielding 1978).

Further studies are needed to resolve these conflicting findings. In the first instance the drugs used, though both tricyclics, were not identical, though similar effects could reasonably be expected. Perhaps if Berney et al. (1981) had used higher doses, a drug response might have been achieved. As it was, they followed the manufacturer's recommendations but did not obtain blood levels. In both studies concurrent treatment was not described in detail and assessment of change was by therapists' rather than independent assessors' impressions.

On the basis of such rather slim data one can conclude tentatively that antidepressant medication may complement the effects of other psychotherapeutic, social, and educational measures in treating school refusal when there are specific indications for use in obvious separation anxiety disorder or depressive disorder. Drugs alone are unlikely to have much effect on entrenched emotional and family problems.

There is a place for residential treatment, usually in a hospital inpatient unit (Warren 1948; Weiss and Cain 1964; Barker 1968; Berg 1978;

Hersov 1974, 1980, 1985). It is indicated when the child's symptoms and behavior are of such severity and extent that other forms of outpatient treatment achieve no response. This is especially the case where the family interaction and environmental factors are so pathological that they support and maintain the child's disorder and so block effective treatment. The maintenance of the child's disorder is sometimes an important aspect of family interaction and the affected child's presence at home may be necessary for family homeostasis. Admittance to a hospital may be the only way to shift the balance in the family and to ensure regular treatment. Inpatient treatment has the benefits of a therapeutic milieu with the opportunity to master separation anxiety (Fleck 1972), learn social skills, and settle into an appropriate school routine.

The experience of hospital admittance can sometimes affect child and family profoundly, activating several dynamic mechanisms at once. The separation of child and family focuses attention on and evokes an affective response to existing pathological attachments. Hospital admittance brings into the open the painful fact that the family has failed to foster the *normal process* of separation as an aspect of healthy emotional and social development. It is also a form of exposure to the feared and avoided situation—namely separation—not unlike the exposure to feared situations that forms part of treatment in circumscribed phobic disorders. Once in the hospital, usually attending school on the premises, the child, with the family, can gain some understanding of the mechanisms and family pathology that maintained the deviant behavior and can adapt better coping strategies. When the time comes, the child can begin to attend an outside school, returning to the secure base of the hospital until he or she is able to return home and continue school attendance normally. In general, patients admitted to a hospital tend to be older, with symptoms of longer duration, greater severity, and resistance to outpatient treatment.

The Association of Separation Anxiety with Other Disorders

In 1964, Klein noted a high prevalence of apparent separation anxiety evidenced as school refusal or inability to attend summer camp in 50 percent of adult inpatients being treated for agoraphobia. More recently, a study of women with panic disorder and agoraphobia showed them to have a significantly higher rate of early separation anxiety than women with simple phobic disorders, but this connection was not seen in male patients (Gittelman-Klein and Klein 1984).

DSM III R (American Psychiatric Association 1987) states that separation anxiety disorder apparently predisposes the subject to develop panic disorder with or without agoraphobia. Retrospective studies of adult patients with agoraphobia conducted in Great Britain (Berg et al. 1974; Tyrer and Tyrer 1974) do not consistently support a specific association between recalled separation anxiety in childhood and adult agoraphobia. Separation anxiety is seen rather as a precursor of neurotic or anxiety disorder in general, as well as of some depressive disorders.

Using a questionnaire about experiences in childhood indicating separation anxiety, Thyer and colleagues (1985) found recently that agoraphobics did not report significantly greater separation trauma than simple phobics. Indeed, agoraphobics spent less time at nursery school and summer camp and reported less fear during overnight visits with friends. Overall, both groups scored in the low range, suggesting that separation trauma was not especially important in either diagnostic category.

Genetic-Familial Studies

Also attracting increased interest is the area of genetic-familial studies, which examines the connections between anxiety and depressive disorders in parents and disorders in children. Earlier family history studies in adults with anxiety neurosis showed an increased rate of anxiety states among first-degree relatives of patients with diagnosed anxiety states. Relatives of probands with agoraphobia have an increased risk for agoraphobia. School phobia occurs more often in the children of agoraphobic mothers, and it has recently been shown that panic disorders in parents conferred more than a threefold risk of separation anxiety in their children (Weissman et al. 1984). Most recently, in a careful comparison study of children of patients diagnosed with anxiety disorder, compared with children of patients diagnosed with dysthymic disorder, children of normal parents, and normal children (Tanner et al. 1987), several important associations were found. Children of anxiety disorder patients were more anxious and fearful, reported more school difficulties, more worries about family members and themselves, and more somatic complaints, and were more solitary than normal children. They were also seven times more likely to meet criteria for anxiety disorder than were the two normal groups. The authors maintain an open mind as to whether the data demonstrate biological factors in the transmission of anxiety disorder or whether the children's reactions are understandable in terms of their life circumstances.

OUTCOME

The outcome of treatment of school refusal is generally good, whatever form of treatment or combination of treatments is used, although so far only two studies using control groups and medication versus placebo designs have been published. Among the descriptive studies, Kennedy's (1965) 100 percent success rate is unusual, but in most treatment series the success rate of return to school is about two-thirds or more (Davidson 1960; Hersov 1960a,b; Coolidge et al. 1964). The outcome seems related, however, to severity of the disorder, age of the child, and time between onset of symptoms and beginning of treatment. Rodriguez et al. (1959) found a poor prognosis in children over age eleven—a 36 percent success rate as against an 89 percent success rate in children under age eleven. The findings tend to support the notion that more serious pathology is found in older children and adolescents and their families (Coolidge et al. 1960).

Weiss and Cain (1964), reporting on the outcome of residential treatment, found that fourteen of sixteen students were attending school after nine months' treatment, while two were still hospitalized. Weiss and Burke (1967) reported a good outcome for school and work in all but one of fourteen patients followed for five to ten years. Half the group still had difficulty in personal and social relationships, however, and several remained unable to sever ties with their families. Berg (1970), reporting on twenty-seven school phobic adolescents treated in the hospital, found on follow-up that 59 percent were attending school satisfactorily, while the remainder were undoubted failures. Of those attending school, one-third were still poorly adapted to home and to social circumstances other than school and home. In a later study, Berg et al. (1976), looking at changes other than school attendance, found that one-third had persisting severe emotional disturbance and social impairment, one-third had improved considerably although they still suffered from emotional disturbance, and the remaining third were almost completely free of problems. In about half, school attendance problems had persisted but later work problems were less frequent. High intelligence appeared to be associated with poor outcome. In a comparison of treatment, Berg and Fielding (1978) randomly allocated two groups of hospital patients to three months' treatment and 6 months' treatment, following up both groups at six months, one year, and two years after discharge. Persistence of emotional disorders into adult life was again found (see Waldron 1976), and length of hospital stay made no difference to outcome in boys, although a longer stay was marginally more effective in girls.

The outcome in adulthood of earlier school refusal is interesting in light of the increasing number of studies linking disorders in childhood and adolescence with their sequel in adulthood. An early study by Nursten (1963) followed sixteen girls into late adolescence and early adulthood. Four required further treatment for absence from school or college, but the rest were attending school or college or holding down jobs, and three were married. Most were able to draw away from their families, but social contacts remained limited and those married were very dependent on their husbands. Overall, they had generally done well. Coote (1982), in a pilot study toward long-term follow-up, using standardized measures of psychiatric disorder, social maladjustment, personality questionnaires, and a fear survey schedule, found that most subjects had difficulties in early adulthood but became more stable in middle life, though one-third showed evidence of current "neurotic" problems. Agoraphobia occurred in a few subjects as part of a more general neurotic tendency.

Warren (1965), in a follow-up study of adolescent inpatients, described sixteen youngsters with school refusal. Of these, four were found later to be handicapped by phobic states, three lived limited lives because of minor phobic difficulties, three had other neurotic problems, and six were quite well. Others have described typical school refusal or phobic problems in an older college population, sometimes with an earlier history of school refusal (Hodgman and Braiman 1965) or cases of work phobia, mainly in males, most of whom had shown in early life a significant reluctance to go to school or overt school phobia (Pittman et al. 1968). Berg et al. (1976), in their follow-up of one hundred adolescent patients, found five agoraphobics, two patients with severe depressive illness, two with severe schizoid personality traits, one schizophrenic, and one severe obsessional disorder in the one-third of their follow-up patients rated as most severely ill.

Tyrer and Tyrer (1974) studied the prevalence of school refusal in 240 adult psychiatric patients and 120 controls matched for age and sex. School refusal, particularly in adolescence, occurred significantly more often among psychiatric patients, and the authors concluded that some children who exhibit school refusal are at risk for psychiatric disorder in adult life but that most will become normal adults. Berg et al. (1974) looked at the prevalence of past school phobia in an adult population of female agoraphobic patients compared with controls. Past school phobia predicted an earlier onset of agoraphobia, but it was concluded that school phobia leads to agoraphobia in only a small proportion of cases and that both conditions reflect a lasting tendency to emotional disorder. It was also found that school refusal occurred in the children of agoraphobic mothers to a greater extent than expected.

More recently, Berg and Jackson (1985) obtained clinical and questionnaire follow-up data on 143 school refusers who were now in their early twenties. It was found that 31 percent had been treated for a psychiatric illness and that one in twenty had received inpatient hospital treatment, while 30 percent scored high on measures of minor psychiatric disorder, which is substantially higher than would be expected in a general population group. The former school refusers had a high prevalence of symptoms of minor psychiatric illness and severe social impairment. Yet this rather pessimistic finding, that school refusal in early adolescence requiring inpatient treatment leads to later increased risk of psychiatric disorders, is counterbalanced by the finding that half the sample studied were not affected by severe problems in later life. Those who made a good improvement when assessed shortly after discharge from the hospital, who were intelligent, and who required treatment before age fourteen had a particularly favorable outcome.

Flakierska, Lindstrom, and Gillberg (1988) report on a twelve to fifteen-year follow-up of a preadolescent group of school refusers compared with a group matched for age, sex, and dwelling area of whom only 14 percent had been in contact with psychiatric services. The outcome was generally good, but the school refusal cases had applied for psychiatric outpatient help in adulthood significantly more often than had the comparison group. Thirty-one percent had done so, and the common diagnosis then was neurotic depression or separation anxiety disorder.

School refusal is a complex syndrome rather than a clinical entity, and in practice a diverse blend is found of intrapsychic factors in the child or adolescent, family relationships and influences, developmental factors, and intrinsic school factors. School refusal appears to be on the increase in some countries.

Recent systems of classification have relegated school refusal to the status of a symptom among other symptoms in the manifestation of separation anxiety disorder. This disorder is found in younger children as the predominant diagnosis along with other diagnoses, whereas in older children and adolescents the school refusal is often a manifestation of a phobic disorder.

The complexity of presentation and psychopathology means that current treatment practice may have to include a variety of treatments.

Finally, genetic-familial studies have documented the presence of affective and depressive disorders in first-degree relatives of children with school refusal and anxiety disorders. Outcome and follow-up studies have shown interesting links between school refusal and disorders in adulthood.

REFERENCES

Aldridge-Smith, J. (1974) Personality in School Non-Attenders. M.Sc. thesis, University of Glasgow.

American Psychiatric Association. (1980) *Diagnostic and Statistical Manual of Mental Disorders (DSM III)*. Washington, D.C., American Psychiatric Association.

———. (1987) *Diagnostic and Statistical Manual of Mental Disorders*, 3d ed., rev. (DSM III R) Washington, D.C., American Psychiatric Association.

Berg, I. (1976) School phobia in the children of agoraphobic women. *British Journal of Psychiatry* 128:86–89.

Berg, I., Nichols, K., and Pritchard, C. (1969) School phobia: Its classification and relation to dependency. *Journal of Child Psychology and Psychiatry* 10:123–141.

Berg, I., Butler, A., and McGure, R. (1972) Birth order and family size of school phobic adolescents. *British Journal of Psychiatry* 121:509–514.

Berg, I., Butler, A., and Pritchard, J. (1974) Psychiatric illness in the mothers of school-phobic adolescents. *British Journal of Psychiatry* 125:466–467.

Berg, I., Marks, J., McGuire, R., and Lipsedge, M. (1974) School phobia and agoraphobia. *Psychological Medicine* 4:428–434.

Berg, I., Collins, R., McGuire, R., and O'Melia, J. (1975) Educational attainment in adolescent school phobia. *Psychological Medicine* 4:428–434.

Berg, I., Butler, A., and Hall, G. (1976) The outcome of adolescent school phobia. *British Journal of Psychiatry* 128:80–85.

Berg, I., Butler, A., Hullin, R., Smith, R., and Tyrer, S. (1978) Features of children taken to Juvenile Court for failure to attend school. *Psychological Medicine* 8:447–453.

Berg, I., and Fielding, D. (1978) An evaluation of hospital inpatient treatment in adolescent school phobia. *British Journal of Psychiatry* 132:500–505.

Berg, I., Casswell, G., Goodwin, A., Hullin, R., McGuire, R., and Tagg, G. (1985). Classification of severe school attendance problems. *Psychological Medicine* 15:157–165.

Berg, I., and Jackson, A. (1985) Teenage school refusers grow up: A follow-up study of 168 subjects, ten years on average after inpatient treatment. *British Journal of Psychiatry* 147:366–370.

Berney, T., Kolvin, I., Bhate, S., Garside, F., Jeans, B., Kay, B., and Scarth, L. (1981) School phobia: A therapeutic trial with clomipramine and short-term outcome. *British Journal of Psychiatry* 138:110–118.

Bernstein, G. A., and Garfinkel, B. D. (1986) School phobia: The overlap of affective and anxiety disorder. *Journal of the American Academy of Child Psychiatry* 25:235–241.

———. (1988) Pedigrees, functioning, and psychopathology in families of school phobic children. *American Journal of Psychiatry* 145:70–74.

Berryman, E. (1959) School phobia: Management problems in private practice. *Psychological Reports* 5:19–25.

Blagg, N. R. (1979) The Behavioral Treatment of School Refusal. Ph.D. thesis, University of London.

Blyth, D. A., and Simmons, R. G., (1983) The adjustment of early adolescents to school transitions. *Journal of Early Adolescence* 3:105–120.

Bowlby, J. (1973) *Attachment and Loss,* vol. 2: *Separation Anxiety and Anger.* London, Hogarth Press.

Broadwin, I. T. (1932) A contribution to the study of truancy. *American Journal of Orthopsychiatry* 2:253–254.

Chazan, M. (1962) School phobia. *British Journal of Educational Psychology* 32:209–217.

Coolidge, J. C., Hahn, P. B., and Peck, A. L. (1957) School phobia: Neurotic crisis or way of life. *American Journal of Orthopsychiatry* 27:296–306.

Coolidge, J. C., Miller, M. L., Tessman, E., and Waldfogel, S. (1960) School phobia in adolescence: A manifestation of severe character disturbance. *American Journal of Orthopsychiatry* 30:599–607.

Coolidge, J. C., Brodie, R. D., and Feeney, B. (1964) A ten-year follow-up of sixty-six school-phobic children. *American Journal of Orthopsychiatry* 34:675–684.

Cooper, M. G. (1960) School refusal. *Educational Research* 8:115–127; 223–229.

Cooper, M. (1984) Self-identity in adolescent school refusers and truants. *Educational Review* 36:229–237.

Coote, M. A. (1982) School refusal: A pilot study towards long-term follow-up. M.Phil. diss., University of London.

Davidson, S. (1960) School phobia as a manifestation of family disturbance: Its structure and treatment. *Journal of Child Psychology and Psychiatry* 1:270–287.

Debiesse, J. (1951) *Compulsory Education in France.* Paris, UNESCO.

Eisenberg, L. (1957) School phobia: A study in the communication of anxiety. *American Journal of Orthopsychiatry* 114:712–718.

————. (1958) School Phobia: Diagnosis, genesis, and clinical management. *Paediatric Clinics of North America* 5:645–660.

Estes, H. R., Haylett, C., and Johnson, A. (1956) Separation anxiety. *American Journal of Psychotherapy* 10:682–695.

Eysenck, H. J., and Eysenck, S. (1975) *Manual of the Eysenck Personality Questionnaire*. London, Hodder and Stoughton.

Eysenck, H. J., and Rachman, S. (1965) *The Causes and Cure of Neurosis*. London, Routledge and Kegan Paul.

————. (1965b) The application of learning theory to child psychiatry. In Howells, J. E., ed., *Modern Perspectives in Child Psychiatry*. Edinburgh, Oliver and Boyd.

Farrington, D. (1980) Truancy, delinquency, the home, and the school. In Hersov, L., and Berg, I., eds., *Out of School: Modern Perspectives in School Refusal and Truancy,* pp. 49–64. Chichester, Wiley.

Flakierska, N., Lindstrom, M., and Gillberg, C. (1988) School refusal: A 15–20-year followup study of 36 Swedish urban children. *British Journal of Psychiatry* 52:834–837.

Fogelman, K., and Richardson, K. (1974) School attendance: Some findings from the National Child Development Study. In Turner, B., ed., *Truancy*. London, Ward Lock.

Fogelman, K., Tibbenham, A., and Lambert, L. (1980) Absence from school: Findings from the National Child Development Study. In Hersov, L., and Berg, I., eds., *Out of School: Modern Perspectives in School Refusal and Truancy,* pp. 25–48. Chichester, Wiley.

Frommer, E. (1967) Treatment of childhood depression with anti-depressant drugs. *British Medical Journal* 1:729–732.

————. (1972) *Diagnosis and Treatment in Clinical Child Psychiatry*. London, Heinemann.

Gittelman-Klein, R., and Klein, D. F. (1971) Controlled imipramine treatment of school phobia. *Archives of General Psychiatry* 25:204–207.

————. (1973) School phobia: Diagnostic considerations in the light of imipramine effects. *Journal of Nervous and Mental Disease* 156:199–215.

————. (1980) Separation anxiety in school refusal and its treatment with drugs. In Hersov, L., and Berg, I., eds., *Out of School: Modern Perspectives in School Refusal and Truancy,* pp. 321–341. Chichester, Wiley.

————. (1984) Relationship between separation anxiety and panic and agoraphobic disorders. *Psychopathology* 17, suppl. 1:56–65.

Glaser, K. (1959) Problems in school attendance: School phobia and related conditions. *Paediatrics* 23:371–383.

Goldberg, T. B. (1953) Factors in the development of school phobia. *Smith College Studies in Social Work* 23:227–248.

Hansard. (1974) Parliamentary Debates. *House of Commons Official Report,* 5th ser., vol. 877. London, HMSO.

Heath, A. (1983) The self-concepts of school refusers. Ph.D. thesis, University of London.

Hersov, L. A. (1960a) Persistent non-attendance at school. *Journal of Child Psychology and Psychiatry* 1:130–136.

———. (1960b) Refusal to go to school. *Journal of Child Psychology and Psychiatry* 1:137–145.

———. (1974) Neurotic disorders with special reference to school refusal. In Barker, P., ed., *The Residential Psychiatric Treatment of Children,* pp. 105–141. London, Crosby Lockwood Staples.

———. (1980) Hospital inpatient and day-patient treatment of school refusal. In Hersov, L., and Berg, I., eds., *Out of School: Modern Perspectives in School Refusal and Truancy,* pp. 303–320. Chichester, Wiley.

———. (1985) School refusal. In Rutter, M., and Hersov, L., eds., *Child and Adolescent Psychiatry: Modern Approaches,* 2d ed., pp. 382–399. Oxford, Blackwell.

Hishiyama, Y., and Furukawa, H. (1982) A statistical study of the refusal to attend school: Social factors and the change in the incidence rate in Japan. *Japanese Journal of Child and Adolescent Psychiatry* 23:223–234.

Hodgman, C. H., and Braiman, A. (1965) "College phobia": School refusal in university students. *American Journal of Psychiatry* 12:801–805.

Honjo, S., Kaneko, T., Nawa, M., Takei, Y., Inoko, K., Wakabayashi, S., Sugiyama, T., Ohtaka, K., Aoyama, T., and Abe, T. (1987) The actual conditions of patients who refuse to go to school: Change from 1972–74 to 1982–84. *Japanese Journal of Child and Adolescent Psychiatry* 28:183–191.

Honjo, S., and Wakabayashi, S. (1988) Family violence in Japan: A compilation of data from the Department of Psychiatry, Nagoya University Hospital. *Japanese Journal of Psychiatry and Neurology* 42:5–10.

Hsia, H. (1984) Structural and strategic approach to school phobia/school refusal. *Psychology in the Schools* 21:360–367.

Johnson, A. M., Falstein, E. I., Szurek, S. A., and Svendsen, M. (1941) School phobia. *American Journal of Orthopsychiatry* 11:707–711.

Jung, C. G. (1913) A case of neurosis in a child. In *The Collected Works of C. G. Jung,* vol. 4. New York: Basic Books, 1961.

Kahn, J. H., and Nursten, J. P. (1962) School refusal: A comprehensive view of school phobia and other failures of school attendance. *American Journal of Orthopsychiatry* 32:707–718.

Kennedy, W. A. (1965) School Phobia: Rapid treatment of fifty cases. *Journal of Abnormal Psychology* 70:285–289.

Klein, E. (1945) The reluctance to go to school. *The Psychoanalytic Study of the Child* 1:263–279.

Klein, M. (1923) The role of the school in the libidinal development of the child. *International Zeitschrift für Psychoanalyse* 9:312.

Klein, D. F. (1964) Delineation of two drug-responsive anxiety syndromes. *Psychopharmacologia* 5:397–408.

Kolvin, I., Berney, T. P., and Bhate, S. R., (1984) Classification and diagnosis of depression in school phobia. *British Journal of Psychiatry* 145:347–357.

Lassers, E., Nordan, R., and Bladholm, S. (1973) Steps in the return to school of children with school phobia. *American Journal of Psychiatry* 130:265–268.

Last, C. G., Francis, G., Hersen, M., Kazdin, A E., and Strauss, C. C., (1987) Separation anxiety and school phobia: A comparison using DSM III criteria. *American Journal of Psychiatry* 144:653–657.

Lester-Smith, W. O. (1951) *Compulsory Education in England*. Paris, UNESCO.

Leventhal, T., and Sills, M. (1964) Self-image in school phobia. *American Journal of Orthopsychiatry* 37:64–70.

Leventhal, T., Weinberger, G., Stander, R. J., and Stearns, R. P. (1967) Therapeutic strategies in school phobics. *American Journal of Orthopsychiatry* 37:64–70.

Lock, M. (1986) Pleas for acceptance: School refusal syndrome in Japan. *Social Sciences and Medicine* 23:99–112.

———. (1987) A nation at risk: Interpretations of school refusal in Japan. In Lock, M., and Gordon, D., eds., *Biomedicine Examined*. Dordrecht, D. Reidel.

Malmquist, C. P. (1965) School phobia: A problem in family neurosis. *American Journal of Orthopsychiatry* 4:293–319.

Mansdorf, I. J., and Lukens, E. (1985) Cognitive-behavioral psychotherapy for separation anxious children exhibiting school phobia. *Journal of the American Academy of Child and Adolescent Psychiatry* 26:222–225.

Millar, T. P. (1961) The child who refuses to attend school. *American Journal of Orthopsychiatry* 48:398–404.

Nichols, K. A., and Berg, I. (1970) School phobia and self-evaluation. *British Journal of Psychiatry* 11:133–141.

Nursten, J. P. (1963) School phobia: Projection in the later adjustment of school phobic children. *Smith College Studies in Social Work* 32:210–224.

Pittman, F. S., Donald, L. G., and DeYoung, C. D. (1968) Work and school phobia: A family approach to treatment. *American Journal of Psychiatry* 124:1535–1541.

Radin, S. S. (1967) Psychodynamic aspects of school phobia. *Comprehensive Psychiatry* 8:119–128.

Reger, R. (1962) School phobia in an obese girl. *Journal of Clinical Psychology* 18:350–357.

Reynolds, D., Jones, D., Stieger, S., and Murgatroyd, S. (1980) School Factors in Truancy. In Hersov, L., and Berg, I., eds., *Out of School: Modern Perspectives in School Refusal and Truancy*, pp. 85–110. Chichester, Wiley.

Rodriguez, A., Rodriguez, M., and Eisenberg, L. (1959) The outcome of school phobia: A follow-up study based on forty-one cases. *American Journal of Psychiatry* 116:540–544.

Ross, A. O. (1972a) Behavior therapy. In Quay, H. C., and Werry, J. S., eds., *Psychopathological Disorders of Childhood*, pp. 273–315. New York, Wiley.

———. (1972b) Behavior Therapy. In Wolman, B. B., ed., *Manual of Child Psychopathology* New York, McGraw-Hill.

Rutter, M., Tizard, J., and Whitmore, K. (1970) *Education, Health, and Behavior.* London, Longman (reprinted Huntington, N.Y., Krieger, 1981).

Rutter, M., Shaffer, D., and Sturge, C. (1975) *A Multiaxial Classification of Child Psychiatric Disorders.* Geneva, WHO.

Rutter, M., Graham, P., Chadwick, O., and Yule, W. (1976) Adolescent turmoil: Fact or fiction? *Journal of Child Psychology and Psychiatry* 17:35–36.

Schmitt, B. D. (1971) School phobia, the great imitator: A paediatrician's viewpoint. *Paediatrics* 48:433–441.

Skynner, R. (1974) School phobia: A reappraisal. *British Journal of Medical Psychology* 47:1–16.

Smith, S. L. (1970) School refusal with anxiety: A review of sixty-three cases. *Canadian Psychiatric Association Journal* 15:257–264.

Sommer, B. (1985) Truancy in early adolescence. *Journal of Early Adolescence* 5:145–160.

Sperling, M. (1961) Analytic first aid in school phobias. *Psychoanalytic Quarterly* 30:504–518.

———. (1967) School phobias: Classification, dynamics, and treatment. *Psychoanalytic Study of the Child* 22:375–401.

Suttenfield, Y. (1954) School phobia: A study of five cases. *American Journal of Orthopsychiatry* 24:368–380.

Talbot, M. (1957) Panic in school phobia. *American Journal of Orthopsychiatry* 27:286–295.

Tennent, T. G. (1969) School nonattendance and delinquency. M.D. thesis, Oxford University.

Thyer, B. A., Nesse, R. M., Cameron, O. G., and Curtis, G. C. (1985) Agoraphobia: A test of the separation anxiety hypothesis. *Behavior Research and Therapy* 23:75–78.

Torma, S., and Halsti, A. (1975a) Factors contributing to school refusal and truancy. *Psychiatria Fennica* 75:209–216.

———. (1975b) Outcome in truancy and school refusal. *Psychiatria Fennica* 76:121–133.

Turner, S. M., Beidel, D. C., and Costello, A. (1987) Psychopathology in the offspring of anxiety disorder patients. *Journal of Consulting and Clinical Psychology* 55:229–235.

Tyerman, M. J. (1968) *Truancy.* London, University of London Press.

————. (1974) Who are the truants? In Turner, B., ed., *Truancy*. London, Ward Lock.

Van Houten, J. (1948) Mother-child relationship in twelve cases of school phobia. *Smith College Studies in Social Work* 18:101–180.

Waldron, S. (1976) The significance of childhood neurosis for adult mental health. *American Journal of Psychiatry* 133:532–538.

Waldron, S., Shrier, D., Stone, B., and Tobin, F. (1975) School phobia and other childhood neuroses: A systematic study of the children and their families. *American Journal of Psychiatry* 132:802–808.

Waldfogel, S., Coolidge, J. C., and Hahn, P. B. (1957) The development, meaning, and management of school phobia. *American Journal of Orthopsychiatry* 27:754–776.

Waller, D., and Eisenberg, L. (1980) School refusal in childhood: A psychiatric-paediatric perspective. In Hersov, L., and Berg, I., eds., *Out of School: Modern Perspectives in School Refusal and Truancy*, pp. 209–249. Chichester, Wiley.

Warren, W. (1948) Acute neurotic breakdown in children with refusal to go to school. *Archives of Diseases in Childhood* 23:266–272.

————. (1965) A study of adolescent psychiatric inpatients and the outcome six or more years later. (II) The follow-up study. *Journal of Child Psychology and Psychiatry* 6:1–17.

Weiss, M., and Burke, G. B. (1967) A five- to ten-year follow-up of hospitalized school phobic children and adolescents. *American Journal of Orthopsychiatry* 37:294–295.

Weiss, M., and Cain, B. (1964) The residential treatment of children and adolescents with school phobia. *American Journal of Orthopsychiatry* 34:103–114.

Weissman, M. M., Leckman, J. F., Merikangas, K. R., Gammon, E. D., and Prusoff, B. A. (1984) Depression and anxiety disorders in parents and children. *Archives of General Psychiatry* 41:845–852.

Weitzman, M., Klerman, L., Lamb, G., Menary, J., and Alpert, J. (1982) School absence: A problem for the paediatrician. *Pediatrics* 69:739–746.

Yates, A. J. (1970) *Behavior Therapy*. Chichester, Wiley.

Yule, W., Hersov, L., and Treseder, J. (1980) Behavioral treatments in school refusal. In Hersov, L., and Berg, I., eds., *Out of School: Modern Perspectives in School Refusal and Truancy*, pp. 261–301. Chichester, Wiley.

II

School Refusal:
A Japanese Analysis

3

Education in Japan: The Issues at Stake at the Dawn of the Twenty-first Century

TERUHISA HORIO

JEAN-FRANCOIS SABOURET

SUMMARY

In Japan, 92 percent of students of school-leaving age obtain a high school diploma. More than half of these continue their studies for at least two years after high school, until age twenty, and it is estimated that virtually all Japanese will be doing so by the early twenty-first century.

Of the universities that offer four-year degree programs, three out of four are private, as are eight in ten of those that offer two-year degrees. Professional higher education, which is entirely private, has experienced rapid growth. In Japan, education is a market in which students are consumers obliged to pay increasingly exorbitant prices for this "service." Their frustration is intensified by the fact that the substance of the knowledge required and the method of assessing it (HENSACHI) favor those who can pay for the indispensable supplementary classes given in the cram-schools known as the *juku* and *yobiko,* which provide special preparation for the competitive examinations. Education in Japan is therefore subject to fee-paying twice over: both school and the parallel academic institutions (juku and yobiko). Although this educational system is often admired from abroad, it is the source of agitation within Japan. The right wing currently in power wishes to transform the educational system imposed by the Americans in 1947 into one where there would be on one hand a particular education reserved for the elite and for future national leaders and on the other school curricula and a school spirit that evoke sinister memories in those who underwent the militaristic education of pre–1945 greater Japan. The issues go well beyond the school context and indicate clearly political and economic trends in Japan. Many Japanese are intensely and actively involved in opposing the educational reforms concocted by the right wing and by profiteers in the education industry.

Education in Japan can be viewed in much the same way as the proverbial glass containing half the possible amount of water. A pessimist would say it is half empty and an optimist that it is half full. Likewise, one can begin to examine Japanese schools from the negative angles already given such widespread attention in other countries: teenage suicide, school violence, bullying, the torment of preparing for competitive examinations, the exorbitant cost of high school and university education, and the intense commercialization of education with the development of the now-famous parallel schools, the juku and the yobiko.

Yet one could also blow government trumpets to the tune of the Triumphal March accompanying the announcement of record numbers of high school students leaving with a diploma under their arm: 92 percent. Who can do better than that? More yet: the trend toward continuing education after age eighteen is stronger every year, and specialists estimate that by the year 2000 almost an entire age group will be engaged in some field of study until they are at least twenty. For the same timeframe France, beset with unending problems of teacher recruitment, teacher salaries, and inadequate educational infrastructures, promises a similar age group an 80 percent success rate in the baccalaureate. By the year 2000 the same 80 percent success rate in France will have been achieved in Japan thirty-two years earlier (1968). French teachers are not obliged to remain in their place of work outside their actual teaching hours, whereas in Japan, teachers, like all civil servants, must be present in their schools for at least forty hours whether or not they are teaching a class.

There is substance for dreams here for many a minister of education. Japan once adopted a slogan taken from Fukuzawa Yukishi (1834–1901), an educator and one of the greatest intellectuals of the time of Japanese enlightenment, who urged the country to "catch up and overtake the West." Japan has not only caught up but in many areas has already overtaken the West. It would be difficult to account for this without the excellence of the educational systems installed in Japan after the Meiji restoration in 1868. No country can achieve economic or scientific success or social advancement for its people without an educational system adapted to its needs at every stage in its history.

How then to present an accurate and objective description of Japanese education, which some people highly prize and others bitterly condemn? What can one say about an educational system that is denounced as an aberration or lauded as a paragon of virtue according to the requirements of discussion? Arguments, facts, and figures are hurled back and forth as though education were a question of political programs in an electoral debate. The heart of the matter is that behind the facts and statistics lies an entire concept of human beings. This is where one must look in any attempt to grasp what the authorities on the one hand and educators on the other understand by and expect from education.

An educational system is a machine designed to produce people: Should it be run for the greater benefit of the state and to serve the objectives of those in power, or should it be used to encourage the development of the personality and talents of each child with the greatest respect for individual rights and personal outcome?

The present educational system in Japan goes back to the years around 1947, when the American occupying army and the Supreme Commander for the Allied Powers were working on a new democratic face for a drained, exhausted Japan. Educational missions from the United States hoped in this way to banish harm permanently from the minds of new generations. This harm had arisen from the education given in Japan's militaristic period, which involved blind obedience to orders from superiors and the gift of self to the sacred person of the emperor-god Hirohito, who acceded to the throne in 1926. All Japan's textbooks on ethics and the Japanese language, including those written just before and during the war, are filled with rhetoric about sacrifice and this code of ethics.

The Imperial Rescript on Education (*kyoiku chokugo*) of 30 October 1890 was recited to all children in primary and secondary schools every day. This document taught that the emperor was the father of the nation, the being to whom every Japanese owed allegiance and total sacrifice when necessary. World War II showed the world to what extremes this ideology of self-giving and blind obedience could be pursued. The rescript was so thoroughly inculcated in all that anyone who attended primary school before Japan's defeat can recite it to this day. Most of the present conservative leaders bear the stamp of this training, and these are the people who today not only have the ideas but, if they belong to the Liberal Democratic party (LDP), also wield power. It is thus justifiable to ask if in some way their nostalgia for the old system of education might not mean that their purpose in reforming education is purely to restore the traditional morality, drummed into generations, that brought disaster to Japan and all of Southeast Asia.

The kyoiku chokugo is not merely of historical value but still operant today. Because it is a source of guidance in the thinking of many politicians and members of educational reform commissions around the prime minister, it seems important to state it here:

> Our Imperial Ancestors have founded Our Empire on a basis broad and everlasting, and have deeply and firmly implanted virtue; Our subjects ever united in loyalty and filial piety have from generation to generation illustrated the beauty thereof. This is the glory of the fundamental character of Our Empire, and herein also lies the source of Our education. Ye, our subjects, be filial to your parents, affectionate to your brothers and sisters; as husbands and wives be harmonious, as friends true; bear yourselves in modesty and moderation; extend your benevolence to all; pursue learning and cultivate arts, and thereby develop intellectual faculties and perfect moral powers; furthermore, advance public good and promote common interests; always respect the Constitution and observe the laws; should emergency arise, offer yourselves courageously to the State; and thus guard and maintain the prosperity of Our Imperial Throne coeval with heaven and earth. So shall ye not only be Our good and faithful subjects, but render illustrious the best traditions of your forefathers.
>
> The Way here set forth is indeed the teaching bequeathed by Our Imperial Ancestors, to be observed alike by Their Descendants and the subjects, infallible for all ages and true in all places. It is Our wish to lay it to heart in all reverence, in common with you, Our subjects, that we may all attain to the same virtue. (Kikuchi 1909)

Japanese troops and officers came back to a country under the authority of the former enemy and found themselves having to learn American-style democracy. The more prominent political figures were imprisoned, some of them tried and even hanged. Of the twenty-five defendants sentenced at the International Military Tribunal for the Far East (a counterpart to Nuremberg) in Tokyo, seven were executed by hanging, including Gen. Tojo Hideki and former prime minister Koki Hirota. Other war criminals judged sufficiently guilty to be classed as Category A by the

Americans were imprisoned and awaiting trial. The Cold War disrupted American policy with regard to these prisoners, however.

It was no longer the time to act against past ideologies but to struggle against a new evil, the ideology gaining ground in the Far East. China fell into the hands of Mao Tse-Tung and the Communists in 1949 (Peking fell on 22 January 1949), and the Korean War began on 25 June 1950. In Japan itself there were powerful left-wing movements, and in exchange for collaboration against communism, the Americans freed a number of political prisoners. Some prospered and took part in the country's economic reconstruction. Kishi Nobusuke even became prime minister (February 1957–July 1960). Sasakawa Ryoichi and Kodama Yoshio, two former Category A war criminals with close links to far-right elements as well as to the Japanese underworld, played a vital role in reorganizing the country's political right wing and developing the Jiminto (LDP), the faction that has now been in power for more than forty years. Many former soldiers or officers, such as Nakasone Yasuhiro, who have neither forgotten nor repudiated any of their ferociously nationalistic ideals, were elected as deputies even before the American occupation ended.

A close look at what these influential rightists have said over the years, particularly with regard to education and its reform, gives some indication of their true intentions in setting up an educational reform commission, as Nakasone did. To gain an understanding of the "education" tactics of these politicians (all trained in the mold and memory of the Imperial Rescript), their strategies must be analyzed in the context of a political stance that goes well beyond education. These same politicians decided to allocate sums exceeding 1 percent of the global national budget to military expenditures and are agitating for reform of the constitution and the educational system. It is a coherent and premeditated overall policy—and the subject of this chapter.

HISTORICAL BACKGROUND

Apart from a brief period when the Socialist party held power, between May 1947 and March 1948, postwar Japan has been dominated by the right wing. The figures speak for themselves. In the legislative elections of 1986 the LDP won 304 of 512 seats. Alternation of power is a concept long since restricted to foreign democracies. In voting overwhelmingly for the LDP the Japanese seem to be saying "Why get rid of a winning team?" Japan is a rich and powerful country;

in 1968 its gross national product was the third largest in the world; today it ranks second. And the strength it is now acquiring even in the United States is beginning to worry many people.

This outstanding economic achievement, whose rationalization goes back to the high-growth period around 1965, however, has had a backlash in human terms. The change has not been confined to the workplace: family life, school, and the areas of traditional sociability have undergone profound upheaval and been sacrificed on the altar of triumphant economics. "Maximum efficiency, minimum personality" could be the key phrase in Japan from the high-growth era to the present. Human relationships have become glacial, and a completely calculating outlook is taken to demonstrate people's adjustment to the modern world.

The younger generations do take a skeptical view of the traditional values and modes of thought of militarist Japan, but social pressures, first at school and then in the workplace, prevent the genesis or development of new values. One would think that in the setting of such wealth, Japan's young people could take wing and do whatever they wanted. Appearances are deceptive: the socioeconomic pressures to which the individual is subjected make such freedom a mirage.

The changes of the high-growth period were deep-seated. Economic development required tremendous labor to be drawn off toward the towns. This was effected under an agricultural law that caused rural populations to decline sharply as people gravitated to urban areas. It also altered existing human relationships, which became atrophied and superficial. Agricultural mechanization continued as television invaded the countryside and the number of automobiles increase. All these elements have influenced children's education.

As early as 1963, a year before the Tokyo Olympics, the economic council recommended to the government that school and society should be restructured so that, on the basis of the principle of personal aptitudes, it would be possible to identify the 3-5 percent of elite individuals it was calculated that Japan desperately needed for the future. To this end, proposals were made regarding means of diversifying the educational system to give greater advantage to early talent. Such demands continue to pressure Japanese schools.

At that time, the Ministry of Education published a white paper on "education and growth." The word *growth* referred not to human spiritual or personal growth but to a vision of things in which people were nothing but a term in a far wider economic equation.

And so every child's school performance came to be measured on a scale that was to become the absolute reference: the famous HENSACHI, a kind of Binet scale of individual abilities leading to a speedy and unequivocal hierarchization of every child and the channeling of each one into an appropriate professional orientation.

Alongside the period of high economic growth there was a parallel boom in school populations. The rate of high school attendance suddenly shot up.

	1960	1970	1980	1985
High school	57.5%	82.1%	94.2%	94.1%
University	10.3%	23.6%	37.4%	37.6%

At this point obtaining a high school diploma became the prerequisite for secure and respectable employment. The 6 percent of students unable to get into high school found themselves viewed with great suspicion and burdened by an inescapable professional handicap.

For the 37 percent who went on to higher education—either two or four years at a university or at one of the elite professional training schools—the problem was not being able to show a diploma but to produce one from the right place. Four years of study at a modest private provincial university where the number of applicants roughly equals the number of places available or four years at Tokyo or Kyoto University do not lead to comparable careers. In this context, education has become a business proposition: parents literally invest in their children's education. Education salespeople offer to take children in hand to prepare and cram for the competitive exams.

The juku and yobiko industry flourishes throughout the country, and after each of these competitive exams, the best among these schools—the Sundai, the Yoyogi Semi, and the Kawai Juku—publish the lists of their students who are accepted at the good universities. The governors of these establishments, cronies of those in power, make sure that their opinions are felt, strongly criticize public schools, and quite simply propose taking the place of public schools.

The yobiko arose from the establishments that were formerly proposed for high school students who had failed university entrance examinations and for whom there was no other post–high school solution available. These establishments took in students repeating high school classes (*ronin*), and their image was originally somewhat negative.

To gain admission to the good universities, one must first get into the best public or private high schools. However, the same applies here as to the universities, and entrance is won only through competitive examination. With the rush on schools during the high-growth period, competition became cutthroat; the juku began at this point to help students prepare for the entrance examinations to the major high schools. Today it is virtually unthinkable to enter any of the reputable universities or high schools without previous study at a yobiko or a juku, regardless of whether one is an exemplary student or one of lesser capabilities. The parallel schools have become the mandatory detour on the road to success at the university and, by extension, professional success.

In contrast to French competitive examinations, Japanese examinations demand a tremendous effort of memory. The correct answers to the numerous questions must be selected from sets of five possible responses. These multiple-choice tests are called *marubatsu shiki,* the noughts and crosses system.

In the yobiko and juku students learn to memorize at a forced quick march, and mock examinations and practice runs are duly computerized and analyzed. Students and their families anxiously pace waiting rooms until they are given the verdict of the omniscient computers and their official prophets/priestesses. All of this is of course extremely expensive, and many parents start saving as soon as children are born to provide for future education costs. Even worse, high school and university costs have escalated in recent years, more drastically for private high schools and universities than for public education. This does not imply that the earlier period of compulsory education involves no outlay on the part of the parents.

THE SCHOOL CURRICULUM SOCIETY

Today, the ability to give accurate and rapid answers in tests is virtually the sole measure of a person's worth. This system leads to the hierarchization of the entire social structure and the terms of each individual's remuneration, as well as one's reputation among other people. The function of Japanese-style competitive examinations is to "label" individuals and slap on them a certificate guaranteeing a form of excellence that does not necessarily have anything to do with the quality of their thinking. A well-known anecdote indicates the thinking prevalent among the Japanese youth of today: during a course at Tokyo University, a student showed Professor Keber a list of names of philosophers from Plato to Heidegger via Descartes, Hume, and Hegel. Professor Keber was asked to name "the first" in order of importance on the list.

Before and during the war, loyalty was the primary virtue in the school system. After a brief interlude during the postwar period, when respect for the individual gained the upper hand, the predominant feature has been numerically measured competition among individuals carried out against a background of interlinked pyramidal social and educational structures. The conservative authorities have twice revised the school system imposed in 1947 by the American reforms commission, in 1963 and in 1971. The prevailing concern in these reforms has been the gradual subservience of education to economic imperatives. Does the educational reform commission set up in 1982 on the initiative of Nakasone follow the same trend as others before it?

THE PROVISIONAL EDUCATIONAL REFORM COMMISSION (*RINKYOSHIN*)

The period of high growth ended abruptly with the oil crisis in 1973. In following years, financial and administrative reforms advocated slashing social welfare and educational budgets to reduce overall expenditures. Parents gradually assumed the burden of what had previously been a state responsibility. The national universities' tuition fees skyrocketed, school food services were privatized, and demands for reducing the size of classes to fewer than forty pupils were shelved.

At the same time, the government tightened control over textbooks, which required a kind of Ministry of Education imprimatur. History books, for example, had until then used the term *invasion* to describe the act of Japanese aggression perpetrated in China (over twenty million deaths ensued). The word was removed and replaced by reference to the *advance* of the Japanese army, which caused outrage and protest by the Chinese government.

In Tokyo's Nakano District, members of the education committee, who are responsible for administering academic matters for the area, used to be elected by local popular vote. The Ministry of Education declared this system of election illegal and tried to take control by appointing the members of this committee. Influential right-wing parents' associations lobbied to have the national anthem sung and the Japanese flag flown in schools.

These actions relate directly to education, but they occur within a broader context of reforms designed to relieve the state of part of its responsibilities in many areas, including telecommunications, railways, and the state tobacco concession. Nakasone's stated aim was to prepare for the year 2000, which, he claimed, required taking stock of the postwar situation (*sengo sokessan*).

These reform projects have been initiated by the all-powerful Japanese financial and economic circles under the direction of Nakasone's cabinet. A consultative body, the "forum on culture and education," has sprung up, with Mr. Ikuba, president of Sony, as its chairman. The "Kyoto world re-thinking club" (*Kyoto zakai*), whose central figure is Mr. Matsushita, has started a series of discussions intended to embrace a long-term perspective on the twenty-first century, including, among other things, economics, society, and education. Then there are the reports issued by the "commission of enquiry on the Japanese economy," a research body whose work draws on that of economic cliques. These are among many influences being brought to bear on the direction of reform.

The educational reform commission is working on ground already leveled for it. Not only its own members, but also those of the "Kyoto club," the "forum on culture and education," and the "commission of enquiry" are driving forces in this process.

Japan's political leaders have established two facts: (1) Japanese society is at the forefront of the major industrial countries for the mass production of high added-valued products; and (2) Japanese society is aging. To stay ahead, society must be subjected to all-out computerization and internationalized. The educational system must therefore be changed. Japanese society in the twenty-first century must be organized around a ruling elite capable of making decisions that will keep the country in the lead, which explains why the provisional commission on education's project for reform emphasizes training elites so heavily. One well-known aspect of Japanese education is the profusion of tests and competitive examinations that candidates seeking admission to a good university have to undergo. The aforementioned members of the elite, who will have been identified at a very early stage, will no longer have to endure the permanent cramming this involves. For them, the government foresees the creation of a single stream from the beginning to the end of secondary school.

This kind of "leader-production" is supported by a moral education that stresses the unalterable aspects of Japanese culture and the importance of tradition. While looking toward the twenty-first century, virtues that are considered immutable and imperishable Japanese values, such as love of one's country, are also being carried forward. This, together with Japan's mastery of the latest technological advances, should enable the rest of the world to understand Japan's superiority. One aspect of

Japanese nationalism was highlighted by a speech in which Nakasone held the black population in the United States responsible for America's weak overall IQ in comparison with Japan, which is a homogeneous empire.

Against this background, what about the concrete problems of Japanese education—delinquency, savage bullying, school refusal, misfits and rejects, corporal punishment? People with this authoritarian attitude refuse to address school problems or the pressure and anguish children undergo. Quite the contrary: they stress that academic results are higher in Japan than elsewhere.

The LDP's undisguised decision to give a say to economic and financial circles on the one hand and to the parallel schools on the other, and to allow harsh criticism of public teaching in general, shows its intentions on two fronts. First, to reduce the pocket of resistance constituted by left-wing unions and the teachers who belong to them, and second, to curtail the education budget in view of the greater freedom and latitude for development granted to the private educational sector. The school fees in private education and the parallel schools, however, are exorbitant in comparison with the public sector. Who is to pay for them? The conservative government is hardly likely to install a vast grant system to relieve poorer families of the financial burden of education. Parents' "training and education" bills threaten to be heavily increased in the end. The breeze of deregulation and "liberalization" blowing in from the United States and the Friedman school still has a bright future before it in Japan.

The conservative government's action in setting up and heeding the numerous reform committees and think tanks in which the private sector is all-pervasive demonstrates its scant respect for the role of the Parliament.

THE IDEOLOGY OF LIBERALIZATION AND EDUCATION IN THE TWENTY-FIRST CENTURY

The present school system is not efficient enough; its output is inadequate—in other words, it is not a profitable operation. In a period of low growth (between 3 and 5 percent) the state has shown its clear intention to diminish its budgetary commitments by handing over part of the educational system to the private sector. Under the pretext of setting education on a footing of efficiency and dynamism, part of the educational system will de facto surrender to privatization.

As far as business and the private sector are concerned, education is a market and a commodity that can and must show a profit. It is only a short step to having the Mitsubishi, Mitsui, or Toyota school all the way from nursery school to university. The education market is all the more promising because it is well known that in Japan parents will do anything to secure a good education for their children so as to give them the best chance of success in life. The juku and yobiko exert every possible pressure to obtain the right to award official school diplomas. This would be tantamount to having them recognized and put on an equal footing with any other secondary school in the country. The parallel school would take over as the main educational establishment.

Official philosophy in Japan consists of linking and combining state nationalism and the nationalistic proclivities of the business sector to the greatest extent possible. Values have now been overturned, however, and the business world considers the state administration no longer as the top of the pyramid but as a collection of outdated structures that hamper their activities. Japanese businesses state that they support the state and its bureaucrats in every field—including the Ministry of Education—who constantly block their spirit of initiative and undertakings. It is hard to imagine that commercializing and trading in education is likely to produce original schools and creative and independent minds. In addition, the public will have to pay for the product at the highest going rate.

WHAT VISION OF HUMANITY DO THE PROPONENTS OF LIBERALIZATION DEFEND?

Postwar education is criticized on the grounds that it is too egalitarian; there should be competition among pupils and among teachers on the basis of aptitude, as in business and industry. Furthermore, it is stated, this measure of worth and competencies is based on a single scale that takes no account of people's diversity or the talents or possible outcomes and progress of different individuals. One of the great champions of this ideology is Kenichi Koyama, whose thinking is clearly expressed in the claim: "The Nikkyoso (main teachers' union) ideology, which stupidly harps on the idea of education without misfits and rejects, is putting the classroom in jeopardy" (Koyama 1978). In his view, the real task is to restore elite education in Japan. He does not hesitate to expound a eugenic vision of humanity when he says, "In today's industrial civilization, those with an IQ of less than 110 are of no use." And: "A solution must be found that would give people with superior hereditary qualities the right to have more than three children, while at the same time preventing all the rest from having more than two" (Koyama 1967). After statements of this kind, worthy of Plato's reactionary thinking in *The Republic,* Koyama and his colleagues have the audacity to go on to talk about education that leads to free and full development, that respects the personality of each individual, and where each individual is given a chance. But what happens to children who develop late? What about handicapped children, those whose development does not follow the rhythm laid down by these pseudo-pedagogues?

Koyama's thinking is fed by the theories of American economist Milton Friedman, who advocates minimum state interference in the private sector. In this view, the state's role is to defend the private sector, and socialist countries pose the greatest threat. For this reason, the minimally involved state that extricates itself from the field of education has to have a huge military budget to defend its ideal of a free society. One of Friedman's books, *The Tyranny of the Status Quo,* has been translated by Kato Hiroshi, an influential member of the Kyoto club, and in the introduction to the Japanese version, Kato states that Nakasone encouraged him to include the book's central ideas in his reflections on Japanese education in the twenty-first century. We are not so far removed from the nationalistic slogan launched by Fukuzawa Yukichi at the beginning of the Meiji era in the nineteenth century: "a wealthy country, a strong army" (*fukoku kyohei*). The new version could be: "a state that protects business, a powerful army, private and elitist schools." The Ministry of Education's opposition is no more than perfunctory, and the time will come when it too will serve business as the mere executor of its decisions in the field of education.

WHAT EDUCATIONAL ALTERNATIVES CAN BE PROPOSED FOR JAPAN?

The education proposed by many pedagogues, researchers, and teachers in the educational sciences in Japan differs considerably from that advocated by Koyama or Kato. The concept of education held by the members of the Japanese Education Association, the Kyoiku Kagaku Kenkyukai (Kyokaku), which was founded in 1937 and whose thousand or so members include many university teachers, is not rooted in the economy and nationalistic aspirations barely disguised in the trappings of Friedman's ideas. (These ideas are a windfall for Japanese nationalists, who can smugly claim that these are trans-Pacific ideas that they are putting into practice, which enables them to advance under better cover.)

The Japanese Education Association's concept of education is based on human rights and children's rights. It centers on the individual, who cannot be sacrificed to any economic strategy whatsoever, even, or especially, if that strategy is bound up with nationalistic preoccupations.

The truth concerns everyone, and knowledge and culture must be oriented toward the universal. A child is not a thing, an object in which parents invest with selfish intent and purely for profit, as though he or she were a commodity. A child must be taught freedom and independence of mind, not be turned by education into a link in a chain of nationalistic merchandising logic. Article 10 of the Declaration of Children's Rights states that children should be taught that culture and knowledge are not private property for the sole benefit of an individual or a country but precious possessions belonging to all and that they should be used as such.

The business world's strident and insistent calls for privatization of education should be countered by stressing the fact that education is a personal matter involving the three-way responsibility of children, parents, and teachers. Far from denying this responsibility, the state should nurture and encourage it in every way. Japan's system of public education needs to be transformed by introducing a spirit of freedom into it.

Admitting that education is a personal matter means recognizing the individual's right in Japan to take in hand something that affects him or her personally to the utmost. Since the beginning of the Meiji era two main concepts have prevailed in the Japanese movement of "enlightenment" (*keimo jidai*). One holds that reforms and decision making should be carried out by an omnipresent and all-powerful state. The Voltairean idea of "everything for the people, nothing by the people" at least reflects a global concern for the people on the part of officialdom, whereas the concern manifest in the first Meiji posture is first and last for the state and its total power. The individual as an autonomous person capable of generating ideas, initiatives, and values barely exists within this scheme. Unfortunately it must be recognized that the same attitude persists, surviving hydra-like all the vicissitudes of history. This state-dominant concept could be called "enlightenment from above."

The second idea, to be emphasized here, concedes every importance to the desires and initiatives of the citizen. It is the direct opposite of "enlightenment from above," so we shall call it "enlightenment from below." Movements to secure freedom and citizens' rights (*Jiyuminken undo*), which are the real ferment of Japanese democracy, are represented within this line of thought.

The kind of education that should be built up in Japan is one in which action is based on respect for human rights and especially the rights of children. Education should provide the opportunity for each individual, in any country and at any age, to develop and acquire knowledge. The acquisition of learning, information, and culture are fundamental human rights. Instead, Japan has turned education into a machine for classifying individuals according to criteria (HENSACHI) that are both lame and profoundly discriminatory. There can be no such thing as education without justice, peace, and concern for truth and equality. Progress lies in this direction, not in the installation of an educational system conceived in aggressive terms as an efficient weapon in an economic war that could lead, alas, to actual war.

These misgivings are justified by the directives issued by the Ministry of Education on 10 February 1989. The ministry has decided to modify school programs throughout the primary and secondary cycles with a view to reinforcing Japanese identity and strengthening respect for the flag and the imperial hymn, which has now become the national anthem. Beginning in 1992, at school assemblies before and after class, teachers are to sing the Japanese national anthem (*kimigayo*) standing facing the flag (*kokki*) in an attitude of respect. Many teachers and democrats who feel an attachment to the postwar constitution fear an escalation of the return to what they call the old demons and to the recurring temptation of nationalism, which in Japan can take many forms. The educational reform undertaken by Nakasone in 1984 attempts to instill in the Japanese an awareness of their identity and culture in order to establish themselves on a solid footing and to stand firm against other nations.

This is all, of course, disguised by rhetoric about an education whose overriding concern is to seek peace and mutual understanding among nations. It is interesting to note that when Jean-Pierre Chevènement was minister of education in France he adopted a policy not far removed from Nakasone's: emphasis on civic instruction and learning the "Marseillaise" in school.

Chevènement seemed to imply that in order to stand up against international economic challenge people must not only have a high level of education but must also feel strongly that they belong to a specific cultural and historical setting, which is just another way of saying they must be nationalists. Does this mean that the economy is a way of perpetuating war by other methods? There is inevitably cause for concern when one sees the eagerness of politicians to reform postwar education under the pretext of adapting more effectively to present-day challenges and producing new human beings for the twenty-first century. Does this not bring a risk of increasing tension? Devotion to one's country and culture—why not? But must this devotion necessarily entail conflict with other countries and cultures? With the advent of the twenty-first century and the installation of educational reforms in many countries, are we not seeing the return of nationalism cleverly concealed under the cloak of such terms as *internationalization*? To the writer Yamanaka Hisashi, the recent provisions concerning school programs are nothing but a reactivation of the ethic that prevailed before and during the war. The system is designed to produce open-minded creative leaders on the one hand and, on the other, obedient Japanese, submissive to all forms of authority—parents, older children, teachers, the emperor.

The ever greater number of rejects produced by the Japanese educational system through school failure, even if the results appear positive to foreigners, the phenomena of bullying, the violence perpetrated at school by teachers toward pupils, students toward teachers, and students among one another (the scapegoat syndrome), the increasingly costly education considered as a consumer commodity of which only watered-down ersatz versions will be offered to lower-income strata of society, thousands of cases of school refusal every year (*tokko kyohi*)— all of these are the open sores of an educational system that denies respect and love of one's neighbors as individuals.

The notion of individual happiness is rarely mentioned in the projects proposed by the cliques and commissions clustering around the conservative power centers and business circles. Happiness is also a benefit to which the Japanese want access. Happiness is a new idea in Japan.

REFERENCES

Horio, T. *Educational Thought and Ideology in Modern Japan: State Authority and Intellectual Freedom*. Ed. and trans. S. Platzer. Tokyo, University of Tokyo Press.
Kikuchi, D. (1909) *Japanese Education*. London, J. Murray. Cited in Elisséeff, V., and Elisséeff, D., *La civilisation japonaise*. Editions Les Grandes Civilisations. Paris, Arthaud.

Koyama, K. (1967) *Introduction à futurologie. (Introduction to Futurology)*.
————. (1978) *Des leçons de la maladie anglaise (Lessons from the English Malady)*. PHP.
Ota, and Horio, T. (1985) *Que signifie la réforme de l'éducation? (What Is the Meaning of Educational Reform?)*
Sabouret, J.-F. (1985) *L'Empire du concours: Lycéens et enseignants au Japon*. Paris, Autrement.

4

School Refusal: Psychopathology and Natural History

AKIRA NAKANE

SUMMARY

A review of clinical research on school refusal in Japan suggests that socioeducational factors play an important etiological role. In addition, specific stages of the psychopathological phenomena in school refusal can be identified. These stages are emerging as a provisional natural history of this disorder as follows: (1) difficulties attending school due to maladjustment at school; (2) maladjustment at home caused by prolonged absence from school; (3) general maladjustment caused by missing opportunities to attend school again; and (4) temporary adjustment to society, but with a predisposition to social failure and personality disorder.

The plight of children with school refusal is now a serious educational problem in Japan. Therapeutic approaches have been taken from various fields, and school refusal has been a frequent topic of discussion at the Japanese Association for Child and Adolescent Psychiatry and Allied Professions (JACAPAP). At the first general meeting of JACAPAP, in 1960, Sumi and his colleagues and Nareta gave presentations on this subject based on the separation anxiety theory. Earlier, Takagi had noticed the problem of children who do not attend school and had conducted a survey of schools in Kyoto and published the results in 1959. Takagi attempted to divide the development of school refusal symptomatology into three stages, each expressed through a characteristic clinical picture: (1) hypochondriacal stage, (2) aggressive stage, and (3) seclusive stage. Takagi's paper was frequently quoted in other articles on school refusal published in Japan, and reactions, both positive and negative, to his proposal of three stages were strong. (The paper also appears in *Acta Paedopsychiatrica*, vol. 30.)

Takagi stated that these stages were typical clinical observations and that not all school refusers progressed through these clinical stages. As times have changed, he argued, more patients now act violently toward their mothers and more give little evidence of a seclusive stage. Most distinctively, Takagi refuted the separation anxiety theory of school refusal. Although initially controversial this opinion has been widely accepted in Japan and stands in marked contrast to DSM III, which treats school refusal as a separation anxiety disorder.

Minagawa, Shimizu, Abe, and Nakane sent questionnaires to researchers and clinicians all over Japan asking whether school refusal should be treated as an independent clinical entity. The responses were evenly divided. When asked what diagnosis should be given, however, no one suggested separation anxiety disorder, indicating the negative view held by Japanese professionals toward the DSM III classification of school refusal.

At the Tokyo Metropolitan Umegaoka Hospital Furukawa and Hishiyama studied the frequency of "school haters" at public junior high schools in Tokyo 1951–1978 (see fig. 4.1). One peak occurred between 1963 and 1966. It then declined to the lowest incidence in 1972, and the incidence rose gradually thereafter. The incidence differed by region; commercial areas and new residential areas showed especially high rates. This difference in incidence also paralleled a similar trend in the incidence of juvenile delinquency. Furukawa et al. suggested that school refusal was linked to socioeconomic conditions. They noted that the factors affecting the incidence were (1) population density and personal economic factors; (2) cultural factors, such as the level of domestic stability, the level of neighborhood security, the amount of information available in homes, and educational standards; and (3) the rate of increase in number of households and in population. They also examined similar surveys throughout Japan and found regional differences in the incidence of school refusal between 1967 and 1978. The national mean rate decreased from 1972 until 1976, as did the rate for Tokyo. After 1976 the rates gradually increased.

Wakabayashi pointed out that statistics from the Nagoya University Department of Psychiatry also showed the lowest incidence of school refusal around 1972–73. Before that date more male than female patients were treated, but the number of female patients increased, and there has been no difference in the incidence rates of the sexes since 1972. This shift in sex difference (increasing numbers of female school

Figure 4.1 *Incidence and Number of "School Haters" among Primary and High School Students in Tokyo, 1951–1978.*

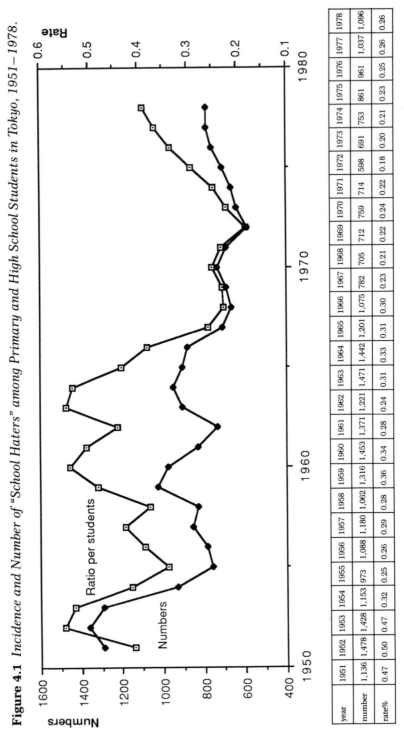

year	1951	1952	1953	1954	1955	1956	1957	1958	1959	1960	1961	1962	1963	1964	1965	1966	1967	1968	1969	1970	1971	1972	1973	1974	1975	1976	1977	1978
number	1,136	1,478	1,428	1,153	973	1,088	1,180	1,062	1,316	1,453	1,371	1,221	1,471	1,442	1,201	1,075	782	705	712	759	714	598	691	753	861	961	1,037	1,096
rate%	0.47	0.50	0.47	0.32	0.25	0.26	0.29	0.28	0.36	0.34	0.28	0.24	0.31	0.33	0.31	0.30	0.23	0.21	0.22	0.24	0.22	0.18	0.20	0.21	0.23	0.25	0.26	0.26

Source: Furukawa, H., and Hishiyama, Y., (1980) *Japanese Journal of Child and Adolescent Psychiatry* 21:300.

refusers) was paralleled by another shift in sex difference, an increasing rate of females entering upper-level schools. Honjo continued to collect data until 1984 and then compared 1972–74 with 1982–84. The number of those under age thirteen at the first contact with psychiatric services decreased in this period, whereas the number of those above age thirteen increased markedly. Accompanying school refusal were such somatic symptoms as headaches, stomachaches, and fevers, unprovoked violence toward mothers, and increasingly poor school records. The number of female patients decreased during this period, contradicting Wakabayashi's conclusion that the increasing incidence of school refusal in females and the increasing incidence of females who enter upper-level schools were linked. Honjo's data show that school refusal is not only based on personal conflicts between mother and child but reflects complex social factors.

Among follow-up surveys, the most significant are long-term studies that investigate social adaptability. Such surveys extend ten years from the first contact with psychiatric services, and the mean age of the subjects at outcome is above twenty. Fukuma's survey in Shimane prefecture found that 68.5 percent of school refusers entered high school as compared to 83.9 percent of the overall student population; 48.8 percent of school refusers entered universities or junior colleges, whereas only 32.5 percent of high school students in the prefecture entered.

Umezawa of Shimane Prefectural Koryo Hospital, which has a psychiatric ward with in-hospital classes for adolescents, surveyed the prognoses of forty school refusers who received residential treatment. Among those who were in the second to fourth years of the follow-up surveys, 31.6 percent were rated as poorly adjusted. As the follow-up period grew, however, fewer were scored as maladjusted. Among those in the eighth to twelfth years of the follow-up, one out of twelve (8.3 percent) was regarded as poorly adjusted. In the first year after discharge from the hospital eighteen failed to attend school or to hold a job. In the second year the number was reduced to thirteen, and at the time of the survey ten were not attending school or holding a job. The study indicates that the findings change according to the length of follow-up. In addition, those admitted to the hospital within eight months from onset of symptoms showed more favorable adjustment than those who were admitted after a longer interval. The mean time between onset of symptoms and admission among the well adjusted was 12.1 months, whereas among the poorly adjusted it was 20.5 months.

Ohtaka of the Nagoya University Department of Psychiatry analyzed forty long-term follow-up cases; 47 percent showed good social adaptation (Group 1), 18 percent had problems but adapted somehow (Group 2), and 35 percent evinced chronic problems in social life (Group 3). Those in Group 1 were able to decide by themselves to enter university or technical school, start a part-time job, or obtain licenses or qualifications. In Group 2, poor sociability and seclusive characteristics persisted, and many dropped out after entering upper-level schools. Patients in Group 3 continued to refuse schooling by either leaving or remaining absent for long periods; most were still receiving psychiatric treatment. These data indicate that the patient's prognosis is related to how closely he or she remains in contact with schools. Most who followed a better recovery course went to high school at night or received qualifications for college admission that allowed them to resume school, thereby readapting themselves to normal life. This reflects the value of education in contemporary Japan.

Watanabe of the National Kohnodai Hospital Department of Child Psychiatry (which also has in-hospital school classes) reported on fifty cases followed up nine to seventeen years after discharge from the hospital. Forty-five subjects had jobs, were helping at home, or were housewives. Twenty-seven cases completed upper-level schools. Five were living at home, some becoming agitated occasionally. Their self-esteem was poor and their self-image distorted because of their lengthy absences from school, leading to difficulties in socialization and strong inferiority complexes.

SOCIAL AND EDUCATIONAL CAUSES OF SCHOOL REFUSAL

Bullying, which causes psychological damage as well as physical harm, has recently become widespread in schools throughout Japan. In one common practice, the peer group ostracizes certain students. The victim is often left alone and unaided—not only by other students but at times by thoughtless or inconsiderate teachers. According to Sato of Kitazato University, 69 percent of those diagnosed as school refusers were bullied at the time of symptom onset. Students have always collectively picked on certain students, and this seems to be closely related to school refusal. Bullying has not been emphasized as a cause of school refusal before because more attention has been given to family pathology, but it clearly shows the importance of social factors in the disorder.

Koizumi points out in this volume that school refusal in junior and senior high school often begins in connection with poor schoolwork. Parents living in big cities in Japan prefer their children to go to private junior high schools so that they will have advantages when entering college. Elementary school children with good school records are thus often obliged to attend extra tutorial classes after school. These students often overestimate their academic abilities and do not value themselves in fields other than academics, such as sports or music, after they enter private junior high school. In private schools most students are hard workers, so many students can no longer sustain the good school records achieved in elementary school. They grow disappointed, becoming candidates for school refusal. School refusal in Japan thus has partial roots in the sociopathological phenomena that surround education. Furthermore, the effect of family pathology in which parents lack integrity and authority over the family needs to be examined.

The symptoms and course of the illness of school refusers are determined by the intertwining of internal factors (the patient's personal psychology) and external factors (such as pressure from those around the patient). Some patients fail to go to school while living at home, no matter how hard they try, but can attend school without difficulty once they move to a relative's home. Some patients who were confined to their bedrooms at home and exhibited violence toward their families regained ordinary behavior and attitudes immediately after admission to the hospital. Social relationships, such as that with a therapist who was a graduate of the same school as the patient, can sometimes have an effect additional to the therapeutic relationship. These aspects of school refusal are unique; they differ from other neurotic cases. Because of these uncertain influences from living conditions and therapeutic settings, researchers and therapists have subtly differing views of the disease and its therapy. School refusers commonly tend to become tense over going to school, not having attended school, and continued family criticism.

THE NATURAL HISTORY OF SCHOOL REFUSAL

School refusal often begins with maladjustment to an unpleasant situation at school. School refusers become tense immediately before going to school, and decide to remain at home. They rapidly decline into neurotic symptom formation and are plagued by a harsh superego for not going to school when they are not physically ill. When they can no longer cope with this tension, they give up trying to go to school and remain at home. This does not alleviate the feeling of guilt, so they avoid leaving the house for fear of meeting neighbors or class-mates. They also avoid circumstances in which they might be told things they do not want to hear or be asked about themselves, and they seclude themselves in their rooms. They react aggressively to parents' criticism and enter a stage in which they cannot adjust at home.

If the genesis of school refusal is not limited to separation anxiety phenomena, what theories should be the basis for treating patients? Before answering this question, let me describe changes in school re-fusers during residential treatment. For the past twenty-five years resi-dential treatment institutions for emotionally disturbed children have helped children return to school in Japan. School refusers have also received long-term treatment on child or adolescent psychiatric wards. Although residential treatment is considered to be effective treatment for long-term school refusal, experience at Umegaoka Hospital, shows that such changes are temporary and that the problem is far more complex.

A basic problem when treating school refusers is that many patients refuse outpatient psychiatric interviews while acting violently toward their mothers. They become severely compulsive and out of control. Residential treatment in psychiatric wards begins by offering emergen-cy refuge from these behavioral problems. Resistance against admit-tance disappears within days after arrival at the hospital. The patients begin to understand why they were admitted and to think specifically about how they can return to school. They thus appear to be quite normal and usually give no impression of serious illness. Such shifts in patients' attitudes generate a temporary resolution of their maladjust-ment at home. Once the patients clarify their conflicts about school through therapeutic interviews and they can interact with their families through the help of family counseling or just by spending some time at home, treatment focuses on helping them return to school.

Most child and adolescent psychiatric hospitals today have in-hospital school classes. When they first go to these classes, patients become tense. Such tension is within the limits of their endurance, however, and allows them to continue to go to class. Once they can adapt to school and everyday life on the ward without trouble, they progress to the next step. They first attempt to go to their original school from the hospital and then try to attend school while living at home. Once it is certain that they can manage satisfactorily to go to school they are discharged from the hospital. At each step, crises occur. Soon after returning to school, they often fail to continue attending classes because of the strain of their unresolved conflicts. This setback damages their self-image and causes trouble between patient and family, negatively affecting the family's new image of the patient. Finding methods to avoid this regressive deterioration becomes a focus of residential treatment.

A patient attending school outside the hospital experiences greater conflict than in in-hospital classes. The patient sometimes returns home instead of going to school, and resists coming back to the ward. If the patient has obsessive-compulsive symptoms, he or she begins to behave aggressively toward the mother again and does not return to the hospital after staying overnight at home. The patient can no longer behave adaptively either at home or at the hospital. Such patients have no intention of ever returning to school and live aimless lives. They frequently start acting out, trying to justify their behavior by making excuses or by blaming others. They lapse into a state of general maladjustment. These patients are typically those students who quit school or who graduated from junior high school without being able to continue their education.

As these patients grow older they start to work part-time, attend high school evening classes, prepare themselves to take a qualification examination for college entrance, or choose correspondence school courses in attempts to enter society. These efforts do not last long, however. Their social adjustment is only temporary and fails when minor difficulties occur, thus showing the underlying fragility of the patient's ego. Some of these patients begin to manifest social problems in late adolescence, derived from insufficient socialization, immaturity and poor control of their emotions, and an inferiority complex as a result of not attending school. Yet other patients work hard, overcome this crisis of general maladjustment, and become productive members of society. However, difficult patients may be diagnosed as having borderline personality disorders because of severe acting out and other characteristic behavior traits. This stage is critical because the incipient personality disorder may worsen. The progress of these stages indicates how vital it is to provide opportunities for schooling until the patients can be truly independent.

For children who do not go to school, feelings of personal inadequacy always remain. This is especially true of junior high school students or older adolescents, who are acutely concerned with their self-value. We should always understand these patients within the framework of adolescent psychology and support their desire to find a solution. The behavior of elementary school students reflects the less mature psychological capacities appropriate to middle childhood. They have feelings of inadequacy only as regards their peers, while they maintain an equilibrium at home that requires the help of over-adaptation by family members. For young people who tend to blame others for their own failures, repeated failure leads to general maladjustment. Those with favorable prognoses avoid repeated failure by involvement in activities, whatever their solutions, achieving some success through making decisions based on their own values.

The clinical picture of school refusal is not simply a state of not attending school, but an abnormal process of prolonged absence from school that leads to additional social dysfunction. Family pathology is not the only cause of school refusal. As the period of absence from school lengthens, maladjustment at home becomes evident and extends into life in general. Acting out becomes a prominent feature and in some cases symptom development follows the course of a borderline personality disorder. Yet in some cases the maladjustment phase does not deteriorate into intractable neurotic defenses and symptoms. To a certain extent the course of the illness is reversible; patients may become working members of society by overcoming their problems and returning to a normal route—school life. The natural history of school refusal appears to consist of the following stages.

1. Difficulties attending school due to maladjustment there: At this stage patients often have psychosomatic symptoms caused by intense conflict and tension. They cannot go to school, suffer guilt about not attending school, and cannot leave home because of feelings of inadequacy.

2. Maladjustment at home caused by prolonged absence from school: Patients begin to make every effort to attend school. Although this halts the course of the neurosis, some patients develop obsessive-compulsive symptoms. They continually rebel against pressure and complaints from their parents, seclude themselves in their rooms, or act aggressively toward their mothers. The neurosis is still reversible at this stage, since it can be favorably altered by efforts to attend school.

3. General maladjustment caused by repeated failure to attend school: When efforts fail and hope for the future collapses, patients often act out, justify themselves, or blame others for their behavior. They spend days without trying to find a solution.

4. Temporary adjustment to society: As they grow older, patients try to adapt to society. This does not last long, however. Failure easily results and patients retain strong feelings of inadequacy. Avenues for

normal social life are still available, but many patients follow the course
of personality disorder.

REFERENCES

Fukuma, H., Inoue, E., Namine, T., et al. (1980) Long-term follow-up of
school phobic children and adolescents (in Japanese). *Clinial Psychiatry*
22:401–408.
Furukawa, H., and Hishiyama, Y. (1980) A statistical study of the refusal to
attend school (1): Social factors and the change in the incidence rate in
Tokyo (in Japanese with English abstract). *Japanese Journal of Child and
Adolescent Psychiatry* 21:300–309.
Hersov, L., and Berg, I., eds. (1980) *Out of School: Modern Perspectives in
School Refusal and Truancy.* Chichester, Wiley.
Hishiyama, Y., and Furukawa, H. (1982) A statistical study of the refusal to
attend school (2): Social factors and the change in the incidence rate in
Japan (in Japanese with English abstract). *Japanese Journal of Child and
Adolescent Psychiatry* 28:183–191.
Honjo, S., Kaneko, T., Wakabayashi, S., et al. (1987) The actual conditions of
patients who refuse to go to school: Change from 1972–74 to 1982–84 (in
Japanese with English abstract). *Japanese Journal of Child and Adolescent
Psychiatry* 28:183–191.
Koizumi, E. (1973) *School Refusal* (in Japanese). Tokyo, Gakuji-Shuppan.
———. (1979) School refusal in adolescence: On educational consultation
(in Japanese). *Japanese Journal of Child and Adolescent Psychiatry* 20:33–
35.
Ohtaka, K., Wakabayashi, S., Enomoto, K., et al. (1986) A long-term follow-
up study of school refusal children (in Japanese with English abstract).
Japanese Journal of Child and Adolescent Psychiatry 27:213–229.
Rutter, M., and Hersov, L., ed. (1976) *Child Psychiatry.* Oxford, Blackwell.
Sato, K., Ito, I., Morita, S., et al. (1987) The issue of "bullying": Neuroses
and psychosomatic syndromes of bullied children (in Japanese). *Japanese
Journal of Child and Adolescent Psychiatry* 28:110–118.
Takagi, R., Kawabata, T., Fujiwara, A., et al. (1965) Nuclear type of school
phobia (1): Symptom formation (in Japanese with English abstract).
Japanese Journal of Child Psychiatry 6:146–186.
Takagi, R. (1963) Mental mechanisms of school phobia and its prevention.
Acta Paedopsychiatrica 30:135–140.
Umezawa, Y. (1984) School refusal and modern society, from the follow-up
study of residential treatment (in Japanese). *Japanese Journal of Child and
Adolescent Psychiatry* 25:85–89.
Wakabayashi, S. (1980) *School Refusal* (in Japanese). Tokyo, Ishiyaku
Shuppan-sha.

Wakabayashi, S., Kaneko, T., Saburi, M., et al. (1982) The relationship between school refusal and social condition in Japan (in Japanese with English abstract). *Japanese Journal of Child and Adolescent Psychiatry* 23:160–180.

Watanabe, T. (1986) The clinical picture of school refusal children after a long-term period: The cases from residential treatment (in Japanese). *Japanese Journal of Social Psychiatry* 9:36–42.

5

School Refusal and Family Pathology: A Multifaceted Approach*

KAYOKO MURASE

SUMMARY

Clinical viewpoints are discussed, derived from the outcome of thirty cases of school refusal the author has treated over ten years: (1) Damaging effects of Japanese high technological society as a background for school refusal; (2) Contributing factors in the child, in the family, and in society; and (3) Factors that determine the success of treatment: how one grasps the child's needs and problems as expressed through school refusal, and how accurately one understands the specific structures of the family, school, and community.

Therapy should attempt to find potential strengths in the child; to avoid encouraging the child to attend school too soon; to foster the child's inner maturation; to find a "window of the heart" to facilitate the therapeutic alliance (by devoting attention to daily routines and hobbies that can be shared with the therapist); to offer the family comprehensive information and support; and to maintain contact with the school.

In this chapter I examine school refusal from a clinical point of view: I review thirty cases of school refusal that I have treated during the past ten years with a known therapeutic outcome. In addition, I describe in

* I express my gratitude to Mr. Kenichi Ito, lecturer and counselor in the Taisho University Counseling Institute, and to Ms. Kyoko Kato, Ms. Fumiko Kurihara, Miss Takako Oyama, and other research students. I give special thanks to Ms. Fumiko Kurihara, who was the therapist for case 13.

73

detail a selected case in which I attempted a multifaceted approach designed for the treatment of cases of school refusal.

Behind school refusal lie the damaging effects of Japanese society at large. In modern high-technology society people tend to be valued only for their productive efficiency, and as a result an increasing number of children feel that they are not accepted for what they are. A complete understanding of school refusal, however, requires consideration of several other elements: (1) factors in the child (personality, infantile conflicts, trauma in early childhood, psychological conflicts in later life, identity crisis in adolescence); (2) factors in the family (emotionally inadequate family relationships, role diffusion and dysfunction in the family, symbiotic relationship between parent and child, unfulfilled object relations); and (3) social factors (administrative influences, such as discrepancies between reality and stated goals when a proposed plan for education oriented toward individuals rather than the group is taken over—by a rationalization—but individually oriented education and training programs are then discontinued.

School refusal is not a specific disease; rather, it is a syndrome with diverse causes. Its incidence among schoolchildren has risen in recent years. The personality development of affected children is jeopardized at an early age, with characteristic manifestations of poor development in verbal expression, severe acting out behaviors, and somatic complaints. Successful therapy depends largely on how one understands what a child is trying to achieve through school refusal, the nature of the problems presented by the child, and how accurately one understands the specific structures of the family, school, and community.

In addition to planning psychological help for the child and parents, the therapist must have a therapeutic perspective that projects effective ways of helping them by defining who will help and when, where help will be given, what specific aspects of the problem will be addressed, and how these therapies will be organized, by grasping the whole picture surrounding the child. This is a multifaceted approach. When approaching this therapeutic challenge, the therapist balances several approaches simultaneously. One generally tries to find potential strengths in the child. At the same time, the therapist attempts to avoid encouraging the child to go to school too soon and to wait until the time to initiate schooling ripens, while watching over and fostering inner maturity. In order to achieve all of these goals, it is essential to nourish the therapeutic alliance by cherishing a "window of the heart" by paying attention to the child's routines and hobbies, which can be shared with others and can become sources of a mutual language with the therapist.

CLINICAL CASES

The syndrome of school refusal commonly coexists with several disorders. The cases listed below do not include patients who were diagnosed during evaluation as suffering from schizophrenia, depression, delinquency, or obvious truancy. Those unable to attend school because of acute obsessional symptoms were diagnosed as having obsessive-compulsive neurosis and left out. Also not included are cases whose parents came for advice because they felt uneasy or dubious about treatment their children were receiving elsewhere. Supportive measures were taken with these parents, but no direct contacts with the children were made.

The characteristics of each case and the components of treatment are shown in table 5.1. Family structure is also noted. The explanation of each category is indicated at the bottom of the table, but the numbers shown in the "style of therapy" column refer to the therapeutic modalities described in the following list:

Types of Therapy

1. therapist———child   therapist for the child only

2. therapist———parent   therapist for the parent only

3. therapist———child   therapist for the child and parent
   ‌   ˋ ˋ ˋ ˎ parent

4. therapist———child   different therapists for parent and
   therapist———parent   child

5. therapist⤹   ⤵child   therapists for the parent and child
   therapist⤴   ⤴parent   alternate occasionally

6. therapist⤸ | child | joint therapist(s) for parent and
   (therapist)‑ ‑ ‑ ‑| parent | child

The "therapist tutor" column indicates whether the therapeutic approach made use of a college or graduate student hired to help the child catch up on schoolwork and to supplement the child's play and activities in the neighborhood. The therapist tutor acts as a domain between that of the therapist and the original home tutor from the school.

The term "life experience group" refers to environmental therapy, one of the types of life therapy practiced. Some recent clients have a

Table 5.1 *Characteristics of Clinical Cases and their Treatment*

Case No.	Sex	Age( )[a]	Concomitant Symptoms	Violence[b]	Harshly teased[c]	Father < Mother[d]	Conflict Between Generations, Brothers and Sisters[e]	Medical Treatment[f]	Provisional Termination[g]	Style of Therapy[h]	Therapist Tutor	Life Experience Group	Contact with School	Window of the Heart
1	F	7(3)	Taciturn	○●	○	○		○‡	4 months	3,6			○	Scribbling riddles w/drawings, making lunch together
2	M	7(3)	Headaches, Stomachaches				○	‡	3 months	2				Appealing to his mother w/needs for affection
3	F	7(4)	Headaches, Continuous				●	‡	2 months	3				Fantastic story writing, smoking
4	M	8(2)	Pain all over the body		●			‡	3 months	2			○	Jogging w/his mother
5	F	10(2)	Anorexia nervosa, taking mother's money			○	●	‡	1 month	3,6			○	Carrying as an amulet a slip of paper with therapist's address & phone #
6	F	11(2)	Taciturn at certain times		○			#‡	2 months	3,4,5			○	Scribbling, sand play technique, crafts
7	F	11(2)	Stomachaches, Anorexia nervosa		●		●	‡	3 months	4				Animals, sports, mischievous tricks
8	F	12 (Cnt fm 8)	Headaches, Stomachaches		○	○	●	†#‡	26 months	3,4,5	○	Yes	○	Cartoons, story making
9	M	13 (Cnt fm 4)	Stomachaches	○●	○	○	●		22 months	3,6	○		○	Vehicle play, fishing, raising animals, eating together
10	M	13(12)	Headaches, Nausea	○●	○	○		#	12 months	3,4,5	○		○	Poem and novel writing, drawing
11	F	12(5)	Taciturn at certain times		○	○	○		18 months	3,4,5		Yes	○	Raising a weed (self image), raising animals, sports, cartoons

No.	Sex	Age	Symptoms				Duration					Interests/activities
12	M	13(4)	Taciturn at certain times, Asthma	○	●	†‡	18 months	3,4,5		Yes	O	Raising animals, sand play techniques, cooking
13	F	13 (Cnt fm 5)	Packing knapsack to leave home	○	○		5 months	3		Yes	O	Drawing, raising animals
14	F	13(3)	Stomachaches	○			3 months	3,4	O	Yes	O	Playing an electric organ, rock music, animals
15	M	13(5)	Headaches, Kidney ailment	●	●	†‡	3 months	3			O	Drawing, making personal computer games
16	F	14 (Cnt fm 11)	Scrupulous about her appearance				2 months	3,4,5			O	Table tennis, cooking, learning to do household chores for ill mother
17	M	14	Running away, stomachaches	○●	○		17 months	3,4,5			O	Writing poems, crafts, sewing
18	F	14(8)	Fever	○	○		8 months	3,4,5			O	Animals, stuffed animals, secret telephone calls, toll calls, lunch
19	F	14(3)	Fever, headaches	●	●	O	3 months	3,4	O			Table tennis
20	M	14(2)		○	●		2 months	2	O			Taking relief in the change in his mother
21	F	15(4)	Allergic asthma, anorexia nervosa	○●	○	O‡	8 months	3	O	Yes	O	Drawing, hugging filthy dogs, tennis, playing piano
22	F	15 (Cnt fm 11)	Pain all over the body	○	●	O‡	9 months	3,6	O	Yes	O	Cooking, reading, table tennis
23	M	15(3)	Headaches	○	*		3 months	3	O		O	Reading philosophy and literature, rock music

(continued)

Table 5.1 (*Continued*)

Case No.	Sex	Age( )[a]	Concomitant Symptoms	Violence[b]	Harshly teased[c]	Father < Mother[d]	Conflict Between Generations, Brothers and Sisters[e]	Medical Treatment[f]	Provisional Termination[g]	Style of Therapy[h]	Therapist Tutor	Life Experience Group	Contact with School	Window of the Heart
24	M	16(9)	Various mental complaints	O		O			2 months	2				The father's understanding the client's feelings, secret telephone calls
25	M	16(3)	Anorexia nervosa	O	O	O	●	O	5 months	2	O		O	Matters concerning motorcycles
26	M	16(3)	Various mental complaints	O	O	O	◖		7 months	3				Subject of religion
27	F	16(3)	Shoplifting with friends		O	O			6 months	3	O			Chinese, subjects on Chinese culture
28	F	16(3)	Headaches		O		O	O†	1 month	4,5		Yes		Sand play techniques, movies, rock music
29	M	15(3)	Headaches			O		O	3 months	2				Classical music, seeing society through a part-time job
30	M	19(7)	MBD	O●			●	O†	5 months	3,4,6		Yes		Table tennis, badminton, painting

[a] The age is that of the time when the client first came; the number in parentheses represents months passed since symptoms began. In some cases—where marked—symptoms have continued for years.

[b] Violence before consultation O; after consultation ●

[c] Especially harsh teasing ●

[d] Father < Mother means weak family participation of father; a * in this column means Father dead.

[e] Relationship between generations (grandparents, aunts and uncles) clearly affecting the family symptoms O; conflicts between brothers and sisters ●

[f] Those treatments before consultation O; those received in the Department of Psychiatry †; Department of Internal Medicine #; elsewhere ‡.

[g] The period it took to return to school, or to initiate a new way of life.

[h] Style of therapy and last four columns explained in greater detail in text.

basic character development that has been arrested, and experiences are not meaningful to them. It is thus useful to return to the period when the developmental disorder began and help regrowth, to try to understand what can be done now, and to find the concrete means available to implement these ideas.

At the Taisho University Counseling Institute, we establish a liberal therapeutic relationship within this framework, based on a comprehensive knowledge of rules and restrictions concerning therapeutic structure and appreciating our responsibility. Time limits and activities are selected according to the patient's needs. Activities include eating together, modifying the physical setting in the institute together, participating in sports or shopping, giving the child responsibility for buying toys and tools after specifying plans and a budget, and group study and learning through cooperative communication (for example, a younger patient telephones an older one with high scholastic ability who cannot leave home, asking about what he doesn't understand). What we call "life experience group activity" is a component of our flexible methods.

Case M: A Multifaceted Approach

Certain daily matters and favorable times may appear trivial in human growth and development but are in fact fundamental. In the process of therapy for school refusers, elements other than the therapist likewise converge and are related organically. Silence or the patient's favorite activities of interest are often a barely visible catalyst for growth. If the therapeutic process is likened to a theatrical play, the therapist can be considered the scriptwriter and director, evaluating the client's problem, offering what is needed, and being responsive and responsible during treatment. In the sense that he or she acts to help and watch over the people and matters on the stage, the therapist can be considered the stage and the *Kuroko* (a stagehand in a Kabuki play). The therapist's role is to understand the patient's position in relation to daily concerns and the people around the patient, to maintain a broad perspective, and to help at timely points hinted at by the patient, in order to strengthen the patient's ability to adjust.

The patient, M (number 9 in the table), had been absent repeatedly from school since age four. During junior high school he would lock the door of his room and eat alone. Both his parents held jobs. When M was in seventh grade, his father came alone to consultation. He listed M's faults, saying that he and his wife were too busy for consultation. The therapist sent a postcard, "Landscape with a White Horse," asking M to meet for a consultation (this tranquil picture conveys an image of traveling within the inner self, and was sent with hopes of traveling with M in the world of his inner mind). M agreed to meet the therapist if she would come to his house. The therapist agreed to visit the patient's home for several reasons: (1) because of the parents' weakening enthusiasm for therapy; (2) in order to decide if the family's loss of interest should be explored in therapy; (3) to make the most of the preliminary indication of the patient's therapeutic motivation; and (4) to ask M to come to the institute.

The sliding door of the small living room was in tatters. (M's room was even worse.) A fat, dirty M appeared and stared at the therapist. Then he kicked her. The parents, flustered, retreated to the kitchen. After the therapist introduced herself, a dirty, fat cat with no whiskers appeared and hopped onto her lap. Startled, M stared at the therapist. The therapist, petting the cat, asked if he liked cats. He said he did, and she continued, "So do I. Animals are honest, aren't they?"

"Yeah."

"Cat's can't shave their own whiskers. You did it, right?"

"Yeah."

They continued talking, and the therapist eventually asked, "Why don't you come for a meeting, to see what therapy would be like?"

M replied, as if it were a favor, "Yeah. I will." (M later reminisced, "I picked up the stray cat when I was in third grade and still following rules. I cared for it like it was my own child. But, as I gave up on people, I got mad at the cat. The cat was afraid of people and hardly ever came out during the daytime. I was surprised when the cat hopped onto your lap because it stayed away from everyone.")

Though he was sometimes late, M began to come for consultation. His parents had lost hope, and his school was also at a loss and did nothing. The therapist set the following goals for treatment:

Therapeutic Plan

a. M was very suspicious toward everyone and had lost his self-confidence. In order to give him another life experience, the therapist will share in activities in which the patient is interested.

b. His social relationships were awkward and he wanted to change them. A therapist tutor will be called in.

   c. The family relationships were fragmented. M felt abandoned by his parents and clung to the house. He had few activities. One of the goals for therapeutic changes in M is that the parents' hope will be restored, reuniting the family.

   d. The therapist will keep in contact with the school, and during the therapeutic process have them let M know periodically that he could go to school.

   e. The parents had already tried consultation and were uncooperative, fearful that their own problems would be identified. The therapist will talk to them regarding subjects related to their inner life, about what might be done now, and will help them put recommendations into practice.

At first, M lived with day and night reversed and missed treatment or was late because of oversleeping, but gradually he came to consultation at the scheduled time. He had suffered an extreme loss of self-confidence, but islands of competence occasionally appeared. For example, when talking about favorite foods he showed refined tastes. In his perceptive remarks about the contradictory attitudes of adults, his intelligence appeared to be above average. Without the love he wished for, however, he pretended indifference.

Hearing of his interest in trains, the therapist read *Railway Journal* and similar magazines, and made a cardboard model of a train that became a toy for M. Though scorning this as "kid stuff," he went to a model shop to buy material. To do so he had to ride a bike for the first time in years, but his obesity made him awkward. He wanted to lose weight, so the therapist suggested sports and changes in his eating habits.

The therapist played table tennis with M. Because of his lack of fitness, M stumbled and fell. Whenever he hit a great smash, he gave a smile. At home, he told his mother that the therapist was better at table tennis than he had expected. This was the first time that M had voluntarily spoken to his mother in years.

Moved by the slight change in M, each parent took the initiative to come to consultation separately. Each criticized the other from his or her own one-sided view. The father claimed that the mother was stubborn and never repented or apologized. He warned the therapist not to be fooled by her. He described her as an able worker but a messy housekeeper who poured everything into her work and religion. It was she who ruined their home. The mother claimed that the father was vain, often drunk, and looked at reality only from the perspective of his own interests. He was justly placed as a "window-side worker" (employees who have lost significance in the office) and remained psychologically dependent on his own mother. According to M, "Father is weak. He spends rashly and likes gambling and drinking. But Mother is so strong and stubborn that she is pushing Father into drinking. Strong women ruin men. I have been mutilated by her for fourteen years." So the three of them insulted one another, and finally each challenged the therapist to try to change the others into stable persons. This was "therapy by commission."

Coincidentally, M mentioned a late-night movie he had seen. His parents had also seen it and were deeply moved. It was the first and last thing this couple ever agreed on. "This is one of the seven wonders of the world," M said. The therapist responded, "They seem to hate each other so, but there is at least one thing they agree about. Maybe deep down inside they are looking for a tie they have lost."

Surprised, M said, "What a way to think about it!"

This episode became a fragile thread that barely held together this awkward, stubborn, but lonely family.

The therapist and M reviewed his eating habits in order to help him lose weight, which pointed up the family's unbalanced meals. In addition, although M gave touching expressions of his feelings, he lacked common sense about living on his own and caring for himself, and he was hindered by his parents' frequent nights out. After talking during interviews about learning concrete life skills, he began to help with household chores. This helped relieve his mother's tension; she had had no help with housework for a long time.

M had had no friends since childhood and was reluctant to join in group activities, saying people frightened him. The therapist decided to invite him to her home. On one occasion, he and the therapist's child went fishing. M caught many fish, one after another, and the therapist's child exclaimed, "You're a fishing genius, aren't you!"

M thought, "His words are spontaneous. Adults' words are always thought out and planned, no matter how nice they are." After this, M went fishing with the father he despised. "Sitting silently with fishing rods, we seemed to understand each other's feelings." It was a delicate communication.

The mother said grimly, "M said to me that 'Mrs. Murase is a working woman, but she made me something nice to eat. Work isn't an excuse.' I've been working hard outside the home, and I'm determined not to lose my opportunities." She began to pay more attention to their life-style, and she kept M's clothes clean.

M complained of nausea when looking at schoolbooks; using the English instructions for a war game he enjoyed, however, he studied basic grammar, learning bit by bit. Using the same instructions, he also studied fractions and decimals. He occasionally sighed, saying, "The ship has left me behind." He told the therapist, "I'll be like this forever. You're either going to give up on me or get old and senile."

His mother said to the therapist, "Some people are just scum. Even his parents have gotten sick of him. You are strange."

The therapist said, "Thinking of both the future and what we can do right now is what is important. M is stubborn, but I am the mother of stubbornness."

M, unconvinced, said sarcastically, "Sure," but his facial expression indicated that he was not wholly adverse to this thought.

Studying during therapy sessions was not enough for M to catch up, so he requested to have a therapist tutor come once a week. This tutor, T, was a gentle male graduate student. T listened quietly to M's angry comments about his life. Eventually, T told M that he himself hadn't played at all as a child because he was always studying for entrance exams. He very much enjoyed fishing, games, trains, and movies with M, who was surprised by this. "He's a bit strange, but maybe people are not that frightening after all," said M.

M no longer cut off the cat's whiskers, and the cat began to join the family. M kept the fish he caught, as well as finches, as pets. Through raising pets, M learned to keep an appropriate distance from others, allowing himself friendship yet not becoming intrusive. Though still afraid of group life, he decided to return to school.

From the start the therapist had contacted the school at the end of each semester. The school had sent M notes telling him he was wel-come to return. His teacher had not urged him to attend school but, thinking that finally the time was right, visited M's home and promised to meet M at the school gate in the morning. M went to school, but he felt awkward and out of place in his ninth grade class and his atten-dance was only periodic.

Just before M was to graduate, his parents said they regretted that they had treated the therapist as if she were doing "therapy by commis-sion" and would simply follow their instructions; they apologized and sat down with M and the therapist for a talk. They decided that, instead of graduating through special interventions, M should continue regular school life and finish junior high school on merit. He transferred into tenth grade in night school, where he met students of various backgrounds and experiences and had a good teacher. He was elected to a class office. M had many experiences, including taking care of a friend who was absent from school, visiting Hiroshima alone and thinking about peace, and playing mischievous tricks with his friends. His parents watched over him leniently. M became a positive young man capable of leadership and attended part-time high school while working. He proceeded to the science department of a national university.

The parents came together to an interview to report, "We learned from you not to give up. We hadn't learned that before, or that a husband and wife must find something good in each other, and help each other. M suffered for a long time and helped us understand it." M's father said this, the mother nodding and smiling next to him.

SUMMARY OF RECOMMENDATIONS FOR TREATMENT

In nineteen out of thirty cases, the father's participation in the family was minimal (Father < Mother in the table). This includes only those cases where this was obvious both physically and psychologically. In the remaining cases, it was difficult to consider the father as a good guardian and the source of authority in the family. Conversely, in these cases the mother was often interfering or overzealous, which was not optimal for the child's mental and physical development or needs. A psychological distance suitable for the child's age was often lacking. From this perspective, although there are several levels of school refusal, children who refuse to go to school are lonely and dissatisfied with relationships around them; they have problems with identity development.

Within the family, the client is seen as psychologically (and sometimes physically) fragile compared with other family members and weak in his or her own defense. School refusers carry the family's problems on their shoulders (some are of three or four generations) and are ill because of them. They then signal others, calling for help. When a family functions too poorly to raise children, their development is barred. The child cannot cope with inner and outer stimuli, is unable to adjust to reality, and becomes reclusive, refusing to attend school.

Experience with the thirty cases listed here indicates that the first meeting generally has a strong effect on the success of therapy. First, the therapist should have information about the patient, but should not allow it to limit his or her view. He or she should stand on the same ground as the patient, but should have a new perspective and be ready to grow with the patient. Concretely, the therapist should find "windows of the heart" in order to establish a therapeutic alliance and consider all aspects of treatment from several viewpoints. The therapist should relate not only with words but with shared activities (sports, studies, and so on). An interest in youth and their currently popular culture and the ready admission of contradictions within yourself are attitudes necessary for success.

Second, clear judgment about whether to accept a case is essential. Other essential issues include whether to refer to a medical or other type of clinic, the level of your own ability, and whether or not your own clinic is a suitable facility.

Third, when with the family, the therapist should appreciate the mental labor and efforts of the family until then and try to listen to them without placing blame. The therapist should create an attitude of valuing the future and cooperation in the restoration of the family.

Fourth, it is useful to classify the nature of the parents' difficulties:

> *a.* They are unable to understand the child's behavior and do not know how to manage it;
> *b.* They have little interest in the child;
> *c.* They are psychologically caught in the child's problem and cannot make a proper judgment about it; and
> *d.* They also have a significant separate problem, which distorts their judgment and relationship with the child.

The therapist can help parents understand the child in response to the dynamics of *a* and *b*. In *c* and *d*, steps to relieve the parents' anxiety come first, although these activities actually overlap. In any case, concrete information, and hope based on actual facts from the assessment, are essential for therapy.

Instead of simply urging the patient to go to school, should the therapist not help the patient reconsider the kind of adult he or she wants to be? In order to do this, a concrete means of assuring adequate time and space for regrowth is needed. The first step is to find the patient's interests, the "windows of the heart" with which to relate, and determine what can actually be done now. Instead of pushing the patient into these measures, it is useful to employ several methods suitable for his or her condition, and not restrict treatment to a relationship with the therapist. Therapist tutors, group activities for life experiences, and other parts of a therapeutic network complement one another and improve chances for a successful outcome.

Periodic contact with the school, based on the patient's and the family's consent is necessary. Visits from classmates, teacher accompaniment on the way to school, and other specially arranged interventions should be woven into the treatment. When and how to do so depends on how accurately the therapist understands the patient and the circumstances.

In cases with substantial family involvement, questions and problems are managed carefully within existing conditions. Change in the child sometimes moves the parents or brothers and sisters to come for consultation and alters the family. There are cases (as in the table) where, though only the mother or father comes to treatment, some change took place in the child or family. In order to facilitate change, the therapist should enable the patient and family to be naturally forthcoming in their conversations.

The patient decides when to terminate therapy. In some cases, for example, many problems remain after the patient returns to school; in others, having given up school, the patient goes through significant character development and becomes able to determine his or her own direction for the future. A therapeutic goal is for the patient to feel that "I faced a problem and tried to cope with it. In the long road ahead, I will deal with it in whatever way is needed."

The treatment for school refusal has several overlapping components: first, supplying the patient with a snug nest in which mental regeneration can occur; second, assuring that the lack of social learning experiences can be made up for; and third, initiating thoughtful planning of the timing and nature of contacts with the school. It is also essential to offer the family a chance to recognize the intense ties between parent and child and to provide opportunities for the child to become psychologically independent from his or her parents.

REFERENCES

Bettelheim, B. (1987) *A Good Enough Parent.* New York, Knopf.
Iida, M., et al., eds. (1983) *Mental Science 6: The Life Cycle.*
———. (1983) *Mental Science 7: The Family.*

Murase, K. (1979) The function of a therapist tutor in child psychotherapy. *Taisho Counseling Institute Bulletin* 2:18–30.

————. (1981) Therapeutic development in child psychotherapy: Aims and termination. In *The Emergence and Development of the Therapeutic Relationship,* ed. K. Shirahashi and K. Ogura, pp. 19–52. Tokyo, Seiwa Press.

Murase, K., and Ito, K. (1986) Japanese family pathology. *Youth and Social Pathology* 11:14–25.

Ogura, K. (1983) The first interview. In *The First Interview,* ed. M. Yamanaka and K. Nozawa, pp. 53–92. Tokyo, Seiwa Press.

Shimosaka, K., ed. (1984) *Crises of Adolescence.* Tokyo, Kanehara.

6

School Nonattendance and Psychological and Counseling Services

EIJI KOIZUMI

SUMMARY

According to a report by the Japanese Ministry of Education (1987), the number of elementary and junior high school children who do not attend school more then fifty days in a school year because of "dislike" of school is increasing. This paper examines the problem of nonattendance at school or school refusal, which is sometimes said to be a particularly Japanese behavior problem. This chapter comments on the rate of occurrence of school refusal, the types of school refusal, psychological mechanisms, and other issues. The factors causing school refusal are complex. Some aspects of school refusal might be related specifically to the Japanese school and social environment.

THE OCCURRENCE OF SCHOOL REFUSAL

A report issued by the Ministry of Education in September 1987 surveyed the number of elementary and junior high school children who do not attend school. The number of children not attending more than fifty days out of the required 210 days in a school year because they dislike school is increasing. In 1986, there were 4,402 pupils in elementary schools and 29,694 students in junior high schools not attending because they disliked school. The current number is about 1.5 times higher in elementary schools and almost 4 times higher in junior highs than the prevalence in 1975.

This paper discusses the prevalence of school refusal, its causes, its various types, and other topics from the standpoint of psychological and counseling services in the education field.

Table 6.1 shows that the numbers reflect the definition of long-term absenteeism, that is, where we set the criterion of number of days of absence to be included. Thus, the occurrence of school refusal shown in

Table 6.1 *Occurrence of School Refusal*

Survey body	Ministry of Education	Directors' committee of prefectural and designated cities' educational research institutes
Survey year	1986	1984
Subjects	All schools	Sample taken from: —2% of public elementary and junior high schools throughout Japan —3% of public high schools
Criterion	Absent more than 50 days in a school year	Absent more than 30 days in a school year
Reason for absence	Dislike of school	School refusal
Occurrence per 10,000 students	Elementary school 4	20
	Junior high school 49	78
	Senior high school (not investigated)	53

table 6.1, 4 pupils per 10,000 in elementary schools and 49 students per 10,000 in junior highs, is tentative and the term "occurrence" is used instead of the usual "prevalence." But the data are valuable, as this is the only nationwide survey done annually.

According to information in a survey by the directors' committee of the Educational Research Institutes of various prefectures and designated cities (1985), the occurrence of absenteeism more than 30 days in a school year due to neurotic school refusal is 20, 78, and 53 per 10,000 students in elementary, junior high, and senior high schools, respectively. These numbers exceed those of the same survey done five years earlier in 1979, amounting to two times as high in junior highs, and 1.7 times as high in senior highs.

Diverse agencies and organizations help schoolchildren with their problems in Japan, because the administering departments differ. Psychological and counseling services in the field of education are operated as a division of education research institutes and educational centers under the boards of education of the local governments. They treat problems related to a student's education and school adjustment, based on requests by a child's parents and teachers.

There are 157 prefectural and designated cities' educational research institutes or other cities' educational centers that offer counseling services in Japan. In 90 percent of these 157 institutes, school refusal is the first-ranked problem, followed by delinquency, maladjustment in the classroom, and mental retardation or delay in speech.

In 1986 these 157 institutes and centers dealt with 9,001 cases of school refusal (table 6.2). These represented 42.9 percent of the total number of 20,963 cases seen by those centers that year, an increase of 11.6 percent over the previous year.

TYPES OF SCHOOL NONATTENDANCE

While working at the educational consultation division of the Tokyo Metropolitan Educational Research Institute, I recognized four categories of nonattendance at school, as shown in table 6.2:

(1) Absence due to physical illness and injury. Most of this group should be excluded from the school refusal category, because it is caused by an inability to attend school. However, some children in this group choose not to go back to school, even though they have

recovered from their physical conditions; these children can be considered school refusers.

(2) Nonattendance due to economic reasons. These cases are negligible in number at present.

(3) Absence because of a familial reason, such as a broken home, neglect by parents, or the irresponsibility of parents. Some parents neglect their children, or do not let them go to school. In this case, help from the department of social and child welfare is required.

(4) Nonattendance due to psychological reasons. These children are the actual school refusers in a broad sense; they may be divided into six subgroups. When school teachers look for reasons for a child's absence, these classifications are helpful, because they are easy to understand and apply.

The percentage of the total number of 9,001 cases of school refusal in each group or subgroup is indicated in table 6.2 in parentheses. The first is neurotic school refusal, with 70.2 percent of the total. Second is the subgroup with mental illness. A child with schizophrenia, depression, neuroses, or other major psychiatric disorder may sometimes, as a result of such illness, be unable to attend school. Among children coming to centers in the educational counseling field, such cases are not common (only 3.3 percent), but this ratio might be higher in mental health centers and hospitals. In the third group nonattendance is due to 'truancy.' It is important for teachers to differentiate type 1 from type 3.

The few cases in the type 4 subgroup include students with the problem of chronic indecision, students who do not admit the value of school and students who refuse to consider seriously going to school. In several cases students seemed to exhibit bravado by ignoring school but then secluded themselves at home and idled away their time. The fifth subgroup is that of temporary nonattendance, caused by a specific event such as transfer to another school or parents' divorce. Once the situation has settled down, the child will usually return to school. Recently, more children who are bullied deteriorate into school refusal. When the bullying ends, school refusal may continue. Some of these cases result in a subgroup similar to neurotic school refusal, which must be distinguished carefully.

The problem of school refusal or nonattendance at school became a subject of academic discussion around 1960 in Japan. First named *school phobia*, according to Johnson's terminology (1941), the concept evolved in subsequent years. However, due to resistance to the inaccu-

Table 6.2 *Types of School Nonattendance**

long-term absence from school
- (1) physical reason (illness, injury etc.)
- (2) economic reason
- (3) familial reason (broken home, neglect by parents, parents' irresponsibility, etc.)
- (4) psychological reason (100%) 9,001 cases reporting† (school refusal in broad meaning)
  - (a) neurotic school refusal (70.2%) (school refusal in narrow meaning)
    - i. separation anxiety type
    - ii. spoiled child type
    - iii. burnout of a good child type
  - (b) mental illness (3.3%) (schizophrenia, depression, neuroses, etc.)
  - (c) truant tendency (8.1%)
    - a. apathetic tendency
    - b. delinquent tendency
  - (d) intentional denial of school (does not admit the value of school) (2.2%)
  - (e) temporary school refusal (7.7%)
  - (f) school refusal based on mental retardation and academic failure (7.4%)

*Percentage shown in parentheses refers to the portion of the total number of 9,001 school refusing children who were consulted in prefectural and designated cities' educational centers in 1986.
†Percentages do not add up to 100 due to rounding.

rate use of the technical word *phobia,* the term *school refusal* became accepted.

School refusal is described as a "phenomenon in which a child refuses to attend school due to psychological reasons and shows a variety of characteristic symptoms" (Wakabayashi 1980). Such symptoms may be comprised of physical maladies (including headaches or stomachaches); obsessive-compulsive behaviors; radical changes of behavior and temper within a day; oversensitive reactions to any suggestion of school attendance; remaining at home during school hours; and similar behavioral problems.

There are many hypotheses concerning the psychological mechanisms involved in the symptom formation and onset of school refusal. Around 1960, when the theories of Johnson and Eisenberg were introduced, the psychopathology between mother and child, especially where it involved separation anxiety, was cited as a cause for school refusal in Japan as well as elsewhere. Personality traits and levels of ego development of these children were discussed. The father's absence or a lack of paternal support was pointed out. The school environment itself was said to be full of problems, especially in recent years. It is impossible to identify a sole reason for school refusal.

Three types of neurotic school refusal became apparent when I analyzed contributing factors and processes in case studies of school refusers in senior high school, in work at the Tokyo Metropolitan Education Research Institute in 1972. They are as follows:

(i) *Separation anxiety type.* When the onset of school refusal occurs in kindergarteners and children in the lower grades of elementary school, it is often derived from separation anxiety. The relationship between mother and child is overprotective and symbiotic in some cases, while in others the mother is rejecting. In the latter cases, as a result of the mother's rejection the child seeks her and clings to her. In addition, grandparents sometimes pamper their grandchildren, encouraging their dependence. As a result, these children may refuse to go to school.

(ii) *Spoiled type.* The onset of this type of school refusal is observed at kindergarten age; there are frequent relapses and they get steadily worse. It might be called the chronic type. In this case the relation between parents and child is dominated by the child. Mothers are acquiescent and overprotective, and very close to the child. Fathers are not always supportive and are often peripheral in the family. Children in such homes like to play by themselves in the house and do not play with friends. Accordingly, they seldom face a frustrating situation, have too much pride, have low frustration tolerance, are emotionally immature, are dependent on their mothers, and lack a self-reliant spirit. When such children encounter a threatening situation, they quickly retreat into the house.

(iii) *Burnout of a good child type* (my description). This is an acute type of school refusal which occurs suddenly in junior and senior high school students. Typically, such refusers have been good children and good students; they have never shown dislike of school before the onset of this single episode of refusal; and they are very compliant toward their mothers.

This relationship between mother and child is dominated by the mother. She is controlling and interfering, and she disciplines the child with great expectations. These children internalize their mother's expectations, repress their own needs, and grow up to be good children. As they seldom make mistakes and are precise, hard workers, the parents and the teachers hold them in high esteem. But in junior high they sometimes experience trouble among their peers and encounter difficult situations in which they cannot cope with others' expectations of their academic achievement. Once they lose self-confidence, following the slightest failure, they reject everything and seclude themselves at home.

The characteristics of fathers in this situation are similar to those of fathers of the spoiled child type: they contribute little paternal support.

This discussion of parents of school refusers is not meant to suggest that the causes of school refusal lie solely in the attitudes of mothers or the problems of fathers. These factors may be important when we think about school refusal, but the causes of the syndrome are quite diverse. Moreover, treatment plans, therapeutic processes, and prognoses also vary, depending on the child's developmental level and the time of the onset of school refusal.

For instance, therapeutic counseling for the student works effectively for the burnout of a good child, and the prognosis is good. However, counseling for spoiled children is quite difficult. When everything is left up to these children, they idle away their time, staying in the house as long as they wish. Therapeutic counseling should be undertaken with the parents in order to help them be united and stand firm toward their children.

This classification suggests the necessity of dynamic assessment for school refusers. We cannot see them as manifesting a single psychological mechanism or pathology, but instead we must view them in the context of their developmental levels and parent-child relationships, as well as within the process of symptom formation.

CAUSES OF SCHOOL REFUSAL

The route of the educational system in Japan can be represented as a single line. This means that after six years of elementary school, all the pupils must enter junior high school. About 94 percent of junior high school graduates go to senior high, and then they proceed to universities or colleges. At school, students are pushed to take various exams, evaluated by the results of standardized academic achievement tests (HENSACHI), and controlled by strict school rules. Their individuality is ignored.

In Japanese senior high school education, the high entrance rate and low dropout rate are noticeable. These may reflect strong aspirations for better and higher levels of education. Both parents and students take for granted that dropping out of school means dropping out of the social structure of life itself. This stifling false belief in education nurtures the emergence of school refusing children and makes it difficult to relieve the situation.

Parents, students, and even teachers should have more flexible attitudes toward education, as well as in their daily lives in general.

Another important factor in school refusal is the social environment in Japan. Academic sectionalism (institutional nepotism) has a long history and persists throughout the governmental and private sectors. The term "academic sectionalism" refers to the practice by officials in government or private business of hiring new employees from their own universities. In order to get a good job with a good company, or any good placement, it is almost always necessary to have graduated from the requisite university. Therefore, the competition is keen from kindergarten through senior high school. This competition causes schools to make their programs conform to the needs of society.

Since 1960, changes in the social, economic and cultural life of Japan have put more pressure on students. This may be why the school refusal rates have increased. These changes also have altered the interactions and expectations between parents and children. The mass media influence the nature and quality of parent-child relationships; this influence may secondarily cause a decrease in mutual parent-child responsibility for the child's education. Children secluded with a family computer do not play with and do not learn from other children. Currently the number of nuclear families is increasing, and the number of children per family is decreasing. Fathers work longer hours to support the family and the society's economic development. Child rearing is left to the mother. As a result, some mother-child relationships develop as too close. Moreover, many fathers unwillingly live alone in small cities when they take up new posts, leaving their families behind in large cities because living in such places helps children enter prestigious schools. The problems of school refusal or violence at home are more apt to occur in such families, and it is sometimes very difficult to resolve them. As we have seen, there are many factors to consider. Each case must be evaluated on its own merits, a demanding task for clinicians.

Recently, we have encountered new difficulties. One is a decrease in cases which can be readily classified according to the previously mentioned three typical categories, and a corresponding increase in cases which can be called mixed or intermediate.

A second phenomenon is the emergence of seemingly conflict-free school refusing children. They are immature, especially in person-to-person social interactions. They easily give up activities without showing any enthusiasm; they fail to face their own problems. In these cases, such behaviors do not turn out to be a truly serious problem, but it takes a long time for these children to recover from school refusal.

A third problem is that some mothers tend to be less devoted to taking care of their children, even if they wish strongly for their children to enter a good university. In these cases, the mother-child relationship has become superficial rather than close, as it used to be. Sometimes, mothers follow popular advice acquired from television. For example, one common opinion was expressed thus: "You cannot push your child to go to school. You have to trust your child, and let him or her decide when to go back to school." Another type of mother believes that her child's school refusal is mainly due to social factors, according to the view of experts whose comments they have heard or read. These experts emphasize the school's inadequate environment. When mothers hear these comments, they feel freed from their guilty feelings. Consequently, the mother lets her child follow his or her own wishes, and again a long time must be spent solving the problem. Who should be responsible for such a situation?

Clinicians have opinions derived from their professional experiences. While these clinicians have theoretical discussions and debate these possibilities, however, school refusing children continue to increase in number, and parents and children are left at loose ends.

This paper attempts to clarify the specific characteristics of school refusal in Japan and contrast them to the features of school refusal elsewhere. In order to achieve these goals, it will be important to have the help of distinguished experts from other countries. If a consensus about school refusal is established, it will be very helpful for us all.

REFERENCES

Educational Research Institutes. (1985) *Survey by the Directors' Committee of Various Prefectures and Designated Cities.*

Japanese Ministry of Education. (1987) *Report of the Annual Survey by the Ministry of Education.*

Johnson, A. M., Falstein, E. I., Szurek, S. A., and Svendsen, M. (1941) School phobia. *American Journal of Orthopsychiatry* 11:702–711.

Kamiide, H. (1980) *Gakko Girai no Kodomo* (Children Who Dislike School). Tokyo, Fukumura Shuppan.

Koizumi, E. (1973) *Tōkokyohi* (School Refusal). Tokyo, Gakuji Shuppan.

———. (1979a) *Shishunki Tōkokyohi Jido no Chiryo/shogun' o Megutte* (Concerning the therapy and treatment of adolescent school refusal children). *Japanese Journal of Child Psychiatry* 20, no. 1.

———. (1979b) Jyōcho Shogaiji no Yogo ni Kansuru Kenkyu (A follow-up study on school refusal). *Gendai no Esupuri* no. 139. Tokyo, Shibundo.

Koizumi, E., et al. (1972) A study on the therapy of emotionally disturbed children. In *School Refusal of Senior High School Students*. Tokyo, Tokyo Metropolitan Institute for Educational Research.

Saito, K., et al. (1965) Gakko Kyofusho no Shūyo Chiryo (Residential therapy of school phobia). *Japanese Journal of Child Psychiatry* 6, no. 2.

Sato, S. (1968) *Tōkokyohiji* (Children Who Refuse School). Tokyo, Kokudo-sha.

Sumi, T., et al. (1960) Gakko Kyōfusho no Kenkyu (A study of school phobia). *Seishin Eisei Kenkyu* (Mental Health Studies) 8.

Takagi, R. (1977) Tōkokyohi no Shinri to Byori (The psychology and pathology of school refusal). *Quarterly Psychotherapy* 30.

Uchiyama, K., ed. (1983) *Tōkokyohi* (School refusal). Tokyo, Kongo Shuppan.

Umegaki, H. (1984) *Tōkokyohi no Kodomotachi* (Children who refuse school). Tokyo, Gakuji Shuppan.

Wakabayashi, S. (1980) *The School Refusal Syndrome*. Tokyo, Ishiyaku Shuppan.

7

School Refusal Viewed through Family Therapy

KOJI SUZUKI

SUMMARY

School refusal is a more serious problem in Japan than in other countries. This chapter describes the present state of school refusal in Japan and introduces our research, discusses school refusal as a phenomenon of family systems by examining clinical observations in family therapy, and presents several case studies.

McGill, who studied Japanese families from 1985 to 1987, defined the refusal to attend school as "social anorexia nervosa." According to him, school refusal is an important matter affecting a child's future, being equal to social suicide in Japanese society." If we consider that in Japan a certificate of completion of compulsory education or graduation from a higher educational institution is considered a requisite for all mature members of society, his observation is correct.

Concern about this problem is acute for Japan. Hirata states that school refusal is the result of three conditions: sudden changes in society, the inability of schools to adjust to these changes, and the inability of families to adjust to them. These social factors, in addition to intrapersonal problems, cause confusion and conflict for children.

SCHOOL REFUSAL AND FAMILY THERAPY

Among the approximately 450 families who have come to the National Institute of Mental Health for family therapy, the number of school refusal cases has increased during the past few years and at present accounts for 60 to 70 percent of the total number of consultations. Most of the refusers are children in the upper elementary grades (sixth, seventh, and eighth grades). Although some families are referred by other facilities, most of them come to the Institute on their own after learning about it from newspaper articles or television programs.

Family therapy has become well known, so referral cases have recently increased. Almost all of the families who come to the Institute have already received some type of help from other consultation services or health centers; these are cases in which little progress has been made despite previous efforts by caregivers. Because of the long period of school refusal, the composure of the family has been shaken as family members sense the danger that the family is disintegrating. Usually, therefore, all members of the family are ready to try to solve the problem and cooperate with the family therapists.

Ordinarily the mother shows the most positive attitude toward the therapy, but we press the whole family to participate. We hold the first interview only after confirmation that this plan has been accepted. This way, the father, whose participation is considered the most difficult to ensure, takes part from the first session. Even those businessmen who seem to fit the stereotype of the "economic animal" take time off from work to come to the Institute. However, the child himself is rarely willing to come and often requires firm encouragement by the parents.

Because there are many differing theories of the causes of school refusal, different types of treatment have been recommended. Both counseling facilities and medical facilities offer consultations on school refusal cases. Usually, both will carry out individual treatment of the child, parallel treatment of child and mother, or an interview of the child with the mother present.

Ryurou Takagi classifies the symptoms of school refusal into three phases: the first phase, in which the child complains of physical symptoms; the second, in which the child acts aggressively towards the parents; and the third, in which the child secludes him or herself. It is usually during the second and third phases that the entire family begins to think about the child's problem and offers its cooperation in treatment.

The second phase is often marked by violence in the home which forces the family to pay attention to the child. A mother frightened by her son's violence seeks the help of the father, who has seldom given thought to family matters, or whose job takes him away from his family. In this way the family begins to change significantly. When a child's condition worsens and the child becomes seclusive, parents begin to suspect illness and to take the matter more seriously. At this point, not knowing how to act toward the child, they lose confidence, become confused, and come to need a therapist. When the problem remains unsolved for a long period and the symptoms and behavior have advanced to the third phase, the family becomes more confused and the conflict escalates, disrupting the family.

Looking ahead over the process of family therapy, and the resultant family situation after the treatment, the effects of the child's refusal to attend school are not entirely negative for the family. Perhaps they sense this when they decide to enter treatment. In fact, such positive effects may occur as a loosening of the rigid interactions between family members and better communication, both of which aid family development.

FAMILY DYNAMICS AND CLASSIFICATION OF SCHOOL REFUSAL

Families who come to us for family therapy are generally those with children in elementary and junior high school. School refusal among high school and college students is rare. Where it occurs, the main complaint is not strictly school refusal, but usually idleness or doubt on the part of parents that the child or adolescent will become independent in the future. Here we shall examine only elementary and junior high school students.

In family therapy the therapist tries to understand behavioral problems within the context of the family and does not necessarily try to pursue original causes of the disorder. Instead, proximate causes of current problems (effects) are sought within the family. The relation between causes and effects is conceptualized as a chain, a circular process in which effects influence causes, continuing the circle. If we review this chain or cycle at the end of treatment, we can see the process through which the behavior of school refusing children stimulates family change.

Of course, there are different kinds of school refusal, and family dynamics vary as well. A classification of families of school refusing children makes it possible to differentiate and identify the dynamics specific to each. Several types of school refusal have been examined by Saito, Umegaki, Inamura, Takuma, and others.

A useful classification has been proposed by Inamura (1980), describing five types of school refusal: acute, repeating, mental disorder, idle, and temporary. The acute type is also referred to as the core, neurotic, or school phobia type, and it is the syndrome seen most often. With this type of child, the entire family is usually cooperative from the moment they first seek family therapy. Accordingly, the recovery is smooth, and most such therapy is finished within ten sessions.

The repeating type is also called the chronic, socially immature, or regressive type. Such a child's refusal to attend school begins in kindergarten or elementary school, commonly right after he or she enters a new school, and it is repetitive and chronic. In this child's family, there is often a long period of latent tension or conflict between the parents, or disagreement between the mother and her mother-in-law. During the process of family therapy, these problems come into the open; because they are chronic, however, they do not usually resolve rapidly. With the repeating type, moreover, separation of the mother and child has usually been thwarted, and there is often a very complex family situation—such as a difficult relationship between the parents, or between the father and child—fostering the symbiotic relationship between the mother and child.

The mental-disorder type of school refuser is unable to attend school because of schizophrenia, depression, epilepsy, or anorexia nervosa, and many children in this category come for treatment for these reasons, finding only after visiting other clinical facilities for initial diagnosis that school refusal is a secondary matter. In contrast, the idle type is a truant child, and the temporary type is a child who becomes unable to attend school because of a transient problem with school, home, or friends. These last two types are rarely family therapy patients.

Thus the common examples of school refusers who seek family therapy are the acute type and the repeating type. Some of the families of these children comprise three generations, but most are simply nuclear families in which both parents are typically well, physically and mentally. The mother usually sticks close to the child and is overprotective and intrusive. Her strong compulsions and anxieties are in evidence. Caught in the mother's world, the child finds it difficult to be independent, even at an age when independence is required. At the same time, the child tries to escape the mother's hold.

However, this mother's intrusive, neurotic behavior is not the only cause of school refusal. There are observable family dynamics that nourish her behavior. The child's own personality and behavior, and the father's attitude toward the child and his wife, also may be contributing causes. Often this kind of mother's behavior protects the child and herself from an autocratic father; occasionally, it even serves to keep the father away from the child. Such behavior also stops husband-wife conflict from becoming worse and provides an excuse for the wife to blame the husband who does not involve himself with the child. Conversely, because the mother is absorbed with the child, the father is able to work without worrying about the child, and as a result he will support the mother's behavior. The child is ambivalent about the mother's behavior, wishing to get free of her hold and at the same time wishing to rely on her. Thus the behavior of all family members is interrelated.

Effects on Family Structure

School refusal is a phenomenon that occurs within the context of the family; the entire family affects it and is affected by it. The following model of the family therapy process should illustrate the main effects of school refusal on the family.

First, one parent may have a strong tie to his or her original home, which tie may obstruct the relationship between husband and wife and promote school refusal symptoms. When this happens, it is useful in family therapy to draw a distinct boundary between the family and the one parent's original home, helping the relationships among the family to improve. In one case, during the course of school refusal, the child's violence toward the mother became worse, eventually causing her to scream. The father, indecisive until then, became aware of his own behavior and started to treat his child with a firm attitude. He also began to give preference to his own family over his parents' family. As a result, he and his wife became more intimate. The treatment of school refusal should address the conflict among three generations, regardless of whether all the generations live together.

Second, there are cases in which school refusal is useful for solving a conflict between the parents. In the repeating type of refuser, conflict between the parents may be evident, but with the acute type, the conflict between the parents is latent, buried because they are afraid of expressing it openly. In these cases, the child's school refusal and violence in the home often reveal the parents' unseen conflict, with one of two results. School refusal either clearly helps the parents become close, or it worsens the parents' relationship; this may result in divorce. One eighth-grade boy was violent toward his father while absent from school; he finally forced the father out of the home. When his father tried to enter the house, the boy locked the door and would not let him in; when his mother tried to help his father, the child shouted, "Why are you sticking up for such a man?" and behaved violently toward his mother. Although this child's behavior and its contribution to his own problems cannot be ignored, episodes such as this within the family system present an opportunity for improving the parents' confused and dissatisfied relations.

Third, in some cases it is useful to foster a parent-child relationship suitable to the child's age. A child brought up by an autocratic father or overprotective mother finds it difficult to become independent even upon reaching adolescence. Often his or her self-assertion takes the form of school refusal. In one family, when children began to assert themselves they became reluctant to attend school, as though such reluctance were a family trait.

As the duration of school refusal lengthens and the child begins to be violent, the overprotective mother has no choice but to be less protective, even beginning to hope the child will leave the family. But because the tie between mother and child in such cases is mutual, if one tries to break away the other will try desperately to maintain the bond, and it will be difficult to adjust their relationship. However, by the time the child returns to school, his or her relationship with the mother has changed greatly. The same is true of the father-child relationship. Such changes in the relationship between the parents and child also affect the parents' attitude toward the child's brothers and sisters. When an older brother or sister begins to refuse to attend school, the younger brothers or sisters enjoy school life more than before, as if they were trying to get the parents' attention. This, in turn, intensifies the elder sibling's school refusal. By drawing the parents' attention away from his or her brothers and sisters, the school refuser protects them from the parents' overprotection. Thus, the brothers and sisters get a chance to discover themselves through their elder brother's or sister's school refusal.

Fourth, there are cases in which school refusal precipitates useful changes in family members, removing chronic obstacles to satisfying relationships by exploring the family members' differing senses of values. Japanese are often workaholics, and there are many fathers of school refusers who think mainly about their jobs, rarely about their families. This type of parent has probably never even considered taking a long holiday from work. Obviously, this kind of father cannot understand a child's refusal to attend school. He considers it laziness and tries to force the child to go to school. When the mother tries to stop his intervention, the father tells her that the child "became like this because you baby him!" However, there are also cases in which the father spoils the child and the mother accuses him. In any case, differences between the parents in values, education, and lifestyle are brought into the open; the workaholic father starts decreasing his time at work, spends time with his family, and gradually changes into a home- and family-centered father. Our family therapy requires the father's participation, probably reflecting the mother's or child's secret wish: "Father, stay home and play with us."

It may seem paradoxical, but school refusal seems to bring the father and mother—who have lost themselves in the whirlpool of modern society—back to their family. It may be a kind of warning for Japanese society which pursues profit so single-mindedly.

Among the several kinds of treatment for school refusers (each with specific indications), family therapy may best be suited to (1) cases in which individual therapy has shown no progress; (2) the repeating type; or (3) school refusal caused by the parents' arguments or distance from each other (in the last case, school refusal helps to keep the parents together). As we have seen, families who seek family therapy seem to be trying to solve a long-term family problem by calling attention to it through the child's school refusal. Therefore, the solution of the family problem and of the child's school refusal occur at almost the same time.

Those who can return to school after one set of ten family therapy sessions (one two-hour session per month for ten months) are considered the acute type. The repeating and mental-disorder types often need two or three sets of sessions. For the acute type, the combination of individual treatment—including play therapy—for the child and treatment for the parents can be effective. On the other hand, for the mental-disorder type, a psychoeducational approach with individual and group tutoring may be effective, by providing a correct understanding of the disorder and how to deal with it.

Furthermore, there are certain suitable times for returning to school, so the intervals between the family therapy interviews should be flexible. Also, the father's participation is necessary, especially in Japan; in the family therapy method of treating school refusal, this is the key to success.

The parent-child relationship in cases of school refusal is what European and American family therapists call enmeshed, symbiotic, or fixated, and the boundary between generations is said to be ambiguous. A strong tie develops between a parent and child when one parent is preoccupied with the child as a result of a distant relationship between husband and wife. As the husband and wife gradually are helped to become closer, this tie to the child must be loosened. We first help the parent who is preoccupied with the child to become more so, instead of pulling them apart. For example, we say to the mother, "Pay more attention to your child. Continue until your child says, 'That's enough, go away,'" giving the mother a paradoxical prescription to "do more." This seems to ease the separation between the parent and child.

School Refusal: Multiple Causes and Treatments

The problem of school refusal is serious in Japan; it has prompted research by many investigators. It is hoped that more researchers will conduct systematic investigations, such as that described in this chapter.

School refusal is presented here as a phenomenon of family systems, and family therapy is described as effective treatment. It is important to remember that causes of school refusal can also be found in larger systems, such as the school system. Family therapists must keep this in mind and maintain close contacts with school authorities whenever necessary. Sometimes it is necessary to avoid becoming deeply involved in family matters and to focus on more practical interventions, such as manipulating the school environment, in order to solve the problem. Although family therapy is a very effective treatment, it is not the only solution. Thus, family therapists should know their own limits, combining the treatment with other social resources.

School refusal and/or absence are very serious problems in Japan, a situation not comparable to other countries. This urgent subject will influence not only the future of the identified patients, but also the future of Japan. I hope that many concerned clinicians will practice family therapy and prove its effectiveness.

REFERENCES

Hirata, K. (1980) Etiology of school refusal. In Takuma, T., and Inamura, H., eds., *School Refusal*. Tokyo, Yuhikaku.
Inamura, H. (1980) A definition and classification of school refusal. In Takuma, T., and Inamura, H., eds., *School Refusal*. Tokyo, Yuhikaku.
McGill, D. (1985) *School refusal as social anorexia nervosa*. Paper presented at the Japanese Association of Family Therapy, Tokyo.
Takagi, R., Fujisawa, J., and Kato, N. (1965) School Refusal. *The Japanese Journal of Child and Adolescent Psychiatry*, vol. 6.

III

School Refusal and School Problems in Other Countries

8

Nonattendance at School and School Refusal in Britain*

RICHARD LANSDOWN

Then the whining schoolboy, with his satchel and shining morning face, creeping like snail unwillingly to school.
—*As You Like It*, II, 7, 145–47

SUMMARY

At any one time approximately 10 percent of British schoolchildren are absent from school. In inner city secondary schools this figure can be as high as 25 percent. Despite efforts by many authorities, the absenteeism rate has remained consistent throughout this century. This chapter presents a picture of what is understood to lie behind nonattendance at school, the primary causes seen as related to sociocultural pressures and factors of school organization. Efforts to increase attendance rates are also discussed.

School refusal is differentiated from nonattendance. It affects fewer than 1 percent of British children and on the whole it is a condition which responds well to treatment.

NONATTENDANCE AT SCHOOL

Part-time compulsory education was introduced in Britain following the Elementary Education Acts of 1870 and 1876. By 1872

* The author would like to thank Professor W. Yule for comments on an early draft of this paper.

about 66 percent of London children aged five to fourteen who were enrolled in schools attended them; by 1906 this figure had improved to 89 percent.

Since 1906 full-time education has been compulsory, the school-leaving age has been raised to sixteen, secondary education has been reorganized twice, society's need for a body of well-educated young people has never been greater, teaching has become a graduate profession, theories of child psychology and education have proliferated, and the rate of nonattendance at school has remained solidly at about 10 percent not only in London but elsewhere in Britain (Galloway 1985). This figure of 10 percent should be seen as if anything an underestimate because it represents children who fail to register in school; it takes no account of the "internal truants," those who, possibly in large numbers, register and then absent themselves from all or some of the ensuing lessons.

The Classification of Nonattenders

British classification has been influenced by the work of Johnson et al. (1941) who first used the term school phobia to refer to what Broadwin (1932) had called exceptional cases of truancy. Hersov's study (1960a), partially replicated and confirmed by Blagg (1979), gave rise to a more or less firm distinction between truants, who are absent from school without parental knowledge, and school refusers, who are absent with parental knowledge although without overt parental consent. (See Hersov's overview in part 1 of this volume for a more detailed discussion of the difference between these two.)

There is, however, a third group who have until recently received little attention in the literature: those children who are absent with the connivance and even encouragement of their parents, a pattern of behavior called by some *school withdrawal* (Hersov 1960b); Kahn and Nursten 1962).

Galloway (1985) attempted further to refine categories of nonattendance in his studies based on the northern industrial city of Sheffield. He outlined eight categories, admitting much overlap between them (table 8.1).

These data point up well some of the differences in etiology, at least in the deprived inner city area that was being studied. As can be seen, there is a much greater rate of reported sickness in children aged five to eleven than in the older age group, whereas the rate of what Galloway called school phobia increased from just under 5 percent to just more

Table 8.1 *Categories of Absence for Persistent Absentees in Three Annual Surveys Assessed by Education Welfare Officers, 1974–1976*

	Percentages* of total numbers of absentees			
	age 5–11		age 12–16	
	boys	girls	boys	girls
Mainly illness	34	36	18	24
Some illness but other factors also present	22	26	15	19
Absent with parents' knowledge, consent, and approval	15	11	13	17
Parents unable or unwilling to insist on return	17	13	22	20
Truancy: absence without parents' knowledge	4	0	15	9
Sociomedical reasons (e.g. infestation, scabies, etc.)	7	11	6	4
School phobia or psychosomatic illness	5	4	8	9
Other/could not be rated	4	3	4	7

Source: *Educational Research* 24:188–196. Adapted from Galloway 1982.
*Columns do not add up to 100 percent, due to rounding.

than that figure. (It should be emphasized that this figure refers to 5 percent of the children who were absent, not 5 percent of all children enrolled.)

While the overall nonattendance rate is a constant 10 percent or so, there is far less reliable information about how many students fall into each category within that 10 percent. Galloway's findings are based on returns from education welfare officers, so they are not, he asserts, likely to be reliable. One has only to look at the published estimates for absence from school due to medical reasons to realize that we are in a marshy area: they vary from 96.7 percent (Bransby 1951) to 25 percent (Reynolds and Murgatroyd 1974). Doctors give higher figures than welfare officers, a hardly surprising fact given that the former are generally asked to see only those who are thought to be sick while the latter are asked to see only those thought not to be.

Part of the difficulty in gaining consistency is the variation in definition of nonattendance. Are we talking about children who take an occasional day off, or about persistent absentees? And if it is the latter, do we mean those who miss 25 percent of school days, or more than 50 percent? If we include all those who take an occasional day we shall have figures approaching half the school population (Mawby 1977). If we look only at persistent absentees, we find estimates of 8 percent missing one-fifth of the school days in Northern Ireland (Harbison and Caven 1977) and about 2 percent of secondary pupils missing more than half the total days in Sheffield (Galloway 1976).

The Educational Context

It is not possible to understand nonattendance at school in Britain without seeing it in the context of the educational system, and that can be understood only against the background of the country's social and political structure.

British society is deeply divided, in many ways. There are divisions in educational administration between England and Wales and the rest of the U.K. (Although 'Britain' is used in this chapter it should be noted that data are derived largely from England and Wales.) There is, however, no reason to assume that broad statements made about one area cannot be generalized. Much more clear cut are the divisions between north and south, between rich and poor, between the articulate and the less articulate. Such divisions exist in other countries, but it is doubtful if they are always as pervasive as they are in Britain.

There are two educational systems in Britain. Most children, 93 percent of those aged five to eleven and 87 percent of older children in England and Wales, go to state schools. The remaining 7 percent and 13 percent go to private, fee-paying schools. Of the latter there is an elite group, confusingly named for readers unfamiliar with the system, known as public schools. The private schools generally offer smaller classes, more traditional teaching methods and curricula, and a higher academic standard than is available in the state system. Pupils are not expected to leave much before the age of 18.

State schools, by contrast, are more heterogeneous. Some are well equipped, with excellent attendance and discipline records; others are dingy, poor in every respect. One characteristic of British state schools is that the majority of pupils leave as soon as possible. Table 8.2 compares Britain with other countries.

Table 8.2 *Percentages of Children Staying on at School after the Compulsory Age of Attendance*

	U.S.	Japan	France	West Germany	Britain
In full-time education to the age of 18 (in France to the Baccalaureat)	72	94	33	29	30
Entering university	48	36	28	20	14
Graduating	24	"the majority"	18	16	13

Source: Information from the embassies of each country, reported in the *Guardian*, 5 July 1988.

It must be acknowledged that in table 8.2 like is not always compared with like: an American graduate may not pass anything like the same academic hurdles as one from Germany; what is called university in Japan may have a different name in Britain. What is more, universities do not provide the only form of post-secondary-school education in many of these countries: leaving school at sixteen to take up an apprenticeship in a craft is not opting out of education. The point remains, though, that staying on at school has little attraction for the majority of children in Britain.

Factors Associated with Nonattendance

Sex. As table 8.1 shows, overall attendance rates are similar for boys and girls. Samples of truants, however—children absent from school without parental knowledge—contain more boys.

Age. This is one of the few areas in which there is a consistent trend: absenteeism increases sharply in the secondary school years, reaching a peak in the last year of compulsory attendance. Galloway (1976) for example found that persistent absenteeism (defined as missing more than 50 percent of available days) was 0.4 percent in primary schools, but it reached 4.4 percent by the last year of secondary education.

Social class. Here again the figures are consistent, although the interpretation of the data is less straightforward. There seems to be an association between attendance and social class, with fewer nonattenders from the higher classes. Fogelman and Richardson (1974), in a report based on a large-scale longitudinal study, showed that only 6 percent of pupils missing more than 15 percent of their school days came from social class I, compared to 20 percent from class V. (Social class in Britain is measured by parental occupation.) Similar results have been reported for Scotland (Mitchell 1972; May 1975).

Differences within social classes may be of more interest than simple between-class divisions, since the former are likely to yield more information on causality: social class is a crude classification which can mask a good deal. An examination of children's family backgrounds has shown that truants tend to come from large, socially disadvantaged families. Tibbenham (1977) reported that overcrowding was more common in families of absentees in all social classes. Rutter et al. (1975) and Galloway (1982) noted a strong association between poverty, gauged by the provision of free school meals, and rates of absenteeism. Knowledge of such provision did not, however, allow accurate predictions of individual children's behaviour.

Before we jump to easy conclusions on hardship and absenteeism it must be acknowledged, as Wedge and Prosser (1973) did, that only a minority of disadvantaged children are persistently absent from school.

Geographical area. The tendency, small but consistent, is for absenteeism to be higher in industrialized towns. Wales, for reasons so far obscure, has a higher proportion of pupils missing more than 15 percent of school than does England or Scotland.

Patterns of absence. An intriguing finding is that there is a cumulative effect over time. Nonattendance tends to increase towards the end of the week, end of the term, and end of the year. Perhaps there is a parallel in the adult who sees Friday afternoon as virtually free time and therefore does not feel compelled to remain at work.

Attainment. By definition most school nonattenders perceive that school has little to offer them compared to what is available elsewhere. It is tempting to assume that the root of the problem is that children with low attainment simply absent themselves. Douglas and Ross (1965), Fogelman and Richardson (1974), and Fogelman (1978) have used longitudinal data to examine this question. There are two conclusions:

   a) There is a significant association between attendance and attainment but only for children from lower social classes.

   b) Children who continue to miss school also continue, not surprisingly, to have lower scores on tests of attainment; but those who return to regular attendance can catch up.

In other words, it is unlikely that there is a direct, causal association with low attainment leading to not attending school; it is more likely that the association is the other way around.

School differences. For many years we were taught that schools have only a marginal effect on children's performance, the Plowden Report (DES 1967) being the last major statement along these lines. The picture has changed somewhat in recent years, following the pioneering work of Power et al. (1967) and it is now acknowledged that the ethos of the school must be considered in any explanation of both attainment and behavior, including delinquency. Also included in the list of effects to which schools make a major contribution is attendance. Reynolds et al. (1980) looked at nine schools and found consistent differences (between 73 percent and 90 percent attendance) over a seven-year period. Rutter et al. (1979) reported on 15- to 16-year-olds in twelve London schools and found attendance rates varying from 65 percent to 87 percent. The authors of both studies maintained that they controlled for economic and social variables.

It may be hard for readers unfamiliar with the British educational system to appreciate the mechanism by which schools can vary so much. What is often not realized is the degree of autonomy that has, up to now, been enjoyed by head teachers even in state schools. The position is changing, but until now teachers have been free to choose their own curriculum within very broad limits and to decide when and how to teach it.

Delinquency. Teachers have been known to sigh with relief when some truants are away, as they are so often the class trouble makers, delinquents whose absence is welcomed. There is a well-established association between delinquency and nonattendance (Tyerman 1958; Hersov 1960a, b; Tennent 1971). An analysis of the data suggests that truants are at risk for delinquency but the association is far from perfect: not all truants offend and not all offenders truant.

Explanations of Nonattendance

There is no point in seeking a single-factor explanation for a phenomenon as complex as nonattendance at school. Those discussed below are introduced as though separate; in fact, there is likely to be considerable interaction among several variables and no one approach will explain all problems.

Family-centered theories argue that children are victims of parental neglect. Data on family size support this view: the larger the family, the more the individual child's needs are likely to be ignored. Family factors can also explain the rise in absenteeism in secondary schools, since some parents encourage older children to stay at home either to keep the parent company or to look after younger children, or to do both.

Some child-centered theorists argue powerfully that not going to school can be seen as a healthy response in those children who have been made painfully aware of their academic frailty. If school offers nothing but humiliation, with the message given that success will never be possible, then absenting oneself is a self-protective measure.

School-based theories fall into two broad areas. The first is that there is something aversive in school; it may be a feared teacher or a bullying classmate. The second is much more general: formal education, especially at the secondary level, is simply irrelevant to a proportion of children and their parents. These children do not actively dislike school, but rather they see educational preoccupations as marginal to their own. School is a place where "They" say that children have to go. As Galloway (1985) put it, writing about families of persistent nonattenders:

> The problem of school attendance was often treated in the same way as a demand for payment of an electricity bill or a hire purchase demand—something to be deferred for as long as possible. For a majority of families, living in multiply disadvantaged, acutely stressful circumstances, school attendance was low on the list of priorities. . . . School was seldom seen as an active source of advice, help and support. Instead, school attendance was normally seen as just one more burden to be borne. (75)

Measures to Counteract Nonattendance

The Education Welfare Service and the Law

The primary aim of Education Welfare officers is to get children back to school. Although many of them have social work qualifications, they are still regarded by some teachers as "kid catchers" and their work often fails to address itself to the more general reasons for nonattendance.

It is the parents' duty to send children to school and legal sanctions have long been available for use against those who fail in this duty. One approach, used in the northern city of Leeds, has received much attention (Berg et al. 1985). This approach involves taking parents to court and then repeatedly adjourning the case on the understanding that the children's progress will be reviewed in a couple of weeks' time. This seems to be more successful with children whose parents have so far consented to their absence; it is less so with the others (and still less so with school refusers). Summing up the attempts to use legal proceedings to get children to attend school, Galloway (1985) sees their haphazard application and poor outcome as discouraging. They are seldom based on a clear understanding of the complexities of the problem and teachers and magistrates "might be more happily occupied in search of the Holy Grail."

Measures within the Education System

Since it is schools from which children absent themselves, it is schools that should change if the problem is to be tackled at its root. So runs one argument. Much can be learned from the highly successful public schools which have a clear aim: to turn out socially poised young people with academic attainments sufficient to take them into high-income occupations. This is what parents pay for and usually this is what they get. British primary schools, moreover, have a high reputation and by and large they, too, know what they want to do and have a clear idea of how to go about the task. However, state secondary schools, having to cater to a population becoming increasingly heterogeneous as it gets older, have a much harder challenge than either the public or the primary schools and there is nothing like the coherence in the secondary sector that one finds elsewhere. As Jones (1980) put it,

Teachers have tried to be all things to all pupils: parents, friends, social workers. They have been confused about the aims of schools, which have in some instances too often ended as a combination of soup kitchen, social club, and welfare agency. The result has immobilized many schools, with the burden of the nonattender adding to the sense of failure. If there is a failure, it comes from not having defined the task of the school and from not setting realistic limits to the task (172)

Nevertheless, the principle remains that if schools are to change they should move in the direction of ensuring that what they have to offer makes sense both to parents and to children. This may imply a change in the curriculum and teaching methods and it almost certainly means that schools will need to undertake a public relations exercise with their parents. Jones (1980) reported on changes in attendance in her London secondary school following a wide ranging review of the school's procedures. The average attendance rose from 77 percent in 1974 to 88 percent in 1977.

The Future

In conclusion it should be noted that even Jones's efforts failed to dent the 10 percent barrier. There are, however, major changes for British education in the pipeline. State schools may now opt out of the control of local education authorities, which means that head teachers and boards of governors will have more power to shape their overall policy. In theory this means a shift toward making schools more accountable to parents; certainly the aim of legislation is that poor schools, which fail to attract pupils, will go to the wall. Whether this will lead to an increase in the attention paid to the missing 10 percent or whether they will be regarded as nuisances obstructing the work of the other 90 percent remains to be seen.

SCHOOL REFUSAL

As the previous section has shown, nonattendance at school is a serious, long-standing problem in Britain, with a poor outlook. In contrast, school refusal is numerically a much smaller problem, affecting fewer than 1 percent of children, and the outlook is optimistic. This does not mean that it is an easy problem to treat, nor that there is agreement on all sides about etiology or methods of coping with it. It has generated twenty-five times as many research articles as any other childhood phobia (Graziano et al. 1979) but as Blagg (1988) concludes in a review article, "confusion still reigns over the nature of the problem and the best way to handle it."

British thinking in this area has been heavily influenced by the work of Hersov, whose main conclusions were confirmed in a replication in Somerset by Blagg (1979). School refusal is seen as distinct from truancy or parental withholding and falls within the sphere of the child psychiatrist or psychologist; that is, it is seen as a condition amenable to treatment focused on the family or the child.

Psychiatric and psychological services are not uniform in Britain. Every local Education Authority employs educational psychologists, in ratios varying from 1 for every 3,000 pupils to 1 for every 10,000, but the role of the educational psychologist varies between and within authorities. A minority see working therapeutically with individual children and families as their main task; others perceive this as an outmoded, economically nonviable approach, leading to a questionable outcome. The latter group prefer to act as consultants to schools, spending very little time with children themselves. Until recently educational psychologists worked alongside child psychiatrists in child guidance services. This system is now waning, being replaced by a much looser network (DHSS 1976) in which the psychologist has greater autonomy.

In many, but by no means all, areas psychologists and psychiatrists are based within the health service, offering child and family therapy. These professionals work as part of the network mentioned above; unfortunately, communication between those working in health care settings and those in education is not always perfect.

The earliest therapeutic approaches were based on psychoanalytic theories (Klein 1945; Sperling 1961), with a shift from an original focus on the child to one on the family system (Skynner 1974). Current treatment is more likely to be based on learning theory.

Yule (1977) identified five groups of school refusers:

1. Children whose refusal starts on entry into school, with whom separation anxiety is usually associated. They respond well to desensitization via a graded return to school.

2. Children whose refusal begins shortly after a major change in schooling. They also respond to a graded return to school if particular attention is paid to what they find stressful.

3. Those whose sudden overt refusal is not associated with educational changes. It is possible that their behavior is linked with a depressive disorder or other kind of illness. More individual work is usually required with these children than with those in the first two groups.

4. Children—of any age—who have been at school for only a short time. They respond to relatively straightforward techniques such as the preparation of a behavioral contract.

5. Those whose refusal is associated with a combination of stresses; for example, bullied children who were already anxious about separation from home.

Yule et al. (1980) describe an approach to treatment in detail. It is

predominantly behavioural yet with close attention to other personal and family factors. . . . there are four steps in an overall treatment approach: (i) establishing a good, trusting relationship with the child and his family; (ii) clarifying the stimulus situations which give rise to anxiety; (iii) desensitizing the child to the feared situations by using imagination, relaxation, or merely talking, whichever is appropriate; and (iv) confronting the feared situations. We prefer, when we have the choice, to adopt a gradual rather than a sudden approach to the latter.

Blagg and Yule (1984) reported a treatment series of thirty adolescents, using behavioral problem-solving techniques. They noted a 90 percent success rate, compared to 37 percent found in children sent to a psychiatric unit and 10 percent in a group receiving psychotherapy and home tuition. The behaviorally treated group needed an average of two and one-half weeks of intervention compared to forty-five weeks for the hospitalized group and seventy-two weeks for those receiving psychotherapy.

The distinction between psychoanalytic and behavioral techniques should not be exaggerated. Blagg (1987) concluded that a comprehensive behavioral approach has much in common with procedures used by successful psychodynamic therapists. The key components of both are a problem-solving strategy, flexibility and sensitivity on the part of teachers, an assumption that the major question is when rather than whether the child will go back to school, and the organization of an immediate return.

Many cases of school refusal are relatively simple in both etiology and treatment and, in any case, they make up only a very small proportion of those children referred to child psychiatrists or psychologists in Britain. Nonattendance for other reasons is a much more pervasive, complex, and difficult phenomenon which has so far proved remarkably resilient.

REFERENCES

Berg, I., Casswell, G., Hullin, R., McGuire, R., and Tagg, G. (1985) Classification of severe school attendance problems. *Psychological Medicine* 15:157–165.
Blagg, N. R. (1979) The behavioural treatment of school refusal. Ph.D. thesis, University of London.
——— (1987) *School Phobia and Its Treatment*. Beckenham, Croom Helm.
——— (1988) School phobia: Common issues in treatment. *Links* 13:38–42.
Blagg, N. R., and Yule, W. (1984) The behavioural treatment of school refusal: A comparative study. *Behaviour Research and Therapy* 22:119–127.

Bransby, E. R. (1951) A Study of absence from school. *The Medical Officer* 86:223–230;237–240.

Broadwin, I. T. (1932) A Contribution to the study of truancy. *American Journal of Orthopsychiatry* 2:253–259.

Department of Education and Science. (1967) *Children and Their Primary Schools* (The Plowden Report). London, Her Majesty's Stationery Office.

Department of Health and Social Security. (1976) *Fit for the Future: Report of the Committee on the Child Health Services* (The Court Report) Vol.s I and II. London, Her Majesty's Stationery Office.

Douglas, J. W. B., and Ross, J. (1965) The effects of absence on primary school performance. *British Journal of Educational Psychology* 35:18–40.

Fogelman, K. (1978) School Attendance, attainment, and behaviour. *British Journal of Educational Psychology* 48:148–158.

Fogelman, K., and Richardson, K. (1974) School attendance: Some results from the national child development study. In Turner, B., ed., *Truancy*. London, Ward Lock Educational.

Galloway, D. (1976) Size of school, socioeconomic hardship, suspension rates and persistent unjustified absence from school. *British Journal of Educational Psychology* 46:40–47.

―――. (1982) Persistent absence from school. *Educational Research* 24:188–196.

―――. (1985) *Schools and Persistent Absentees*. Oxford, Pergamon.

Graziano, A. M., DeGiovanni, I. S., and Garcia, K. (1979) Behavioral treatment of children's fears: A review. *Psychology Bulletin* 84:804–830.

Harbison, J., and Caven, N. (1977) *Persistent School Absenteeism in Northern Ireland*. Belfast, Statistics and Economics Unit, Department of Finance.

Hersov, L. (1960a) Persistent nonattendance at school. *Journal of Child Psychology & Psychiatry* 1:130–136.

―――. (1960b) Refusal to go to school. *Journal of Child Psychology and Psychiatry* 1:137–145.

Jones, A. (1980) The school's view of persistent nonattendance. In Hersov, L., and Berg, I., eds., *Out of School*. Chichester, Wiley.

Johnson, A. M., Falstein, E. I., Szurek, S. A., and Svendsen, M. (1941) School phobia. *American Journal of Orthopsychiatry* 11:702–711.

Kahn, J. and Nursten, J. P. (1962) *Unwillingly to School*. Oxford, Pergamon.

Klein, E. (1945) The reluctance to go to school. *The Psychoanalytic Study of the Child* 1:263–279.

Mawby, R. I. (1977) Truancy: data from a self-report survey. *Durham and Newcastle Research Review* 8:21–34.

May, D. (1975) Truancy, school absenteeism, and delinquency. *Scottish Educational Studies* 7:97–107.

Mitchell, S. (1972) The absentees. *Education in the North* 9:22–28.

Power, M. J., Alderson, M. R., Phillipson, C. M., Schoenberg, E., and Morris, J. M. (1967) Delinquent schools. *New Society* 10:542–543.

Reynolds, D., Jones, D. and St. Leger, S. (1980) *Schools that Fail*. London, Routledge & Kegan Paul.

Reynolds, D., and Murgatroyd, S. (1974) Being absent from school. *British Journal of Law and Society* 1:78–80.

Rutter, M., Yule, B., Quinton, D., Rowlands, O., Yule, W., and Berger, M. (1975) Attainment and adjustment in two geographical areas. (III) Some factors accounting for area differences. *British Journal of Psychiatry* 126:520–533.

Rutter, M., Maughan, B., Mortimore, P., Ousten, J., and Smith, A. (1979) *Fifteen Thousand Hours: Secondary Schools and their Effects on Pupils*. London, Open Books.

Sperling, M. (1961) Analytic first aid in school phobics. *Psychoanalytic Quarterly* 30:504–518.

Skynner, R. (1974) School phobia: A reappraisal. *British Journal of Medical Psychology* 47:1–16.

Tennent, T. G. (1971) School Nonattendance and delinquency. *Educational Research* 13:185–190.

Tibbenham, A. (1977) Housing and truancy. *New Society* 39:501–502.

Tyerman, M. J. (1958) A Research into truancy. *British Journal of Educational Psychology* 28:217–225.

Wedge, P., and Prosser, H. (1973) *Born to Fail*. London, Arrow Books.

Yule, W. (1977) Behavioural treatment of children and adolescents with conduct disorders. In Hersov, L., Berger, M., and Shaffer, D., eds., *Aggression and Antisocial Behaviour in Childhood and Adolescence*. Oxford, Pergamon.

Yule, W., Hersov, L., and Tressider, J. (1980) Behavioural treatments of school refusal. In Hersov, L., and Berg, I., eds., *Out of School*. Chichester, Wiley.

9

Treatment of School Phobia in Children and Adolescents in Germany

HELMUT REMSCHMIDT

FRITZ MATTEJAT

SUMMARY

Though school phobia very often emerges against a background of affective and anxiety disorders in the child or the child's family, it is not clear whether school phobia has a unique etiology. The important factors in the development of school phobia are the child's personality, the family circumstances and relationships, different trigger conditions (such as parental crisis), and secondary psychosomatic or other complaints.

A patient-centered family therapeutic outpatient or inpatient approach, using family contracts, has been successful for the treatment of school phobia. This therapeutic procedure utilizes the following principles: a stepwise, integrative approach; the interruption of secondary dynamics; and clear directions and plans for all persons and institutions involved with the child. The choice of treatment modality used—inpatient, outpatient, or day hospital treatment—depends on four criteria: (1) the age and developmental stage of the child, (2) the severity of school phobia, (3) the family relationships and stresses, and (4) the family's capacity for cooperation.

This therapeutic approach has been successful for about two-thirds of all patients treated as outpatients or inpatients.

There is general agreement among child psychiatrists that separation anxiety is the main clinical feature of school phobia (Johnson et al. 1941; Eisenberg 1958; Weber 1967). According to DSM III, states of school phobia are classified under the heading of separation anxiety disorder (309.21), using the following diagnostic criteria:

A. excessive anxiety concerning separation from those to whom the child is attached (there are nine additional symptoms belonging to A)
B. duration of disturbance of at least two weeks
C. not due to a pervasive developmental disorder, schizophrenia, or any other psychotic disorder
D. if 18 or older, does not meet the criteria for agoraphobia.

Within the multiaxial classification scheme (Rutter, Shaffer, and Sturge 1976), states of school phobia may be classified under the heading of adjustment reaction (309.2) or as a disturbance of emotions specific to childhood and adolescence.

Several investigators have stated in recent years that, in many cases, an overlap of school phobic disorder with affective and anxiety disorders can be found (Kolvin et al. 1984; Bernstein and Garfinkel 1986). Some authors look upon school phobia and school refusal as a behavior symptomatic of depressive states (Glaser 1967; Cytryn and McKnew 1974).

Yet not all cases of school phobia include symptoms of depression and separation anxiety, in spite of the fact that the majority (about 75 to 80 percent) do (Gittelman and Klein 1984; Waldron et al. 1975). These results indicate that school phobia is not a unique and exclusive condition, and it is therefore important to carry out a careful differential diagnosis before beginning therapy.

The following conditions have to be excluded (DSM III): overanxious disorder, avoidant disorder of childhood or adolescence, pervasive developmental disorders, schizophrenia, major depression, conduct disorder with truancy, and phobic disorder. As this paper deals with therapy, it is not our aim to go into more detail concerning diagnosis and differential diagnosis. But it must be emphasized that a careful differential diagnosis is necessary. Clinicians and researchers in the field agree that the following criteria are characteristic of children and adolescents with school phobia (Berg et al. 1969):

(1) A strong history of school refusal. However, in most cases there are no problems in learning and no antisocial behavior.
(2) Associated emotional and/or psychosomatic disorders. These symptoms have a close relation to school attendance. They are usually not present during holidays and the weekend.

(3) The parents are well informed about school refusal, separation anxiety, and the emotional and psychosomatic symptoms.

(4) There is no history of antisocial behavior.

Within this paper, we use the foregoing criteria for diagnosis, including assessment of family relationships and all other circumstances around the child. It is difficult to give clear epidemiological figures. The prevalence of school phobia reported in the literature varies considerably. The main reason is that there are various degrees of school fears, aversions, and refusal, and therefore the criteria used to identify school phobia may vary significantly. Older studies report between three and ten cases per 1,000 school beginners (Leton 1962). When we use the diagnostic criteria which we report here, the actual prevalence lies approximately between 0.5 percent and 1.5 percent (Granell de Aldaz et al. 1984). It is unclear, at least in western countries, whether school phobia has become more frequent during the last years or whether clinicians and scientists have paid more attention to this interesting condition. There is some evidence of a growing prevalence in Japan.

ORIGINS AND CAUSES OF SCHOOL PHOBIA

As already stated, school phobia has no unique etiology. There is evidence that different conditions and mechanisms play a role in the development of this disorder. First, there is a close relationship to the nature of family interactions, especially a strong symbiotic bonding between the child and the mother. Second, there are symptoms of anxiety disorders, phobic disorders, and affective disorders, but this relationship cannot be found in every case. Third, there is no doubt that developmental stages play an important role in the manifestation of school phobia. For instance, the first manifestation may take place when the child initially goes to kindergarten, and very often there is a relapse at the beginning of primary school and also sometime during adolescence. Fourth, certain conditions inside and outside of school can facilitate the manifestation of school phobia, but are not causal in etiology.

Children with school phobia have difficulty developing independence and autonomy. Outside the family they are mostly withdrawn and socially isolated; especially at school, they feel threatened and insecure. However, in relation to the parents, such children are very pretentious and powerful.

Family Situation and Relationships

Very often the child's mother has a depressive personality structure. She has a strong tendency to develop a symbiotic relationship with her child, especially when the partnership with her husband is unsatisfactory or if she is the only parent in a one-parent family. In families with both parents, the father is largely passive and plays no central role in education. Such families may be characterized by the statement that the child is more important for the mother than is her husband. The child receives ambiguous instructions and is not adequately guided by the parents; on the contrary, the parents are often dominated by the child, and the generational boundaries are not maintained.

A variety of different conditions may trigger the manifestation of a school phobia. We have observed the following conditions: parental crisis with the danger of their possible separation, illness of the mother, birth of a sibling, changing school, difficulties with other children at school, illness of the child, and death of an important family member who had a close relationship to the child.

Moreover, there may be a wide range of symptoms secondary to the central conflict of school phobia. First, there are many somatic symptoms (such as headache, stomachache, or nausea) which suggest to the parents that the child is sick. This results in many examinations by doctors, who determine that the child is physically healthy and, in principle, able to go to school. But the family cannot accept this conclusion. The parents defend the child's somatic symptomatology and do not feel understood by doctors or other therapists. The child remains absent from school, so the social isolation grows, and the child develops guilt feelings which facilitate depressive symptomatology.

There are at least three theoretical models which integrate and interpret the etiological factors:

(1) *The psychoanalytic model.* Within this model, the main mechanism is the displacement of anxiety and aggression from family to school. Anxiety and aggressive impulses that were primarily directed to family members are projected onto people and an institution outside the family, namely the school.

(2) *The behavioral model.* In this model, school phobic behavior can be understood as a reaction of avoidance. According to a thorough behavioral analysis, different features of anxiety situations have to be taken into account, as does the response of the parents who reward the avoidance reaction through their own behavior.

(3) *The family model.* This model initially analyzed the mother-child dyad, but it has extended the view to interactions of the whole family, especially including the role of the father. The family itself is looked upon as a dynamic system in which each person interacts with the others according to the configuration of this unique family. The child's symptomatology plays a central role in the family system, which can be characterized by insufficient boundaries between parents and child and the inability of the parents adequately to confront the child with reality. The result is an imbalance within the family, giving unusual power to the child, but leaving the child in a position of anxiety, withdrawal, and social isolation outside the family.

Of course, these three models do not exclude one another. Each puts the focus on different aspects which often have to be combined within the course of a successful therapy.

GENERAL PRINCIPLES OF THERAPY

Table 9.1 shows some general principles of therapy in school phobia. For each area that has to be influenced, there are different goals. The areas needing change are: (1) symptomatology of the patient, (2) personality and social behavior of the patient, and (3) family interactions and attitudes of the parents. The general line of therapy is to reduce separation anxiety by influencing the child, as well as the parents, and to help the child achieve more autonomy and self-confidence. In addition, it aims to help the family attain some kind of reorganization by developing clear roles within the family and increasing the parents' competence to facilitate the child's education.

According to our experience, it is extremely important to intervene in all three areas and not to use a narrow approach focusing only on the therapy of the child or on counseling the parents. In order to organize and start active therapy, we have found several principles very useful.

A stepwise, integrative approach. After a careful diagnostic evaluation, the initiation of therapy depends on the symptomatology and assumed etiological factors. In cases with depressive symptomatology, for instance, an antidepressant medication is combined with a family therapeutic approach. In other cases, where separation anxiety is not so prominent, but where there is pronounced anxiety in relation to school, a behavior therapeutic approach is preferred.

Table 9.1 *General Goals of Therapy for School Phobia*

Areas of Intervention	Goals of Therapy
Symptomatology of the patient	(1) School attendance (2) Reduction of separation anxiety (3) Reduction of depression and anxiety
Personality and social behavior of the patient	(1) Reduction of dependence on parents (2) Reduction of social anxieties and social isolation (3) Stimulation of self-confidence and autonomy in the child
Family interaction and attitudes of parents	(1) Establishing natural boundaries between parents and child (2) Influencing anxiety and/or depression in parents (3) Development of clear generational structures and roles within the family by active facilitation of the child's education

The best therapeutic method is an integrative approach, which allows the combination of different therapeutic methods taking into account age, developmental stage, family conditions, and diagnostic features of the individual child. We thus combine different methods, beginning with simple steps and going on to more complex ones. In the beginning of this stepwise establishment of the therapeutic process, the therapist takes over a supportive role for the family as well as a controlling one. These functions are given back to the patient and his family according to the progress of therapy. In other words, both the demands on and the responsibility of the parents and the child increase with time.

The therapeutic technique has sequential components; there is a strong predominance of supportive and structured measures during the first period of therapy. When the child and family have become oriented and gained more security and confidence, it is then possible to approach the basic conflicts within the family. In the case of clear depressive symptomatology, a tricyclic antidepressant medication for the child is very useful.

The interruption of secondary dynamics. When the child has missed school for a long time, we find, as a rule, an escalation of the secondary dynamics within the family. For this reason, it is useful to get the child to school again as soon as possible. To reach this goal, it is necessary to inform the parents that the child does not have a somatic disorder and to focus on the positive personality traits and abilities of the child. The therapist supports the parents as they make clear decisions and helps them bring the child to school again in a stepwise fashion. For instance, the child should first learn again to enter the school building, then to stay for half an hour or one hour during a lesson, then to stay longer, and so on.

Clear directions and plans for all persons and institutions involved. At the beginning of therapy, it is extremely important to inform all involved persons and institutions about the child, his or her disorder, and some of the principles of therapy. For instance, school refusal is very often looked upon as a conduct problem or as naughtiness on the part of the child. Somatic complaints of the child are often misunderstood as symptoms of a somatic disorder. For these reasons, it is necessary to inform all those who have anything to do with the child (such as teachers or physicians); of course, this can be done only with the family's consent.

Preparation for Therapy

In principle, there are three settings for the treatment of school phobia: outpatient treatment, inpatient treatment, and day-hospital treatment. In order to decide which modality is the most appropriate for a specific case, the following criteria are important:

(1) Age and developmental stage of the child. The younger the child, the better the prognosis and the better the chances for successful outpatient treatment. It is, for instance, usually not appropriate to use inpatient treatment for kindergarten children or children entering the first grade.

(2) Severity of school phobia. The longer the school phobic symptomatology has existed, the less favorable is the prognosis for outpatient treatment. In chronic school phobics who have refused to go to school for many months, inpatient treatment will be inevitable, especially when there have been several unsuccessful outpatient treatments. During the first episode, outpatient treatment should be attempted. Besides the duration of school refusal, several further criteria can be used to assess the severity of school phobia; these include the extent of depressive and/or psychosomatic symptoms, the degree of social isolation, and the intensity of separation anxiety. It is also helpful to use a global assessment score (for example, see Shaffer et al. 1983).

(3) Family relationship and stresses. The relationships within the family, and an estimation of relative family stresses, are as important as the severity of the child's school phobia. In this respect, different factors are relevant:

- the living conditions of the family and the integration of the family within the community;
- the physical and mental health of the parents;
- marital conflicts of the parents; and
- educational attitudes and style in relation to the child.

The importance of these factors underlines the view of school phobia as a family problem. In some cases, for instance, separation anxiety is also a prominent feature motivating the parents' behavior. But even in cases without manifest separation anxiety in the patients, they show at least an attitude of overprotection toward the school phobic child.

(4) Cooperation of the family. A very important condition for the success of therapy is the cooperation of the family. Within this field, at least three aspects are important.

The objective framework of therapy. There are some basic questions that have to be answered before therapy can start: How often is the family able and willing to participate in therapy sessions? How many family members are able and willing to participate in outpatient therapy? Is one of the parents able to control the child during his attempt to reenter school?
Cooperative ability. The capacity for cooperation depends on intelligence, personality, the capacity for introspection, and the engagement of the parents. It is important to adapt the kind of intensity of therapy to the abilities of the parents.
Cooperative readiness. The readiness for cooperation depends to a large extent on the kind and intensity of suffering of all family members. But not only is the intensity of suffering as such important, but also the kind of problem definition agreed upon by the family members. For example, it is easier to start and continue therapy with parents who desire support in the education of the child and in reducing the family's anxiety and depression. On the other hand, it creates far more difficulties for the initiation and successful outcome of therapy if the parents are not able to give up their opinion that the child is physically ill or if they expect the support and help of the therapist against the teachers and the usual requirements at school. In the latter case, it is always

difficult to instruct teachers about the special conditions of the disorder. Table 9.2 shows some important aspects of the parents' problem definition in relation to the prognosis of therapy.

Beginning Therapy

The beginning of therapy is most difficult if the family is extremely resistant to all suggestions for treatment. In such extreme cases, it is sometimes necessary to separate the child from the parents. Otherwise, it is possible to plan the treatment together with the family.

Before starting treatment, it is necessary to discuss all results of the diagnostic evaluation thoroughly with the family. This session should be used to reassure the parents and to give them a clear understanding of the problem and the different means for its solution. It is necessary to help the parents find a realistic view of the child and of their own behavior. After reviewing the problem definition, it is important to discuss with the family the treatment which seems best for their situation. Very often, a rapid decision has to be made whether an outpatient, inpatient, or day patient treatment is most appropriate.

Of course, inpatient treatment is the therapy of choice only in severe cases. Normally, we prefer outpatient treatment, starting very soon after the first manifestation of school phobic behavior. If there is an agreement on inpatient treatment, it is important to define the whole framework of treatment at the very beginning. It is also necessary to tell the family that during the process of therapy several problems may arise. It is self-evident that treatment is a heavy burden for the parents of a school phobic child, and there is always the danger that they will interrupt the therapy. Therefore, this problem must be discussed beforehand.

If inpatient treatment seems necessary, but the parents are not able to accept this, we propose a probationary outpatient treatment and a contract in which the type of therapy and the obligations of the parents, the patient, and the therapist are fixed. There is also a paragraph within the treatment plan which states under which conditions outpatient treatment will be no longer sufficient, and under which circumstances we will convert to inpatient treatment. In most cases, we start outpatient treatment with a behavior modification plan, with the general expectation that the child should be supported strongly in order to reenter school within a few weeks. The family and the therapist help the child to overcome his or her fear and reward all steps of approximation to the school building and the school situation.

Table 9.2 *Problem Definitions as Indicators of Favorable Conditions for Therapy*

Level of Problem Definition		Example	Expected Treatment	
				Favorable Therapy Conditions
Interactional		The parents present their own problems concerning assertiveness or separation difficulties in relation to the patient	The parents want guidance in respect to the patient or family therapy	↑
Symptomatic	Psychological symptoms including school refusal	The parents are concerned because of psychological symptoms, e.g. depressive mood of the child	The parents want a psychiatric or psychotherapeutic treatment of the child	
	Somatic symptoms	The parents think that the child suffers from an organic disease	The parents want a somatic treatment of the child	
Secondary		The parents complain about the presumably unjustified pressure which the school or youth welfare office puts on them	The parents want support against the demands of the school or other official agencies	↓ Unfavorable Therapy Conditions

If this plan is not successful, there is usually enough confidence between the family and the therapist to enable the family to accept inpatient treatment.

Outpatient Treatment

The majority of children, especially those who live under favorable family conditions and are younger than ten years of age, can be treated by outpatient therapy. In many cases, school phobic behavior is the expression of an acute crisis in the child and/or the family. It is often possible to start treatment soon after the first manifestation of school phobic behavior, especially if parents cooperate. Outpatient treatment typically includes three components:

- behavior therapy
- antidepressant medication if significant depressive symptoms are present, and
- individual psychotherapy for the patient or family therapy, including at least the two parents and the child, combined with separate sessions for the child alone and the parents alone.

Therapeutic Contract

At the beginning of treatment, we formulate a therapeutic contract between patient and parents on one side, and the therapist on the other side. The contract is based on the principles of behavior therapy with simultaneous attention to family dynamics.

In the contract, the patient and parents take on the obligation to achieve specific objectives and to accept control by the therapist. But this is not the only goal of the contract. At least as important are the implicit components of the contract. In this respect, it is important that all participants take over special responsibilities: the patient accepts the obligation to go to school (or at least to try to do so), the parents agree to support him or her in the realization of this goal, and the therapist takes over control (which is given back, in a later phase of therapy, to the parents and child). So the contract has two sides: to confront the patient with clear demands, controlled by the therapist, and to support the patient, including clear parental support. Thus the agreement takes cognitive, motivational, and behavioral aspects into consideration.

(1) *The cognitive aspect: orientation and security.* The contract has to be simple and understandable in order to stabilize the family and give the child and family some security. The following principles are important:

- Explanation of a clearly structured concept of treatment: the explanation includes information about the difficulties of treatment, the possibility of relapses during the treatment course and the necessity for continuous cooperation during the entire period.
- Simple and understandable treatment goals that reduce the complexity of family relationships by concentrating on their most important aspects.
- Clear definitions of the therapeutic goals, which can be tested (examined).

(2) *The motivational aspect: enhancement of self-confidence and motivation.* Although the therapist primarily determines the structure of the cooperation, it is very important to include, as much as possible, proposals by the family in the therapeutic process. Doing this can enhance the self-confidence and motivation of the parents and the child. In other words, the contract has to be as individual as possible for the patient and family, but at the same time it must be structured according to formal principles presented by the therapist. Such a balance can both detect and enhance all positive motivations for change and also foster new motivations during later phases of treatment.

(3) *The behavioral aspect: positive orientation toward success.* It is important to define all conditions and goals of therapy in such a way that there is a high probability that the child and family will fulfill them. If the patient or family is in any doubt about goals or demands, it is better to start on a lower level than on a higher level in order to avoid failure. Only in this way will the contract be able to fulfill its function, namely to cope with loss of motivation and to develop new hope and self-confidence in the patient and his or her parents.

During the course of treatment, demands and goals are changed in relation to the success of the child and the family. During later phases of therapy the contract may not be necessary. The message of the contract is: "You are not yet able to control your behavior, therefore other persons are required to do this for you." When the patient is able to cope with his or her problem, the contract is no longer necessary; on the contrary, it could be an obstacle.

Antidepressant Medication as Adjunct

If the child or adolescent shows a depressive condition (for instance, signs of major depression), we use tricyclic antidepressants during the first month of therapy. They help the child to overcome his or her depressive mood and feelings of inferiority and guilt as well as to become more self-confident and active. The medication also helps us talk to the patient and obtain information about his or her emotional situation. We have no evidence that antidepressants have the adverse effects of masking the basic conflicts and problems of the patient.

Individual and/or Family Therapy

We use a combination of individual therapy for the child and family therapy for the child with both parents. From time to time, it is also necessary to have some sessions with the parents alone. We usually start by discussing, with the whole family, the main principles of the therapeutic contract. The next family sessions are concentrated not only on the symptomatology of the child, but also on many other topics, such as conflicts within the family, living conditions of the family, conflicts with siblings, the school situation of the child, and so on. The more the school phobic symptomatology can be controlled by strict regulations, the more it is possible to include in family sessions discussion of the family conflicts and problems. In this way we make a gradual transition from the structured principles of the therapeutic contract to a more conflict-oriented family therapy.

In some cases with either extreme psychopathological features or pronounced social isolation of the child, intensive individual therapy of the child may be the most important component of the therapeutic program.

The following case history demonstrates our approach to therapy of school phobic children and their families.

A CASE HISTORY

Symptomatology and History

This twelve and a half-year-old boy, Hans, was referred to our outpatient clinic for severe phobic anxieties concentrated on school. The boy was afraid of going to school and finally showed school refusal. He was very worried about declining in his school performance and several times expressed suicidal ideas. In the morning, he often complained about headaches, stomachaches, and heart palpitations. During his last visits to school, he had to be accompanied by a family member. But finally, his symptomatology was so pronounced that he was no longer able to attend school, either alone or accompanied by one of his parents.

Han's mother had suffered from depressive states since he was six years old and was treated with antidepressants. She also complained of feelings of inferiority and related both complaints to her husband, who worked out of town and was seldom at home, leaving her alone with responsibility for the education of their two children, Hans and his brother, who was two years older. The latter did not have any psychiatric symptoms.

There were no problems in the pre- and perinatal history. At the age of eight weeks, Hans was referred to a children's hospital because of apnea while crying. The doctors thought that he suffered from a heart anomaly, but none was found. During the first years of his life, Hans bonded closely to his parents, especially his mother. His parents did not report significant separation anxiety in kindergarten or in the early years of elementary school.

The parents' reaction to the acute school phobic symptomatology was different. While his father remained quiet and was not excitable, his mother was very disturbed by his anxiety and especially his suicidal ideas. During the first interview, she was distraught and cried.

There was no abnormality in the physical examination or the EEG. It was difficult to interview the child alone because of extreme separation anxiety with panic attacks. It was also evident that there was pronounced sibling rivalry with his older brother. Hans felt that his brother was always preferred by his parents. While talking to us, he tried to control his emotions and showed signs of dissimulation and tendencies toward rationalization. On psychological testing, Hans showed a high IQ and no signs of neuropsychological deficits. On projective tests, the strong bond with his mother was evident.

Treatment

After completing the diagnostic procedures and considering the differential diagnosis, we discussed the diagnostic results with both parents and the child. We recommended inpatient treatment to them. Both parents were very anxious and disagreed with this recommendation, and finally they refused to allow it. After the interview, there were holidays for a week; Hans's parents said they would be able to control him and prevent a suicide attempt. During the first therapy session after the holidays, his parents told us that there had been no somatic complaints and no pronounced symptoms of anxiety during the holidays. But after school began again, the full symptomatology returned. This symptom sequence was important, as it enabled us to confirm the diagnosis of school phobia and to exclude a primary depressive state.

Treatment began immediately after the holidays and comprised eighteen one-hour sessions during eight months. The first fourteen sessions were held weekly, and the remaining sessions took place after three weeks, four weeks and six weeks. Four months after the end of treatment, we obtained follow-up information with a telephone call.

Hans and his mother attended all sessions, while the father participated in five and the elder brother in one session. The first sessions always began with a discussion of the therapeutic contract and then reviewed Hans' symptoms and emotions and the family relationships. The therapeutic contract was used only during the first five and one-half months; it was no longer necessary during the last two and one-half months (the final four sessions), by which time the focus of therapy was the family rather than the problems concentrated around school attendance.

During the first sessions, we told the family clearly that outpatient treatment would only be possible if we succeeded in getting Hans back to school again. This was important in order to avoid development of secondary symptoms while he was home. In order to reach this goal, we were able to use a proposal by Hans: he said he would be able to go to school for one or two hours a day, explaining that his main problem in school was the long duration of the day.

The first contract, which Hans and his parents accepted, ran as follows:

1. Hans accepts the task of going to school each day for at least the first two school hours. After success in this, he will try, in a stepwise way, to stay for three and finally for four hours.

2. If Hans fulfills this task, we will continue with outpatient treatment. If he is not able to fulfill it, inpatient treatment will be necessary, starting with a new therapeutic contact.

3. Both parents have the task of discussing this contract with his teachers in order to avoid any difficulties.

The contract was signed by the patient, both parents, the therapist and the co-therapist. The first contract was changed stepwise during nearly each session, in the following ways:

A) After Hans was able to visit school for at least two hours, the potential inpatient treatment was replaced in the plan by the obligation for Hans to phone the therapist if he failed in some way to fulfill the contract.

B) If Hans fulfilled the minimal requirements and accepted the next steps, we extended the time Hans spent at school.

C) In the beginning, the time which Hans spent at school was very important. During the course of therapy, we realized that Hans disturbed his mother and put pressure on her by crying and complaining on the way to school. He also had enormous problems leaving his home and visiting friends. We acknowledged these additional problems in the contract.

D) When new elements were integrated into the contract, Hans at first was required only to observe himself and to register the behavior in question. The modification of these attitudes and behaviors was the next step.

E) After the patient's first successful steps, the parents' activities were altered. First, they no longer accompanied the boy on his way to school. Second, we worked with the parents to better separate their role as parents and the role of Hans as child. During this process, specified in a contract with the parents, it was also necessary to activate the father and to engage him in tasks that had been carried out until then exclusively by the mother. Step by step, responsibility that had been taken over by the therapist was given back to the parents.

Results of Treatment

School visit. Hans was able to extend the time he spent at school step by step during the first eight weeks. In the ninth week, he stayed at school an entire day. This, however, was the last week before Christmas, and after the Christmas holidays, he had a relapse. As we expected this development, we informed the parents in advance to help them cope with the situation. After the Christmas holidays, it took three weeks before Hans stayed at school for all of his classes. There was no further relapse and our follow-up information indicated that his school attendance was stable.

Psychosomatic complaints. His psychosomatic complaints (headache, stomachache, cardiac palpitations) disappeared shortly after the beginning of therapy. Instead of expressing psychosomatic complaints, he cried on his way to school and urged his mother to allow him to stay at home. This change of symptomatology is very common in school phobic children. As the symptomatology was included in the contract, it was possible to modify this behavior within a few weeks.

Anxiety. Hans's anxiety could not be reduced during the first stage of therapy. On the contrary, Hans reported an intensified anxiety. Probably this was the case because during treatment his tendencies toward dissimulation increasingly disappeared, so he had more access to his emotions. These reports about his subjective states gave us the chance to discuss family problems in a more detailed way. As we did this, and after he completed the contract, his anxiety was no more prominent than before.

Changes in his parents' behavior. At the beginning of treatment both parents found it difficult to talk about their behavior in his presence. It was evident that his mother had difficulty finding an appropriate attitude toward her son. She was unable to control him and to stop his dominance and unending requests. At the same time, she felt left alone with all these problems by her husband. Her husband had to be motivated; when he was, he agreed to take over several responsibilities that had until then belonged solely to his wife.

After we discontinued the contract, we continued family therapy for two and one-half months, but less frequently than before. During these family sessions, it remained clear that the parents had enormous difficulties talking about their relationship and also that they did not profit as much by treatment as Hans did. Hans, however, became more extroverted and oriented himself more toward his peer group outside the house. He had no problems leaving the house, meeting other children, or leaving his mother. There were limits in the therapy as it related to his mother because she did not accept therapy for herself, although she showed marked depressive symptomatology. In the end, the treatment outcome was not as good for the parents as for the child. As we have said, four months after the end of therapy Hans had no psychosomatic complaints and was able to go to school without any problem.

INPATIENT TREATMENT

The principles of inpatient treatment are similar to those of outpatient treatment, but they involve some modifications of the therapeutic procedure:

- It takes longer to reintegrate patients into school, because school phobia is more severe in inpatients.

• Separation of the parents and child through hospitalization makes many things easier, but it also causes problems for the patient and the parents—including interruption of treatment, the child's homesickness, and occasional activation of psychosomatic complaints.

The admission procedure is important for the whole process of treatment. As a rule, there is strong family resistance against hospitalizing the child, because separation itself is the family's main problem. This new separation is an enormous burden for the family; it is thus important to prepare them for the child's admission and to inform them about possible problems during the course of treatment.

First Phase of Therapy: Family Background (1–2 Months)

The first and longest phase of inpatient treatment is concentrated on the analysis and modification of the family background problems on one side, and the individual problems of the child on the other side. The question of school attendance is not so important during this phase.

Therapeutic work with the child focuses on the following goals:

lowering the child's dependence on the parents (homesickness, separation problems);
helping the child become independent;
helping him or her cope with social anxieties; and
helping the child become more assertive (training in relation to other patients, sometimes with patients who suffer from different conditions).

Depending on progress toward these goals, the patient becomes more self-confident and less depressed. If there are marked symptoms of depression, tricyclic antidepressants are administered.

The therapeutic measures are the same as during outpatient therapy. Behavior modification techniques are combined with individual psychoanalytically based psychotherapeutic sessions. These methods are supported by occupational therapy. As soon as possible, the children are sent to the hospital school. This is a special school for sick children and is located in the same building as the clinic. The school has special conditions and experienced teachers who can manage such phobia problems. During this first phase of therapy, we hold regular sessions with the parents, mostly without the patient.

Second Phase: Reintegration into School (2–4 Weeks)

The next step is for the patient to attend school outside the hospital. If the child comes from the same town, he or she will be able to return to the original school. If this is not possible, it is nevertheless necessary to practice attending a "normal school," not too far from the hospital. This is important because the transition from the hospital school to an external school often creates significant problems that can be managed only by intensive support of the child by the experienced staff of an inpatient clinical setting.

The reintegration to an external school must be prepared carefully, with a detailed knowledge of all associated risk factors.

Initially, control over the route to school and all questions concerning school and related social situations is taken over by the staff; control is given back to the child incrementally according to his progress.

Third Phase: Reintegration into the Family (2–24 Weeks)

As soon as the child is continuing to attend school, we can test whether this progress can be transferred to the child's home and family. Reintegration into the family is a process that also requires careful, stepwise procedures. During this phase of therapy, all functions that had been taken over by the therapist are given back to the parents. In therapy with older children and adolescents, it is useful to have joint family sessions with the parents and the patient. With younger children, it is sometimes preferable to have sessions with the child and the parents separately.

Fourth Phase: Outpatient Aftercare (At Least 6 Months)

The inpatient therapy of school phobic children and adolescents is not completed with the discharge of the patient. It is always necessary to continue treatment through outpatient aftercare in order to avoid relapses. Many children who are free of symptoms at discharge find their symptoms emerge again as soon as they return to their parents.

The type and intensity of aftercare differs from case to case. If the family lacks motivation for intensive aftercare, we at least offer an appointment if any difficulties come up again.

FOLLOW-UP AND PROGNOSIS
OF INPATIENT TREATMENT

The inpatient treatment program described has already been evaluated, whereas assessment of the outpatient treatment program is not yet finished.

In a partial evaluation of the inpatient program for children with severe school phobias, a study of twenty patients was carried out with a follow-up interval of nineteen months. The following results were obtained (Kammerer and Mattejat 1981): In one-third of the patients, full therapeutic success was obtained, defined as stable school attendance without relapse since discharge. Another third of the patients also attended school continuously at follow-up, but stable school attendance was possible only after a relapse. The last third of the patients interrupted therapy or could not be treated successfully. If patients are excluded who did not really participate in therapy, a full therapeutic success could be registered in 44 percent, and unsuccessful treatment in 12 percent. The results are similar to those of other authors (Berg et al. 1976).

If we look at the age distribution of the three categories of therapeutic outcome, all children with full therapeutic success were younger than thirteen years old at the beginning of treatment. In this group, there was no interruption of therapy and no patient with an unsuccessful outcome. However, in the group of children and adolescents who were older than thirteen years at the beginning of treatment, the outcome was not as favorable. In adolescents with school phobia, there is always a danger of the condition being prolonged or developing into a phobic condition or depression. This does not disagree with the view that school phobia has a low predictive value for psychiatric conditions in adulthood (Baker and Wills 1979). School phobia is similar in this respect to other nonspecific neurotic conditions of childhood and adolescence. According to our experience, however, continuity into adulthood is more likely the older the patients are and the longer the condition exists.

The outcome of our outpatient treatment is more favorable than the results of inpatient treatment: in approximately 60 percent of cases a full therapeutic success was observed (continuous school attendance without relapse). In 20 percent of the patients it was necessary to transfer the patient to inpatient treatment, and in another fifth it was not possible to achieve stable cooperation and therapy was interrupted. We also have evidence from case histories that patients who interrupt therapy are prone to continued psychiatric disturbance into adulthood. We have observed cases in which school phobia was followed by generalized phobias and by compulsion neurosis.

We draw the following conclusions:

(1) The earlier a school phobic condition is diagnosed and treated, the more successful is the therapy. If the condition is treated in the very beginning, nearly all cases can be treated successfully. The older the patient is, and the more chronic the condition, the less favorable is the therapeutic outcome. It is evident that parents, teachers, and others caring for school phobic children should be informed that early treatment is the best method for preventing further complications and psychiatric disorders during adolescence and adulthood.

(2) Therapeutic success is dependent on the cooperation of the parents. Patients and parents who interrupt therapy are a special problem group who need more scientific study and help. We have had favorable experiences using the concept of a provisional outpatient treatment contract; we have also had success with alternative and complementary therapeutic methods (such as day hospital treatment, treatment by mobile services, and home treatment) for severe cases. Using these new therapeutic modalities, we reach families who initially had refused inpatient or outpatient treatment (Remschmidt and Schmidt 1988).

REFERENCES

American Psychiatric Association. (1987) *Diagnostic and Statistical Manual of Mental Disorders,* 3d ed., rev. (DSM III R). Washington, D. C., American Psychiatric Association.
Baker, H., and Wills, U. (1978) School phobia: Classification and treatment. *British Journal of Psychiatry* 132:492–499.
Berg, I., Nichols, K., and Pritchard C. (1969) School phobia, its classification, and the relationship to dependency. *Journal of Child Psychiatry and Child Psychology* 10:123–141.
Berg, I., Butler, A., and Hall, G. (1976) The outcome of adolescent school phobia. *British Journal of Psychiatry* 128:80–85.
Bernstein, G. A., and Garfinkel, B. D. (1986) School phobia: The overlap of affective and anxiety disorders. *Journal of the American Academy of Child Psychiatry* 25:235–241.

Cytryn, L., and McKnew, D. H. (1974) Factors influencing the changing clinical expression of the depressive process in children. *American Journal of Psychiatry* 131:879–881.

Eisenberg, L. (1958) School phobia: A study in the communication of anxiety. *American Journal of Psychiatry* 114:712–718.

Gittelman, R., and Klein, D. F. (1984) Relationship between separation anxiety and panic and agoraphobic disorders. *Psychopathology* 17, suppl. 1:56–65.

Glaser, K. (1967) Masked depression in children and adolescents. *American Journal of Psychotherapy* 21:565–574.

Granell de Aldaz, E., Vivas, E., Gelfand, D. M., and Feldman, L. (1984) Estimating the prevalence of school refusal and school-related fears. *The Journal of Nervous and Mental Disease* 172:722–729.

Hersov, L. A. (1960) Persistent nonattendance at school. *Journal of Child Psychology and Psychiatry* 1:130–136.

Hersov, L., and Berg, I., eds. (1980) *Out of School: Modern Perspectives in Truancy and School Refusal.* Chichester, Wiley.

Johnson, A. M., Falstein, E. I., Szurek, S. A., and Svendsen, M. (1941) School phobia. *American Journal of Orthopsychiatry* 11:702–711.

Kammerer, E., and Mattejat, F. (1981) "Katamnestische Untersuchungen zur stationären Therapie schwerer Schulphobien." *Zeitschrift für Kinder- und Jugendpsychiatrie* 9:273–287.

Kolvin, I., Berney, T. P., and Bhate, S. R. (1964) Classification and diagnosis of depression in school phobia. *British Journal of Psychiatry* 145:347–357.

Leton, D. A. (1962) Assessment of school phobia. *Mental Hygiene* 46:256–264.

Remschmidt, H., and Schmidt, M., eds. (1988) *Alternative Behandlungsformen in der Kinder- und Jugendpsychiatrie.* Stuttgart, Enke.

Rutter, M., Shaffer, D., and Sturge, C. (1976) *A Guide to a Multiaxial Classification Scheme for Psychiatric Disorders in Childhood and Adolescence.* London, Institute of Psychiatry.

Shaffer, D., Gould, M. S., Brasic, J. R., Ambrosini, P., Fisher, P., Bird, H., and Aluwahlia, S. (1983) A children's global assessment scale (cGAS). *Archives of General Psychiatry* 40:1228–1231.

Waldron, S., Shrier, D. K., Stone, B., and Tobin, S. (1975) School phobia and other childhood neuroses: Systematic study of the children and their families. *American Journal of Psychiatry* 132:802–808.

Weber, D. (1967) Zur Differentialdiagnose und Polygenese der Schulphobie. *Praxis der Kinderpsychologie und Kinderpsychiatrie* 5:167–171.

10

How Children Respond to School in Denmark

REIMER JENSEN

SUMMARY

Although children may go to school and stay there all day, they can still refuse all school activities. They may be present with their bodies but not with their minds. This is revealed in their behavior and lack of involvement in schoolwork, especially homework.

In a Danish study 279 children were interviewed in order to study their attitude toward school. At all age levels some children felt what can be called school fatigue or reluctance; this affected girls almost as often as boys, with no clear correlation to grade level except a higher frequency among children who were about to leave school. On a single day 20 percent of the girls and 21 percent of the boys surveyed admitted that they were tired of going to school. Some children disclosed that they had stayed away from school and their absence was not registered as school refusal but rather disguised in different ways. Not all children who said they suffered from school fatigue were identified as such by their teachers; on the other hand, teachers sometimes misinterpreted behavior disorders as school fatigue.

When children lose interest in school activities they can escape into their fantasy world. This is illustrated with a clinical case. Difficult problems in research methodology for the investigation of school fatigue are discussed.

Children at preschool age usually look forward to beginning school. It is appealing for them because it means being a big girl or boy. Very often they admire older sisters and brothers or they are impressed with what older children in their neighborhood can do; thus, entering school is

equated with obtaining prestige. In their imagination children are taking an important step into a new world. They can experience this as
exciting, but they can also find it threatening or even dangerous. Moving into this stage in their lives might imply the possibility of having all
of their unmet needs and wishes fulfilled. If the newcomers have heard
older children, with some years of school experience, express negative
feelings about school life they might be hesitant and skeptical; yet they
are probably still curious about the experience of going to school.

For teachers who meet the first graders, and for parents who accompany their children to school on the first school day, it is exciting to see
how they react to the new situation in their lives. It is obvious that some
of these newcomers are able to enjoy what is offered to them in school
and continue to be interested in attending. However, some children lose
their enthusiasm about going to school all too soon. For adults, it is
discouraging to see how rapidly this can happen. It is possible that these
children had unrealistic ideas about school. Or perhaps they realize that
it is very difficult for them to learn what other children in their group
manage to learn much more easily, quickly, and successfully.

SCHOOL FATIGUE: A DANISH STUDY

After a few years, some children no longer like school. They
find schoolwork boring and homework stressful. Their self-esteem
might be diminished or damaged because they realize the discrepancy
between what they are expected to do and what they really can do.
When children disengage themselves from school, lose interest in
school activities, and feel all kinds of schoolwork to be an unbearable
burden, we describe this as school fatigue or school reluctance.

In a Danish study on this topic (Petersen 1988), 279 children from
third to ninth grade were interviewed. Measures were obtained during
September in one year, and during the following February.

Children at all ages seem to know what school fatigue means. Many
children have experienced this reaction to school and some of them
retrospectively date the experience back to first grade. However, the
number of students who admit that they are or have been tired or
reluctant to go to school varies greatly from school to school and from
grade to grade. When all the students were asked to indicate on a single
day whether they felt tired of school, 20 percent of the girls and 21
percent of the boys surveyed stated that they were suffering from school
fatigue. It was expected that there would be more boys than girls, but

this hypothesis was not verified. Moreover, it was anticipated, on the basis of observations of daily life in school, that school fatigue would increase as the pupils moved upwards in the school system.

The number of children suffering from school fatigue was larger at grade nine, which is the last compulsory year in school, than in all other grades; however, there were fewer children with school fatigue among students from grades seven and eight than there were among students from lower grades.

In this study the diagnosis of "school fatigue" was based on the child's own experiences, as well as on the behavior manifested by the child. The first criterion was a self-report by the child, whereas the other criterion was observations both by the child and by other people, including teachers, parents, and other children.

As there are so many different ways of experiencing, revealing, and hiding school fatigue, it is understandable that there are discrepancies between how children themselves evaluate their attitude toward school and how their friends and teachers estimate their engagement in school.

In this study there were some disagreements between teachers and the students who indicated that they suffered from school fatigue. Only half of those who complained were identified by the teachers, boys three times as often as girls. It is possible that girls can disguise their negative attitudes toward school more easily than boys, or boys might send out different signals than girls. Conduct disorders, more common in boys, might be wrongly interpreted by teachers as school fatigue. Teachers identify accurately almost all students who describe themselves as not suffering from school fatigue. Teachers identified 88 percent of this group correctly, but in 12 percent they described the students as being tired of going to school, whereas the students did not feel that this was the case (or they did not admit it).

The study revealed clearly that school fatigue can change with time. Some children have a negative feeling about going to school over a long period of time, while other children move back and forth between positive and negative attitudes to school attendance.

DIAGNOSTIC CRITERIA FOR SCHOOL FATIGUE AND SCHOOL REFUSAL

When children resist attending school it can be evident in different ways. Staying away from school is just one way of revealing feelings about school. If a child does not want to go to school or does not like it, he can pretend to be sick, or sicker than he actually is, in order to be allowed to stay home. Everyone has had this experience: one doesn't feel well, but it is unclear whether the symptoms are the onset of illness or something which can be overcome in a few hours. All parents know that children commonly have complaints of some kind or other.

It is sometimes difficult to differentiate between illness and conscious school refusal or anxiety about going to school and leaving home (school phobias). Some of the interviewed children admitted that they had skipped school for several hours or stayed away from school at some time, and this was not identified as school refusal by the school. The diagnosis of "school refusal" requires an investigation of the causes behind a child's absence from school.

However, a child might manage to get to school in spite of the fact that he or she does not like or want to attend school. Coming to school with a very negative attitude toward school life and schoolwork might be a disguised form of school refusal. The child disengages him or herself from all school activities in spite of his or her physical presence in school. Absence from the school building is one end of a continuum of which the other end is an intense interest in school. Between these points there are many degrees of engagement in schoolwork.

It is possible for a child to be physically present in school but mentally absent, so that he or she fails to gain anything from attendance. A child might subsequently become hooked on a stimulating topic and thus lose the opposition to school; such an opportunity only exists, however, if the child is physically present in the school building.

The Role of Fantasy in School Fatigue

A child can be present and counted as a school attendant but might be very far away from what is going on. A very bright ten-year-old girl recounted during her psychotherapy sessions how she managed to be present in school without being engaged in what was going on and often not knowing anything about it.

She described a fantasy in which she opened the door to the closet in the classroom and entered a fairy-tale country which was a mixture of the Tivoli Garden in Copenhagen and Disneyland in the United States; she felt like Alice in Wonderland. She did not hear anything of what was going on in the classroom.

When her name was called, she had to hurry back through the door in the closet. Of course, she could not answer the questions she was asked. She was confused, and her ignorance of what the teacher and her fellow students had been discussing became apparent to everyone in the classroom. The teacher felt that she was a dull and lazy student and gave her very low marks. She was not identified as a school refusing student, yet she was almost never mentally present in school.

For different reasons, which I will not review here, she spent a great deal of her time functioning on a fantasy level. This can be an effective way of escaping a world of reality overloaded with conflicts and experienced as boring. Most schoolwork is supposed to take place on a reality level. Learning processes activate primarily the conscious parts of mental life, even if some topics are echoed in the unconscious parts of a pupil's mind. When this happens it might strengthen the learning process, but it can also divert learning to a sidetrack.

Variable Attention in the Classroom and Its Sources

All teachers know from their classroom experience that children cannot work with full concentration, over a long period of time, at a high level of mental activity. They decrease their attention from time to time, or even discontinue the learning process for a while. To what degree this happens in an individual child depends on many factors, some of which follow:

1. The child is not interested in the subject matter taught in school.
2. The teacher is not engaged in the subject and teaches in a boring manner.
3. The child is preoccupied with conflicts with other children or with parents.
4. The child is fixated on inner conflicts.
5. The child has lost all motivation for learning and growing.
6. The child deliberately chooses to seek prestige among peers by opposing teachers and not responding to expectations set by parents and schools or other authorities.

There are thus a number of factors which can drain a child's motivation for active school attendance. The child's available energy is absorbed in activities other than schoolwork; when school refusal is viewed in this way, it is difficult to measure.

It is easy, of course, to determine whether or not a child is present in school. It is not so easy, however, to find out why a child is absent; it is much more difficult to find valid indications of the level of a child's engagement in what is going on in school. Moreover, this level might change from day to day and even from one hour to the next. Yet this engagement is a measure of what we get from the money we spend on schools and the energy teachers spend in their endeavor to educate children and adolescents.

In order to profit from education in all countries, clearly, children must be present. But this is just the first step. The next is to engage them so that they can keep going and not escape from school on a mental level and thereby avoid the entire learning process. Realizing the purpose of going to school is a complicated phenomenon. In a study in Denmark, adolescents sixteen or seventeen years old were given the opportunity to discuss their experiences while exposed to the Danish school system for almost ten years (Jensen and Petersen 1977).

It seemed unknown to most of them that the government had formulated a purpose for schools. However, they had some vague ideas about what they wanted to obtain by going to school. Their more farsighted goals seem to be little related to their present situation, and not in accordance with what they actually did in school or the courses they wanted to take in the near future.

Research methods used to investigate school refusal, in the broad sense of the term used here, are difficult to administer and coordinate. Observations of children and adolescents in classrooms must be linked to clinical methods, so that the students can feel free to speak about their attitudes toward school, teachers, and schoolmates and also express feelings about their own experiences and the meaning they find in school attendance.

We do not have the resources to run large-scale research projects covering all these aspects of school involvement. Another complicating factor is that children who refuse to go to school usually have other problems, too. These problems may overlap so that school refusal or school fatigue may be just one aspect of a problem situation or a psychosocial pathology. We need to describe and analyze single cases very carefully and to demonstrate how the many aspects of children's and adolescents' experiences at home, in school, and in their peer groups influence their attitudes toward school.

If such data can be followed up in longitudinal studies, we will know more about the function of schools both when they succeed and when they fail to keep children interested in learning, growing, and preparing for adult life in their community, whether adapting to it or attempting to change it.

REFERENCES

Jensen, R., and Petersen, R. (1977) *Unges syn på skolen* (Adolescents Look upon the School). Copenhagen, Gyldendal.
Petersen, R. (1988) *Skoletræthed (School Fatigue)* (Copenhagen, Gyldendal.

11

School Refusal and School Problems in Brazil

SALVADOR CELIA

SUMMARY

In developing countries such as Brazil, school refusal has to be viewed in a broad sense that includes refusal to attend school, school phobia, and school failure—which often causes children to drop out altogether, with consequent loss of self-esteem.

While cases comparable to those in the developed world are also found in Brazil, the predominant clinical and educational problem there is school refusal among poor children. In the underprivileged classes, the school population drops to 40 percent of the initial figure by the second year of school and to no more than 6.4 percent by the end of the eleventh year.

A number of explanations have been advanced: from the medical standpoint, malnutrition is responsible; the sociological view blames the persistence of social stratification. From the psychological perspective, clinical data point to either cognitive deficiencies arising from faulty exchanges between the child and the environment, or to the inadequacy of school for children whose cognitive potential is intact but who require special educational mediation between school and their outside environment.

It is important to make the most of children's potential abilities, and health services must work hand in hand with the school in order to forestall and alleviate problems whose sociopolitical dimension cannot be ignored.

In every country in the world, whatever its political structure, school is considered an essential factor in the development of children, citizens, the community, and the country as a whole. Virtually all countries have enacted child-protecting legislation to ensure the opportunity for schooling, but in many areas theory and practice lie far apart and there is in fact a high incidence of nonattendance. This is in some cases due to a lack of schools, in others to a lack of incentive to attend. Sometimes children go to school but do not manage to stay there because of high rates of failure to be promoted and high dropout rates, which constitute what we call school failure.

A number of countries show particular concern for understanding and identifying the causes of school refusal and school dropout. British and American studies, for example, have found that at least 10 percent of school-age children are absent from school at any one time. Many are long-term absentees for medical reasons which are often linked to psychological factors.

Hersov differentiates between school refusal and truancy. He observes that children who present the "school refusal syndrome" begin by giving somewhat vague objections to going to school or by being reluctant to go; finally they refuse either to go to school or to stay there. This conduct may be accompanied by evidence of intense anxiety or even panic when the time comes to leave for school, and the child pleads to be allowed to stay at home.

Hersov also observes that acute onset of school refusal is especially frequent in younger children, while in preadolescents the process starts in a more insidious manner. Both situations present a wealth of symptomatological elements, and in many cases there is a severe underlying psychopathological condition (severe neuroses, borderline states, psychoses).

It is difficult to make an accurate assessment of the prevalence of school refusal, but studies give figures ranging from 1 percent to 10 percent of the population sampled or followed by psychological services. The increasing rate in Japan today is especially alarming.

Addressing the conceptual value of the term "school refusal," Hersov notes that the term does not belong to any specific theory but allows for the inclusion of intra- and interpersonal factors and mechanisms centered on the child and his or her family and life in the school system. In addition, in some countries school refusal may be precipitated by sociocultural factors such as competitiveness or poverty, which we know bring in their wake, among other symptoms, impairment of self-esteem in children and adolescents.

SOCIOCULTURAL INFLUENCES IN BRAZIL

A great many disparities are apparent in Third World countries, particularly in Latin America. The studies I shall present here were carried out in Brazil, which has tremendous social problems arising from the fact that it is a developing country practically the size of a continent and with a population of 136 million.

Any reference to "school," "childhood," "old age," or "family" must be qualified explicitly in the Brazilian context, because the extreme social inequality in the country means that these terms have no homogeneous meanings. One cannot speak about childhood in the singular, because there are many kinds of childhood in Brazil; nor about the Brazilian family, since there exists a variety of types of family organization with different styles of life, depending on the social class in question.

One does, however, come across some cases of classic school refusal with an elaborate symptomatology, similar to those described in the developed world. I refer in particular to children from the middle or upper-middle classes and to those from backgrounds of greater wealth, whose etiologies are very similar to those found in developed countries, including an underlying and often masked depressive picture.

This symptomatology is frequently observed in children sometimes referred to as "mini-businessmen," who live an intensely competitive life. In addition to normal classes, they spend time in out-of-school activities such as foreign language lessons, computer courses, and various sports. Even during these activities they are never able to let go, to relax, and to socialize; they often go on to become all-around athletes.

However, for a much larger number of Brazilian children and adolescents, school refusal is caused by a pathogenic sociopolitical structure that nurtures such symptoms as loss of self-esteem, insecurity, and antisocial behavior as well as the ultimate expression of school refusal, school dropout. In some cases children would like to go back to school, but because of their previous failure there, their personal or social circumstances prevent them from trying to do so.

As shown in Figure 11.1, the pyramid formed by data on age-related school attendance is extremely interesting: in 1981, out of a population of twenty-four million children from seven to fourteen years of age, seven million were not in school. Only 6.4 percent of the children who had entered elementary school (an eight-year cycle) finally completed their three-year secondary schooling. This is the pattern in the "public school" attended by the vast majority of Brazilian children, which is in urgent need of reorganization.

Figure 11.1.*Age-Related Changes in School Attendance in Brazil*

	Class	Percentage of First-Year Class Entering
2d cycle	{ 3d year	6.4
	{ 2d year	—
————	{ 1st year	—
	{ 8th year	17.0
	{ 7th year	—
	{ 6th year	—
	{ 5th year	—
1st cycle	{ 4th year	27.0
	{ 3d year	—
	{ 2d year	40.0
	{ 1st year	100.0

For many years now we have been hearing a great deal about the democratization of schooling in Brazil and the theoretically ensuing increase in the school population; this is presented within the framework of an educational policy and philosophy that aims for "education for all." However, the increase of educational possibilities has turned out to be a mirage. For children from disadvantaged backgrounds, access to education is uncertain, inefficient, and discriminatory in comparison with that for children from the privileged classes.

As the problem has intensified, it has become a subject of study for a number of disciplines, including medicine, psychology, education, and sociology.

From the medical standpoint, neurologists have shown particular interest in the analysis of brain dysfunctions and the effects of malnutrition. In the 1980s, medical practitioners and educators reacted strongly against the medicalization of school failure, which was considered as "a means of explanation designed to clear the school system, as well as family and social conditions, of any blame, and to lay responsibility for low school performance squarely at the individual organic level" (Sucupira 1985). Blaming malnutrition for school failure is a simplistic and misleading attitude that stands in the way of self-criticism and the potential for change on the part of the school as a social institution.

A number of sociological studies show that school failure can be explained by the fact that school is an instrument for the reproduction of social structures. Manfredo Berger clarifies how, in Brazilian society today, education can be manipulated according to the interests of the dominant classes, while the socially underprivileged strata are "educated" to accept and maintain the status quo.

From the psychological viewpoint, it seems obvious that learning is the result of integration of the organism and its milieu and that the school environment is of fundamental importance in the process of knowledge construction if teacher-pupil interactions are to have a facilitating and stimulating effect.

Recent studies in Brazil have attempted to evaluate the cognitive abilities of children living in the slums and marginal areas around the major cities. Two of these reflect interesting divergent positions (Patto 1984). A study done by the University of São Paulo, under the direction of Zelia Ramozzi Chiarottino, takes the position that poverty is injurious to the child's intellectual development because of the lack of environmental stimulation (physical or social) essential during certain phases of development. Cognitive deficiencies result from inadequate exchanges between the child and its milieu.

The second study, carried out by the Federal University of Pernambuco, and directed by Terezinha Carraher, claims that children from underprivileged backgrounds do not present defective cognitive functioning and rejects the theory of cultural deprivation. It no longer looks exclusively to the child's own processes to find the answers but goes beyond that approach to take into account the conditions surrounding the learning process. According to this team, what prevents the acquisition of knowledge is not cognitive deficiency but deficiencies within the school context itself. From the standpoint of these researchers, "the public school is incapable of producing learning, not because its intake consists of children with cognitive deficiencies, but because of faulty evaluation, ignorance of the processes of human development, and the use of teaching methods that are irrelevant, misguided, and tied in with culturally biased contents" (Patto 1984).

From a purely educational standpoint, the contributions of Paulo Freire stand out. Freire proposes transforming school education to include educational elements relevant to the child's social context and turning the school into a mediator between the pupil and the world of culture. This is designed to avoid both the deterioration of the curriculum and passive, uncritical acceptance by the child. The curriculum contents transmitted by the school are often completely irrelevant to the social reality in which the Brazilian child lives. Particularly anomalous

ilar to those found among children and adolescents in the developed countries. We have also observed that in developed countries, children from the underprivileged classes—who live in unfavorable conditions just as they do in Brazil—present similar symptomatic manifestations. However, we feel that it is of the utmost importance to underline the sociocultural etiology of these symptoms as described above. Prophylactic measures at the institutional and community levels are the only possible means of improving and reversing a situation that is clearly structural and is linked to the politicosocial organization.

However, we cannot ignore those cases that require specialized psychological care. They must be given the opportunity to attend health services where they can receive psychiatric attention, such as individual or group treatment, family or milieu therapy, and therapeutic community treatment, backed up whenever necessary by medication.

Finally, I would like to pinpoint an extremely valuable resource that is not always used. This is the potential for joint work by the health center and the school. It is essential that mental health professionals get out of their treatment centers and into the schools, to work together with the teachers and staff of the school counseling services. The practice of school counseling is familiar to families and children, and this can be extremely helpful in preventing and alleviating problems that arise.

In Porto Alegre, in addition to making the most of school counseling, we are currently carrying out two combined health and education projects—using a health center plus a school—in which we work with theater workshops. This provides children and adolescents with an opportunity to enjoy creative make-believe and to benefit from the sociability of group interactions. For children and adolescents with problems of acute introversion, passivity, or aggressivity, we have set up a "therapeutic companionship" program. This involves using a student trainee, supported and supervised by mental health professionals, to develop a six- to eight-hour-per-week project designed to establish a relationship that will improve the child's socialization and at the same time increase his or her confidence, sense of security, and self-esteem.

As we see, the causes underlying the school refusal syndrome are many and varied, and the problems are complex and sometimes serious. I feel that only a broad view of the phenomena involved can help us to acquire a greater understanding of the affliction and increase the possibilities of prevention and treatment. It is a difficult task that can succeed only through joint political actions with both health and education as goals, and which can be adapted to the realities of each region or country.

REFERENCES

Brandão, Z., Baeta, A. B., and Da Rocha, A. D. C. (1983) *Evasão e repentência no Brasil: A escola em questao.* Rio de Janeiro, Achiamé.

Fichtner, N. H. (1983) A escola e o desenvolvimento da personalidade. *A criança e o adolescent da década de 80.* Porto Alegre, Artes Médicas.

Globert, C., Fichtner, N., Celia, S., et al. (1988) *Saúde mental e competência escolar.* Porto Alegre, Projeto IACAPAP.

Hersov, L. (1985) School refusal. In *Child and Adolescent Psychiatry: Modern Approaches.* 2d ed. Ed. M. Rutter and L. Hersov. London, Blackwell.

Nosella, M. de L. C. D. (1981) *As belas mentiras.* 7th ed. São Paulo, Moraes.

Patto, M. H. S. (1984a) A crianca marginalizada para os Piagetinos Brasileiros: Deficientes ou não. *Cadernos de pesquisa* 51: 3 November 1984.

——— (1984b) Pré-escola: A criança a familia e oi professor. *A criança e o adolescente da década de 80.* Porto Alegre, Artes Médicas.

Shirahashi, K. (1988) Keynote Speech. Senday IACAPAP Seminar. Senday, Japan, April.

Sucupira, A. C. (1985) Hiperatividade, doença ou rotuló? *Fracasso Escolar, Uma Questão Médica?* São Paulo, Cortez.

Suzuki, K. (in this volume) School refusal viewed through family therapy.

12

School Failure in France

COLETTE CHILAND

SUMMARY

Children have not always had the opportunity to attend school, nor even today is it possible for them to do so in all parts of the world. Yet it seems that those who do go to school are not always able to benefit from the experience.

I will not address the problem of school failure in response to particular events or as a sign of the onset of illness in a pupil with a formerly satisfactory school record; my attention will be focused on the enormous rate of school failure among children from disadvantaged sociocultural backgrounds.

On the whole, education in France is successful in that many children attend school before and after the compulsory period of education (six to sixteen years of age). It is public, secular, and free. Private school education is possible during this period, but only the state university can award the national examination certificates.

Failure to acquire adequate reading skills in the first year of primary school is a heavy handicap for the rest of a child's academic life. Nevertheless, the programs are set at a level beyond the abilities of many children, since half repeat at least one year of primary school studies. At the secondary school level, the junior high school Collèges d'Enseignement Secondaire (CES) still require considerable reorganization to enable them to meet the needs of mass education, and the universities also fail to produce the results that could be expected of them. The causes and solutions to these problems are the subject of much debate. Reform requires new textbooks, funding, and changes in attitude.

Although education is today a matter of concern everywhere in the world, the issues and approaches differ greatly from one country to another. Developing countries are faced with the problem of providing enough schools and qualified teachers to be able to offer the opportunity for education. There are still some countries, unfortunately, where fewer than 50 percent of children are lucky enough to go to school. The problem is quite different in the developed countries, where it is compulsory for all children to attend school for an increasingly long period (today it is nine years in Japan, ten in France). Many children do not consider this lucky at all, and their attitude is expressed differently in different countries. The Japanese are greatly alarmed by the problem of school refusal, which in its wider sense comprises several different categories. According to the Inamura classification used by Suzuki in this volume, the five types of school refusal are the acute type (which seems to correspond to what we call school phobia in France), the repeating type, the mental disorder type (including schizophrenia and other disorders), the idle type (truancy), and the temporary type. The Japanese are also deeply concerned about the vicious bullying suffered by some schoolchildren, who are sometimes literally tortured and are too terrified to confide in anyone. They sometimes see no way out except school refusal or, in some cases, even suicide. It would appear that no effective means have yet been found to combat this fearsome, recent explosion of violence, which is exacerbated by intense competition and controlled on other fronts (the leader who manipulates his schoolmates and makes them his henchmen or bodyguards is usually an excellent pupil). According to Yamazaki et al. (1989), the failure to stop it might be attributed to a lack of team spirit and cooperation among teachers.

In France we see cases of school phobia whose origins are in individual and family pathology (see Lebovici, this volume) rather than being derived from social change, as in Japan, where neither the family nor society has yet managed to come to terms with the social upheaval of the last few decades. We encounter cases here too of school violence, intimidation, and extortion among schoolchildren, and violence in certain secondary school establishments, but these are only sporadic events. The greatest cause of alarm in France is the problem of *school failure*.

We will not examine school failure as a phenomenon arising from individual pathology, where it is associated with life events (divorce of parents, or a death, for example), in a child who has until that point had a satisfactory school record; nor when it follows absence due to illness, if family and teachers have not made an effort to ensure that the gaps in learning caused by absence from classes are made up; nor when it indicates the onset of a severe pathological condition (incipient schizophrenia).

Instead we will consider the very widespread school failure, affecting a great number of children, which seems to be a social phenomenon rather than a matter of strictly individual pathology. It is particularly frequent among children from a disadvantaged sociocultural background.

Before looking at school failure, however, we must understand the French school and in what respects it is successful.

SCHOOL IN FRANCE: ITS SUCCESSES

Schooling for all children is a fait accompli. School attendance is compulsory between the ages of six and sixteen, and there are no exemptions. Parents who failed to comply would incur harsh sanctions, such as withdrawal of family allowances, which act as a serious deterrent.

Children do not only attend school during the compulsory period. The *maternelle,* or nursery school, which was originally set up for poor children, is attended by many children from the age of two onwards, and by almost all children between four and six. The exception is in some country areas where no maternelle exists; there are only preschool classes for children five years old and older. After the age of sixteen some adolescents go straight into the work force, but the majority continue their education. Either they enroll in vocational training courses, with a view to obtaining a diploma of basic skills, such as the Certificat d'Aptitude Professionnel (CAP) or the Brevet d'Etudes Professionnelles (BEP) vocational studies certificate, or they continue their general studies with a plan to obtain the *baccalauréat,* a certificate of high school education which is attainable after twelve years of school, theoretically at the age of eighteen. These twelve years are divided into five years of primary and seven years of secondary school; of the latter, four years are spent in the CES and three in the high school level lycée. Some students obtain their baccalauréat before the age of eighteen, and many do so at a later age, because they have repeated classes. It is important to note that the baccalauréat is the only qualification needed for university entrance: anyone who has it has the right to register at a university. There is no other entrance examination, except for people who do not have the baccalauréat and wish to resume their studies after having worked for a period of at least two years; even for them, there is no competitive entrance examination.

This picture glosses over the competitive aspects of school in France. I thought competitiveness was quite marked here, until I discovered what it means in Japan. Our children attend only one school, which is often a public school but can also be private (either state-accredited and often denominational, or else nonaccredited). They do not have to attend a second school to prepare for competitive examinations for admission to secondary school, to the lycée, to the university, or in order to gain entrance to the best institution at each stage.

However, the marks obtained in school are extremely important to parents, teachers, and children alike. Although the practice of academic ranking in primary school theoretically stopped in 1968, it still exists in practice. While there is no barrier to entrance at the ces level, the same is not true of the lycée. At the end of the first secondary (ces) cycle, which is the ninth year of school, students are oriented, or given vocational guidance. The exact significance of the word *guidance* must be understood clearly here. It ought to mean that the child is helped to choose a school on the basis of his or her abilities and inclinations. What happens in fact is that guidance conveys the impossibility of continuing general secondary studies to those, many with a great variety of aptitudes, whose marks have not been high enough. The only possibility open to these children is vocational training, and while they can all gain admission to one school or another, there is often not enough room at the school of their choice. The attitude may be expressed, "You want to be an automobile mechanic or an electrician. Right, you'll be a boiler-maker." This approach is going to produce generations of workers who will either refuse to work in the profession for which they are qualified or who will be miserable in the work they do.

Although the baccalauréat ensures the right to attend any university, each university is only allowed a fixed number of entry-year students. Since selection is forbidden, students are not offered admission on the basis of their academic record or their reasons for wanting to register for particular courses. Selection takes place on the basis of what I call the footrace: it is essential to be among the first in the queue on registration day—which means that would-be students or their parents literally spend the previous night lining up in front of the door. If I were Minister of Education I would be ashamed of this system. Its survival can only be explained by the fact that, however disastrous, it is still politically preferable to anything that might smack of selection, a word whose very mention immediately brings students into the street.

However, there is very severe selection before students may enter *les Grandes Ecoles* (Ecoles Normales Supérieures, Ecole Nationale d'Administration, and Ecoles d'Ingénieurs—Ecole Polytechnique, Ecole Centrale). In order to pass this examination, the students attend intense preparatory classes. While some take advantage of these additional classes, others complain about the rigorous demands placed on them. If they succeed in the examination they are exhausted and drained, and if they fail they are plunged into despair. Only a happy few are able to go through the experience unscathed. In medicine there is a comparable competitive examination, the *internat,* which takes place at the end of the course, instead of at the beginning.

French public primary and secondary schooling is free, and while there are registration fees to pay at the university, these are very low— less than 1,000 francs (about $160 U.S.) a year. Universities are state institutions; several private Catholic universities do exist, but they cannot deliver national diplomas. Living costs are the main problem facing students: grants or scholarships are few and not high enough to cover maintenance. Many, if not most, students hold jobs while they are at university—and these are not "odd jobs" like the Japanese *arbeito.*

Teachers are civil servants, recruited on a departmental scale for preprimary and primary school, and on a national basis for other levels. The current minimum required training is four years of post-baccalauréat study. The status of civil servant guarantees security of employment: as such, these workers cannot be dismissed for reasons other than very serious professional misconduct, which is extremely rare, and they are therefore sure of being kept on even if they turn out to have little aptitude for teaching or to have pathological personality features.

SCHOOL FAILURE

Let us examine the implications of school failure at various levels of education. In nursery schools the notion of failure does not apply, because most fortunately there are no programs, marks or sanctions. It must be said that these have long been the pride of the French school system, the setting for educational innovations and a place of great freedom. The atmosphere is a happy one and children receive highly individual attention. Teachers choose to teach at that level because they are particularly interested in very young children; for a long time there were only women teachers in pre-primary schools, but in recent years they have been joined by men. This seems to have had positive results; it is a sign of our times that an interest in small children is no longer exclusive to women, and that men do not feel that contact with toddlers is a threat to their virility. A regrettable tendency can be observed here and there, however, toward labelling children and reacting negatively to any clumsiness in writing or drawing. We now find requests for "writing reeducation" for children who have not yet even begun systematic learning of the written language; in some instances, moreover, incorrect conclusions about a child's intelligence are made on the basis of his or her drawing ability. It should nonetheless be noted that as early as at the age of four (see Lentin 1972) marked differences can be observed in the level of language skills among children according to their family background. This seems to be a crucial time to take measures to prevent later failure in primary school, because the level of spoken language is extremely important in learning to read.

After that comes compulsory schooling: in the September of the year in which they turn six, children must go on to primary school. From then on there is a program of learning to be accomplished each year, and the cornerstone of this education is reading. Is age six too late or too early to learn to read? Some people are convinced that children should start as early as three, by dissociating learning to read from learning to write, and using talking typewriters (see Cohen 1977). This is an opinion I find untenable; in my view the experiments described are really situations in which children have been placed in an enriched setting which included the talking machines. Countries that have the lowest percentages of children with difficulties in learning to read, such as Sweden (less than 5 percent), are those in which reading is not taught systematically until children are seven years old. It is also true, however, that in Swedish phonetic transcription of the language is much simpler than in French or English, and the country has an unrivalled school system.

Not all pupils have acquired sufficient reading skills by the end of the first year of school (the Cours Préparatoire, or CP). That is, they are unable to read a simple text at adequate speed, without mistakes or hesitations, and understand its meaning. These three components (speed, precision, and comprehension) must be assessed separately: if they are combined in a single overall score, the source of the child's difficulty is masked. A good attitude would be one in which the child is able to stop in front of a word or letter he or she does not understand, think about it and say "I don't know." The ability to slow down and exercise personal control is something solid and satisfactory, whereas children who do not possess this capacity settle into an attitude of "anything goes," whereby they always manage to give some kind of an answer, no matter how inappropriate or nonsensical it might be. Children like this become set in faulty reading habits which become increasingly difficult to correct.

So far I have not mentioned *dyslexia,* because the term is one which gives rise to conflict. It could be taken in a descriptive sense to mean reading difficulties, but many authors have attributed an etiological significance to it. Dyslexia, or specific reading disorder, has been contrasted with secondary difficulties (absenteeism, low intellectual level, social conditions, and so on), and it is implied that dyslexia is a specific disorder of organic origin. A good deal of mileage is gained from the anatomical-pathological examination of fewer than a dozen brains of dyslexics (see Galaburda 1986), which show slight asymmetry with some ectopia in the area of the *planum temporale.* Other explanations include heredity, involving genes for reading, as well as references to a higher incidence of perinatal problems. Proponents of the latter throw in dyslexia, attention deficit disorders, learning difficulties, and minimal brain dysfunction together. It is perfectly conceivable that if all instances of educational mishandling were set aside, there would remain a core group of children whose difficulties in learning to read could be traced to individual pathology in which organic factors are one component among many. The fact remains, however, that children who have reading difficulties confront us with a phenomenon far more widespread than that.

It was calculated in 1962–63[1] that of a sample of sixty-six children aged six, 40 percent had good reading results, 20 percent had average reading skills—which were inadequate for these children easily to follow first-year teaching in the Cours Elémentaire (CE1, second year of primary school)—and 40 percent had totally inadequate or nonexistent reading ability (see Chiland 1971). We followed up the children in this sample for twenty years and were able to determine the long-term effects of this failure to acquire adequate reading skills in the first year of primary school on our subjects' subsequent schooling (see Chiland

---

1. These figures have improved somewhat since then, no doubt thanks to growing awareness of the problem and the efforts made to counter it. These include, in particular, the creation in some schools of Psychopedagogical Assistance Groups (GAPP), consisting of a school psychologist, a special education teacher, and remedial education specialists.

1978; 1983). Twenty-three of the sixty-six finally obtained their bac-calauréat; not one of them was among the 20 percent who had attained only average reading skills at the end of the first year of primary school. All but two had been good readers[2] at the beginning of the second year of primary school. The two exceptions were both from upper-social-class backgrounds; one was given remedial reading classes from the first year onwards, while the other was kept on at the lycée, despite repeated flunking, through his father's influence.

Reading failure occurs mainly among children from the sociocul-turally underprivileged classes; the parents' cultural level is more sig-nificant than family income. In fact, given similar income status, the parents' cultural level is decisive, and when children have identical intellectual levels, their sociocultural background plays a determining role.

Another way of measuring the extent of the phenomenon is to see how children proceed through the various stages of schooling. The French Ministry of Education document *Scolarité de générations suc-cessives*[3] shows that, for the eleven years of school, of children for whom there are complete studies (children born between 1952 and 1962):

- 55 to 60 out of 100 children entering the first year of primary school (CP) at the age of 6 entered the second year of secondary school (CM2) when they were 10 years old;
- between 9.6 and 17.6 out of 100 children entering the CP at 6 went into the senior year of high school (lycée) at age 17.

All the others were held back by failing at least one year and having to repeat it; some never made it to the lycée at all. These studies, further-more, make no mention of the level of the children within the various classes, which would give an even bleaker picture of the situation.

The figures given also illustrate the problems of failure in secondary school. When students continue to secondary school (Collège, or CES) there are special sections known as sections d'enseignement spécialisé (special education sections) available for a certain number of children whose intellectual level is below the norm. Others cannot be admitted because their intellectual level is normal, even though their academic level is such that they are unable to follow the program in the *sixième*— the first year of secondary studies, which corresponds to the sixth year of school. No satisfactory solution has yet been found for this type of

2. I use the word "readers" here to indicate reading ability, not necessarily enjoyment of it.
3. *Etudes et Documents du Ministère de l'Education Nationale* 81:236.

school failure after primary school. Most of the affected pupils are usually directed to a professional route.

In both the CES and the lycée far too many students have little or no interest in their studies. They do not refuse to attend school, although they might skip classes and be truant upon occasion. Despite their physical presence, they nonetheless reject schooling: they reject what they are taught, and despite sanctions (detentions, in particular) they refuse to learn their lessons or do their homework, and may or may not present disciplinary problems. Once again, we return to the family context, and here it is not just a question of the family's sociocultural level, but also of family dysharmony, family breakdown, single-parent family situations, and the entire field of family pathology in every sociocultural setting. There is also the new phenomenon of substance abuse. Adolescents use drugs ranging from tobacco and alcohol, to soft drugs such as hashish, to hard drugs, especially heroin. School failure has become just one element in an alarming picture that includes delinquency arising from the need for money to procure drugs.

At the university we come to what could perhaps be called elite failures, because even if these students do not entirely fit the description of what we would consider ideal university students (except for a proportion that I would put at somewhere between 10 and 20 percent), they have nevertheless acquired basic academic instruction and passed their baccalauréat. Even so, the results are nothing like what could justifiably have been expected. Although there are no selection procedures for admission, there is a selection at the end of the first year for some courses, including medicine, and here there is an enormous dropout rate: 50 to 60 percent of first-year students fail even to sit for their examinations in science, humanities, social science, law, or economics. Only a very small proportion complete the studies they begin.

CAUSES AND REMEDIES

For children whose parents are not in a position to transmit culture to them, school provides the major opportunity to acquire it. Only a few take full advantage of this chance, while the majority do not do so at all or do so to a very minor degree; the net result is the perpetuation of social stratification.

Explanations for this have been advanced from the sociological standpoint (Bourdieu and Passeron 1964) as well as from the political angle

(Baudelot and Establet 1971), according to which school in France is said to be an instrument of capitalist state policy. On the social front, the originality of French educational policies lies in the existence of relevant laws and decrees, as well as budget appropriations to uphold them. But when it comes to the question of attitudes, individual psyches must be taken into account. How is it that teachers contribute to the preservation of social stratification when a great many of them consciously derive their vocation from a desire to help children acculturate? Of course, poverty and unemployment do exist, and schools cannot solve every economic problem; nonetheless, teachers should realize that they unwittingly give positive reinforcement to middle- and upper-class children simply because they like to see children arrive at school clean, smelling nice, fresh and scrubbed, well dressed, polite, well bred, and who handle language easily and show a lively curiosity. It is perhaps less easy to feel the same attraction and approval, or to be as positively inclined toward a child who is dirty, ragged, and foul smelling, with a runny nose, infested with fleas and lice, who speaks badly if at all, and who seems to have no interest in anything. It is not a common idea among teachers that school, far from depending on parents to keep an eye on their children's classwork, should on the contrary be self-sufficient. School should offer more—infinitely more— to the culturally disadvantaged child. There is a great waste of educational time that could be used to create the enriched setting to which I referred earlier. Advantage could be taken of the school cafeteria or the evening supervised study periods for children whose parents both work. Presiding over these groups is viewed as little more than guard duty when it could be used to provide extra help for children who need it.

The problems are different at the CES level. The provision of secondary education for all children is relatively recent, dating only from World War II. Only a minority of children previously had access to it, and secondary education has yet to make the adjustments necessary in its programs, methods, and teacher training to enable it to adapt to mass education.

Going to school might have appeared to be an opportunity for social advancement that ought to be seized when such an education was not accessible to all. Now that it is not only accessible, but compulsory it is no longer inviting to children and adolescents, who even in disadvantaged social circumstances enjoy amusements that are easily available and require nothing of them other than passive participation. Television is the classic example. Sitting alone in front of the television the whole day long is no benefit to anyone: it is only of some advantage if it can be used as a source of exchanges between the children and their parents.

In conclusion, I would like to underline the conditions essential to any education reform. Obviously, legal texts must be changed, but unless this is backed up by adequate funding, it will remain moot. Any reform is costly, and it is impossible to carry out reform and simultaneously cut expenditures. This is simply a contradiction of terms, and it considerably deflates the claims or promises of political rhetoric. Finally, all reform depends on changing attitudes and, as we have seen, bringing about change is no easy task.

REFERENCES

Baudelot, C., and Establet, R. (1971) *L'école capitaliste en France.* Paris, Maspero.
Bourdieu, P., and Passeron, J.-C. (1964) *Les héritiers: Les étudiants et la culture.* Paris, Editions de Minuit, édition 1966.
——— (1970) *La reproduction.* Paris, Editions de Minuit, édition 1971.
Chiland, C. (1971) *L'enfant de six ans et son avenir,* 5th ed. 1988 Paris, Presses Universitaires de France.
——— (1978) L'enfant de six ans devenu adolescent. *Revue de Nevropsychiatrie Infantile* 12:697–707.
——— (1983) Les facteurs de chance. In *Les bons enfants,* ed. M. Soulé, pp. 9–19. Paris, ESF.
——— (1987) L'école maternelle. In *L'enfant et sa santé. Aspects biologiques, épidémiologiques, psychologiques et sociaux,* ed. M. Manciaux, S. Lebovici, O. Jeanneret, E. A. Sand, and S. Tomkiewicz, pp. 551–560. Paris, Doin.
Cohen, R. (1977) *L'apprentissage précoce de la lecture.* Paris, Presses Universitaires de France.
Etudes et Documents du Ministère de l'Education Nationale 81, 1 *Scolarité de générations successives.*
Galaburda, A. (1986) La dyslexie et le développement du cerveau. *La Recherche* vol. 16, no. 167, pp. 762–769.
——— (1988) Dyslexie et anatomie de l'asymétrie et de la dominance. *Les Cahiers du* CTNERHI. *Etre dans l'incapacité d'apprendre (Learning Disabilities and Brain Function).* 41:17–19.
Koizumi, E. (in this volume) School nonattendance: A view from educational centers.
Lebovici, S. (in this volume) School phobia: A psychoanalytic view.
Lentin, L. (1972) *Apprendre à parler à l'enfant de moins de six ans.* Paris, ESF.
Murase, K. (in this volume) School refusal and family pathology: A multifaceted approach.

Nakane, A. (in this volume) School refusal: Psychopathology and natural history.

Plaisance, E. (1986) *L'enfant, la maternelle, la société*. Paris, Presses Universitaires de France.

Suzuki, K. (in this volume) School refusal viewed through family therapy.

Yamazaki, K., Inomata, J., Makita, K. and MacKenzie, J. A. (1989) Culture japonaise et caractéristisques des manifestations névrotiques dans l'enfance et l'adolescence. In *Nouvelles approaches de la santé mentale de la naissance à l'adolescence pour l'enfant et sa famille,* ed. C. Chiland and J. G. Young. Paris, Presses Universitaires de France.

13

Rejection of School
in France

RENÉ DIATKINE

SUMMARY

Going to school and benefiting from what is taught there implies a specific psychic activity which, in our civilization, takes on an important role in the achievement of individual autonomy. A child or adolescent who is responsive to schooling is one who is capable of freely developing mental play around themes proposed by teachers or suggested by books. From the primary school level onward, it should be possible to carry out this playful activity without someone who acts as a counter-phobic object. Examples are given of rejection of schooling at the start of pre-elementary education, when children begin learning to write, and at adolescence.

When parents come for a consultation because their child has developed a negative attitude toward school, the child sometimes presents mental characteristics that can be worrisome not only for their obvious immediate effects, but also for their medium- and long-term implications. In other cases, however, these are no more than the reactions of adolescents forced to go to school as long as it is legally required; these students get no satisfaction whatsoever out of school. They often feel degraded by what they see as being kept in an unbearably protracted infantile state. It is a difficult undertaking to keep children affected by school failure in school until they reach sixteen years of age, but it is an undertaking that should not be relinquished. Some particularly gifted teachers are sufficiently imaginative to turn this obligation into a useful experience. It also sometimes happens that once the legal requirement is removed and they leave school, these adolescents regain their enthusiasm, find work, and their intellectual curiosity is secondarily reawakened.

Unfortunately, though, not all youngsters who reject schooling follow this pattern, and child and adolescent psychoanalysts often find themselves confronted with very difficult situations requiring intervention.

Rejections can begin with the child's earliest experience of schooling. Although it frequently appears at the start of preschool education and generally fades out of its own accord, it can reappear at the start of formal learning, again in preadolescence, and yet again in adolescence. One has to wonder if there are factors common to these specific negative reactions—which lead to failure in early learning—and to all the psychic activities that constitute school phobias or pathological outcomes in adolescence. Can any structural analogy be discerned between psychic events occurring at such different ages and in such different psychic contexts? Asking this question is one way to approach possible predictive factors in child psychiatry.

These problems can be examined more clearly if we first define which feelings and attitudes enable a child to be at ease in school and interested in what is offered there.

I will tackle the question from a psychoanalytic viewpoint, without taking for granted that children or adolescents get a great deal out of school, whatever might be said about an innate tendency to strive for knowledge. The central idea running through my reflections on the rejection of schooling is the hypothesis that a great part of intellectual and language activity is developed when the child, in the absence of the mother or mother substitutes, develops the psychic organization necessary to avoid the experience of object loss and the internal disorganization that this could entail. The mental image of the external object is given a cathexis distinct from the initial cathexis of the perceived object, although of the same intensity. This avoids a state of continuous yearning in the child. When the child is able to designate an absent object through spoken language (in favorable circumstances this occurs by the end of the second year) reference to an image develops together with the beginnings of complex speech (when the utterance contains at least two elements, according to Cabrero). At the same time, the child becomes sensitive to the relevance of phonetic contrasts—that is, the arbitrary constituents of language. Absence is in this way compensated for by the passage from signal to sign, from analogy to symbol; the balance created, however, is delicate and easily threatened by the renewal of anxiety and depressive affects.

Play is already apparent in cooing and babbling, and the use of phonetic contrasts renews it again in utterances that arise out of the intensity of the child's earliest desires. When the infant soliloquizes, with its mother listening from a distance—to take the situation described by Winnicott as the capacity to be alone in the presence of mother (Winnicott 1958)—it is taking the first steps along the path of playful psychic activity that will later develop into narrative language. When the speech act refers to a past or fictitious event, it is independent of any immediate necessity. It allows object loss to be avoided, but it becomes ineffective when there is a recurrence of anxiety for one reason or another.

THE START OF SCHOOLING: NURSERY SCHOOL

In France children attend nursery school at an increasingly early age. This is a social phenomenon likely to be far more productive than raising the school-leaving age, and it can be hoped that early educational methods adapted to this particular young age will enable a greater number of children to achieve success in primary school and go on to higher education.

Entering a structured school situation during the third or fourth year of life entails a decisive modification of the child's mental functioning. During the first years of its existence, the infant was either in the company of its family, cared for during the day by a mother's helper, or sent to a day care program. Whichever was the case, it was surrounded by a small number of adults and children, and its place and role were clearly defined. The child is often the youngest member of the family; it may have had to find its place in relation to older children and face the birth of the next infant, but its identity was not involved (I disregard here the problem of twins, which are a special case). If the child was looked after by a mother's helper, despite obvious differences life was organized more or less along the same lines as usual. Traditionally, day care programs have tended to create the most individual relationships possible with infants, toddlers, and preschoolers, including by assigning a particular caregiver as responsible for each child.

The structure of classroom groups, however, is radically different. Even when class numbers are not excessive, the subject finds him or herself confronted with many other children of the same age and only one person, the teacher, to look after the entire group.

In the beginning, this new person establishes an individual relationship with each child, holds each one in his or her arms, and has close contact with each. At other times, the teacher addresses all the children together, without attributing any particular role to one or another. The beginnings of the first year at nursery school are difficult, whether the child is younger or older than three. When they arrive in the morning the children are reluctant to be separated from their parents, cry after they have gone, and either make a great deal of noise or take refuge in a mutism adapted to the occasion. These difficult moments, in which the children seem lost in a hostile universe, are repeated day after day for many long weeks, and some parents eventually give in and keep the children at home. For the majority, however, the situation sooner or later improves and at some point during the school year they finally get over their initial anxiety and are content in class. They have not been traumatized by this painful experience; they have, instead, undergone a significant change. This change can be examined from the perspective of cathexes and of language.

The mental image of the teacher becomes part of the child's psychic universe, while his or her relationship with the teacher as a person is included among the characteristics of the classroom: this requires, among other things, respecting a physical distance. Although some closer contact is necessary for a while to get started on a new task, communication is essentially verbal. At a later stage eye contact with the adult—by means of which the adult is "present" in the classroom— is sufficient for a hesitant pupil not to feel left alone and therefore disorganized.

These new patterns reflect a psychic readjustment that could be described as a redeployment of the capacity to be alone with a loved person, with organization carried a step further. Through this gradual adaptation children find a certain pleasure in setting the limits of their own autonomy, which enables them to accept an adult's suggestions without feeling invaded. The image of the teacher undergoes cathexis similar to that of the images of each of the parents. This displacement— or projection from internal objects—is subject to secondary elaboration and makes the primitive ambivalence less sharply drawn. It follows the vicissitudes of this elaboration. When all goes well, cathexis of the teacher and the psychic activities proposed facilitate the diversification and flexibility of mental functioning. If splitting is too rigid it can lead, on the contrary, to the adult being seen as a persecutor and to rejection of everything he or she proposes.

If events turn out satisfactorily, there is a change in the child's behavior toward the parents. The child can start to contradict them, using the authority of the teacher as a backup. The child no longer calls on the parents to witness everything that happens to him or her or tells them everything that goes on in school; indeed, the child answers questions laconically. By now the child has seen the differences in the respective organizations of family and school; he or she is aware of holding a different place in each of the two groups and of the fact that there are incompatibilities between the two systems. The schoolchild has the whole nursery-school period for his or her narcissism to adapt to this new situation, to accept the presence of others and not to be undermined by rivalries, disloyalties, and overturned alliances. At the same time the child's private domain is widened: now there are things that can no longer be said to parents, others which must be kept even from the nicest teachers, and still others yet which are no business of his or her schoolmates. Each frontier has its own outline, although this is by its very nature a movable limit. All of these mental activities call into question, to some extent, the feeling of self-unity: still, the discoveries made in the realm of knowledge and imagination at nursery school (what is conveyed by cultural transmission) buttress this unity by sustaining the pleasure of mental functioning.

This redistribution of cathexes is projected into language. When a child enters school in the third or fourth year, his or her language is in a constant state of fluctuation. Some children already speak very well, possess a wide vocabulary, and are capable of a considerable variety of syntactic manipulations. Others have not yet reached that stage and have some difficulty mastering narrative language, but all of them already use language in several different registers. In the small groups they have lived in until this time, utterances were accompanied by familiar sign language or gestures which were exchanged within a narrow and relatively constant framework. Despite the shortcomings of the language, communication could be made subtler through a lingering idiosyncratic component. This very personal language, together with intimate little words and physical contacts, is related for the most part to present or familiar objects. Only a few privileged children had stories told to them, whether read from books or improvised. Going to nursery school introduces a new element: when the teacher addresses the group he or she uses language in its universal form, with all its precision, paradigmatic and syntactic contrasts, and complexities of syntax. Although it is spoken language, utterances intended to be understood by the whole group require a structure analogous to that of narrative and written language. The interplay of phonetic contrasts and syntactical complexities is necessary for the child to understand instructions and proposals addressed to the group and for the child to respect the distance inherent in the classroom situation.

The ability not to reject schooling is forged during this transition from personal, intimate language with familiar referents to universal language—which transition constitutes the second stage of the child's experience at nursery school. When the teacher uses this new form of language to transmit the most elementary and least affect-charged instruction (such as, "now everyone get up and leave the classroom quietly"), the new mode of communication is acceptable to the child for two reasons. First, the enunciator is not the child's mother, yet the teacher's mental image is derived from the mother; second, the child's ability to understand this order (like that of all the other pupils) is linked to classroom situations that offer a quiet pleasure in mental functioning, enabling the child to manage without any need for the parents' physical presence.

The somewhat dry form of this utterance puts it among the many forms of separation procedures which, from the perspective I have adopted here, are part of the development of the use of imagination and the acquisition of knowledge. It falls within the realm of the protagonists' interacting images of the situation. As we mentioned earlier, for some fortunate children, this psychic activity had already been started through bedtime stories, which allow the child to be separated physically from the parents while listening to a story in which separation is reenacted in a playful register. The teacher's universal language combines story-language—that of the tale—with the one used for instructions given to all the children; these instructions organize the children by conferring on each his or her role in separation-related activities. If the child has not been able, before starting school, to organize the ability to withdraw without anxiety into his or her own intimate psychic space, with its subtle, fluctuating frontiers, there is a danger at some point of cathecting the teacher as someone who is depriving the child of his or her mother. A splitting of the maternal object results in a persecutory projection onto the teacher, and if this is sustained, school phobia of indeterminate duration can set in. It is usually barely perceptible as such: what is apparent is that instructions are not heard, and that the child seems uninterested in what is said in class; thus, the child's agitation is considered hyperkinetic. This situation, which is a fairly frequent one, can often be handled within the school context itself, as long as the teacher is not overly concerned about it and does not lose interest in the child. Experience has shown that such "institutional" treatment through the school is most valuable, because it enables a dangerous crisis to wind down to a favorable outcome and makes it possible afterward to draw the appropriate practical conclusions in a calm context.

The experience of nursery school plays a role in ensuring school acceptance in later years. It is the period in life when a child can discover a great many new forms of mental functioning without being asked to prove that he or she can give back what is being taught by giving a right answer. It is a time of expansion of intellectual activity without any negative consequences. Unfortunately, such a lack of monitoring of knowledge runs counter to habits transmitted from generation to generation, and this often prevents recognition of the specificity of the nursery school's role.

PRIMARY SCHOOL

Almost all children are enthusiastic about going up to "the big school," but not all of them are happy once they get there. A child accepts primary school with pleasure as long as the child is able to imagine that the teacher is talking to him or her when addressing the whole class, even though the child knows this is not quite true. This fairly sober "delusion" must be sufficiently bound up with playful psychic activity that it requires no testing; otherwise, the child can become opposed to schooling. Such a child needs the intervention of an outside person in order to avoid becoming depressed or daydreaming. He or she gains the attention of the adult present by breaching what minimal discipline exists; or, he or she expresses an irresistible need to be in contact with another pupil, either by chattering or by showing aggression. In other cases, children are simply inhibited, and their inhibition disappears when the teacher pays particular attention to them. Conflict that takes maladaptive behavior a fraction beyond this point makes the children inaccessible to schooling: not only are they unaware of what the teacher says to them, but they cannot utilize the school situation, and prostration or agitation are their only possible responses.

The inability to cathect the teacher with a sufficient degree of imaginative elements often results from a disturbance in the child's evolution during the first few years of life. To be able to handle the play activities required by primary education, the child must have lived in conditions stable enough to strengthen his or her narcissism and elaborate conflicts with the parental imagos. Beyond the various phases of organization of the Oedipus complex, the separation processes must have progressed from the tragic death-anxiety phase to imaginary variations on the same theme. Even though an increasing number of children have discovered before they learn to read that literature offers agreeable variations on the conflict between generations, the fear of incest, and death anxiety, everything can be called into question again at the point where the child begins to learn to read. It can happen, for a great many reasons, that learning turns out to be difficult, and that adults stop reading stories to children in order to prevent them from acquiring lazy habits. A misguided insistence that the child read independently can quickly make the child hate the activity when it gets difficult. Yet a positive cathexis of things that can be constructed beyond what is actually perceived is essential, not only for a child to be able to tolerate school, but also for a child to remain interested in what is being taught and to redo exercises correctly.

We have seen the imaginative activity that must be brought into play for the child to avoid becoming depressed about being just one among twenty-five or feeling nonexistent. A corollary of this attitude is the child's ability to be interested in the situations suggested—in which he or she is never directly concerned and which invariably refer to an imaginary situation—however realistic and melancholy the texts offered may be. At one time it was thought that for children's interest to be aroused it was necessary to refer to their everyday experiences, including life at home or familiar street scenes. This idea of situating children in their habitual surroundings is certainly not to be rejected out of hand, but neither is it sufficient in itself to ensure the child's interest.

Responsiveness to schooling, then, means accepting—or better still, enjoying—the teacher's proposals as a springboard for mental activity whose focus has no direct bearing on the subject's own set of problems. This acceptance brings with it an additional freedom, namely that instruction, the texts read (whether by the teacher, the subject, or other pupils), and what is written on the blackboard are not cathected as wounding objects, liable to intrude into the subject's psyche. Without necessarily considering the situation of children today a tragedy, the idea of intrusion by adults and their so-called gifts must be borne in mind constantly in any reflection on the rejection of schooling. One frequent and sadly commonplace occurrence in family life sheds paradigmatic light on what happens in class. A school age child looks as though he or she is doing nothing; he or she may even seem bored. The father or the mother suggests doing an exercise, learning the next day's lesson, or perhaps helping with something in the house. The child may not answer at all or may respond in a dilatory fashion, with a response like "later." This response irritates adults, who think the child is lazy, and the usual misunderstanding arises. The parents raise their voices, the child fumes and grumbles. After that, there is a third stage in which communication is restored and the child does what he or she was asked. An attentive observer reconstructs what might have taken place. The child, who seemed to be unoccupied, was indeed in the clouds; he or she may have been in one of the secret dream worlds characteristic of children of that age, or perhaps the child was simply in a vacant state of mind. In any case, the adult's injunction, when uttered, created and violated a limit.

Acceptance or rejection of schooling at the primary level depends on whether or not the child achieves access to the language taught there: the story language, written language, and mathematical language—in other words, whether or not the child becomes a reader. The pupil's psychic structure must take a stance with regard to passage from the language of action to the language of the story, with its references to people, places, and events of which the child has, or should have, a mental image. Every narrative includes, in addition, a secondary comment on the child him or herself. From the child psychoanalyst's point of view, there is a structural analogy between the imaginary narrative—of which the fairy tale is the most unadulterated example—and the informative text introducing abstract relationships that permit the acquisition of knowledge. It is easy to see a progression in the mental work of the very young schoolchild from familiarity with stories to the use of numbers. This progression starts with analogical transcription (a "king," a "queen," a "prince," or a "princess" are only simple displacements) and it proceeds from the disguised imago, to access to the abstract symbolism of elementary mathematical concepts and the arbitrary nature of orthographic signs.

In order to be received, the story, whether told or read by the subject or by someone else, requires psychic work that comprises a system of discrete and shifting cathexes. When not alone doing silent reading, the child must be interested in the person by whom the story is read or told, through identification with the original narrator. He or she must recognize the storyteller, who is at first confused with the narrator but who then becomes increasingly distanced from the reader. The storyteller knows what is going to happen but does not reveal the outcome. The child has to bear the suspense of not knowing the end of the story (a fact which partly explains children's attachment to repetition and undeviating similarity, and later their liking for the care taken to ensure that the hero should remain alive and ever-youthful at the end of each episode). The child is helped to bear the uncertainty by the heroes themselves, who know even less than he or she does about what is in store for them. The child must distinguish the various characters from one another and recognize their dialogue from their direct or indirect style. He or she is sensitive, without being unduly affected by them, to elements which in some way evoke aspects of him or herself.

The description of this process would be incomplete without mention of the final operation by which the child is turned into a reader. There comes a day when the child takes a book and plunges alone into the world of the story, which becomes part of his or her intimate personal space. Another debate is now opened up. This introjection, which henceforth organizes part of the child's imaginative existence, is not effected without a certain degree of violence towards adults. This is another step, after the very early capacity to be alone with the mother and well before the reworkings of adolescence, in which the subject indicates to parents that they must not enter the pockets of private life that are being created during the course of these processes. Once again, they must not be overly curious, but they must be present nonetheless. The outcome of this process determines the future.

When all goes well, as is very often the case, this process is only a first stage, which enables the child to reestablish relations of a different type and cathect teachers without projecting unelaborated parental imagos on them. Parents and teachers can sometimes be intrusive, even if it is only by obliging the schoolchild to read, and very often by asking questions about the things the child holds most secret—the thousand and one joys and delights of sadism and anxiety, subtly distilled into rebellious elements that are tolerable in the most gripping stories. Reading is not done to order, and indiscreet questions are answered only in a conventional or disorganized manner.

The various overlaid transparencies of the text set off the subject's psychic elaborations into activities whereby the ego's relations with its object-representations unfold and recombine. If the child has not at an early stage set up a defense system to protect him or herself from being invaded by depressive affects when he or she is alone—alone at a desk, alone in class among fellow pupils—his or her psychical process is often vulnerable and the child most commonly finds refuge in inhibition. This means that the most normal child can at some time or another be a "nonreader," or at least can be incapable of being interested in what is said in class. Each child—and each teacher—knows without being told that during difficult moments he or she is no longer able to read at all, or can only take refuge in reading matter that he or she has chosen (material not necessarily of a high standard) but also that this does not mean the child is sick or suffering from depression. Although he or she is more easily protected by a kindly adult presence, in which case the grownup acts as a counter-phobic person, the child is still subject to comparable variations in psychic organization. This occurs, however, without the child's being granted the natural right to transient deterioration and disorganization. Misunderstanding sets in. Some talk of laziness, others fear that these blank periods might have entailed gaps in the child's knowledge and propose repeating the year for pupils whose basic skills seem inadequate. The net result is often a narcissistic wound that is only worsened by a school system in which competition prevails. This explains why the transformations of adolescence are liable to go badly and the fact that a variety of different forms of school rejection can arise.

PREADOLESCENCE AND ADOLESCENCE

Although adaptation to schooling and the mental work involved leads gradually to a point at which both internalization of parental imagos and moments of relative autonomy in relation to parents are possible, until the threshold of adolescence the parents must remain present or within short distance. It is for or despite them and for or despite teachers that the child gets good or bad results at school.

Long before puberty, all these "intimate world" areas tend to coagulate, and the secret debate on the degree of autonomy takes over. The onset of physical maturity and puberty then makes it difficult to accept tender feelings toward parents. Since all of these radical changes are well known, we will only examine some of their effects on the subject's interest in schooling. Most adolescents no longer resolve upon a particular course to please their parents, but choose one more dependent on their own wishes. The persistent conflicts with parental imagos are unconscious—and their conscious offshoots are no longer recognized as predominant.

If, during childhood, the adolescent has built up a secondary-process psychic activity that has enabled him or her to discover the pleasure of mental functioning, he or she manages one way or another to cope with ruptures without being broken down by them. School or university work will be carried out according to his or her own responsibility and inclinations, with all the normal ups and downs that this budding autonomy entails.

When events have not taken such a favorable course, situations involving rejection of schooling are likely to occur. Broadly speaking, these take three main and fairly distinct forms.

1. *Egosyntonic* refusal is the kind of rejection mentioned earlier with reference to adolescents who are obliged to stay in school at least until the legal school-leaving age of sixteen. This group includes many pupils who have weakened at some point because their mental play has been momentarily overcathected and hence inhibited, and who have then suffered the narcissistic wound of school failure officially recorded by the authorities. As I pointed out above, such school failure may have no more than a very minor bearing on their adult lives.

2. School phobias can reemerge in psychic structures that are very different from one another. Their common denominator is massive projection—onto the subject's image of the school—of his or her depressive affects linked to the rupture of adolescence.

3. Far more serious than these two is the form that involves an impossibility which can take on a stable configuration in adolescence. This is the impossibility of organizing the steps necessary for the subject to abandon the idea of immediate fantasy realization of his or her early desires, and to elaborate the psychic means of attaining, by modifying them, the object of desires given shape by the ego ideal. The subject's school life begins to be disorganized by absences, first from particular classes and then from school altogether. This is sometimes followed by the appearance of delusions or schizophrenic dissociation.

"I don't belong here, nor in my family" was a phrase repeated by a thirty-year-old schizophrenic patient who had been ill since adolescence. "Where do you belong, then?" he would be asked. "In section C" (the honors science class) was his invariable rejoinder. His disorder had indeed begun with a fall-off in the lycée equivalent of ninth grade and he had repeated the year in the hope of getting back into the honors group which had seemed to be the natural course indicated by his brilliant performance until then. He had lost the ability to organize his thinking in the way others demanded of him, without having lost any of his intelligence.

REFERENCES

Winnicott, D. W. (1958) The capacity to be alone. *International Journal of Psycho-analysis* 39:416–420.

IV

Clinical and Research Strategies

14

School Phobia: A Psychoanalytic View

SERGE LEBOVICI

SUMMARY

School phobia is a neurotic symptom characterizing the organization of an incapacitating childhood neurosis. In this respect it is a very distinctive form of what is called school refusal. This study examines the displacement and projections peculiar to it, which point to an obvious failure of repression and organization in the latency period. Through these characteristics, school phobia provides a direct indication of a rather particular organization of the family system: the affected child finds separation from the mother impossible, as is true in any panic attack. Accepting this specificity does not imply rejection of the contributions of other disciplines to our knowledge about these conditions or their treatment. However, the fact remains that the presence of the phobia and the inability to go to school and/or stay there clashes head-on with adult common sense, particularly that of the parents, and this clash provokes violent reactions that can only serve to reinforce the symptom and the school refusal it entails.

Since Johnson and her colleagues particularized the clinical framework of school phobia in 1941, a distinction has been made between children and adolescents who do not want to go to school and those who cannot go and/or stay there—the school phobics. This phobia is the problem I will examine here. In recent years, however, doubt has been cast on the opposition between school refusal and phobic difficulties in attending school (see Hersov, this volume).

It is my view that while some explicit clarification of its clinical and prognostic specificity is required, this clinical framework should nonetheless be maintained. What is important, among other things, is to see whether school phobia necessarily leads to diagnosis of a true phobic neurosis or if it only corresponds to a symptom that can be understood satisfactorily in terms descriptive of the behavior it involves and the psychopathology that organizes it.

Finding the answer to this question provides a contribution to clinical knowledge about school refusal and, in this hazy area of child psychiatry, identifies those specific characteristics of these behaviors that are both significant and distinctive to clinicians. It is also an attempt to situate the discussion on the symptomatological, nosological, and psychopathological level at a time when the description of the anxiety and its connotative neurotic symptoms has come under criticism on many scores.

First, the classifications in use in child psychiatry are in question, especially the revised American classification known as DSM III R and the World Health Organization's proposed Tenth Revision of the International Classification of Diseases (ICD–10) as they attempt to take account of the anxiety and symptoms in separation anxiety. The DSM III R classification lists school refusal among the diagnostic criteria for separation anxiety disorder, but in its concern for maintaining an atheoretical stance, it makes no reference to the idea of neurosis, which would be too exclusively associated with psychoanalysis.

Second, other theoretical approaches to phobic anxiety are proposed: we are talking about the distinction between "social" phobias and panic attack. The latter has neurobiological and cognitive bases, is possibly related to depressive symptomatology, and can be treated behaviorally or with such drugs as anxiolytics or antidepressant medications.

In other words, school phobia comes under converging attacks which reject its specificity and consider it as just another form of school refusal. The trend is all the more pronounced because it coincides with protest against the "psychiatrization" of school problems. It happens that the latter tendency often suits parents who hope that this approach will avoid any critical examination of family organization, whose characteristics are quite distinctive in cases of school phobia. It is also true that the school system is often tedious and disheartening, at least for those who are unsuccessful in it, and refusal to attend school goes along with rebellion in preadolescents who are kept there against their will.

I attempt here to define the framework of school phobia and justify reference to this clinical and psychopathological framework, using psychoanalytic theory and practical observation as a means to understanding it.

CLINICAL LIMITATIONS OF THIS STUDY
AND A DESCRIPTIVE APPROACH

I will not include under school phobias the avoidant attitudes characteristic of adolescents whose behavior is tinged with a certain degree of poor reality testing and who are on the brink of psychosis.

At the other end of the chronological scale, young children's fear of being separated from their mother over the first few days of kindergarten, for example, does not seem to warrant the diagnosis of phobia. This is because the fear of separation is expressed directly and cannot be construed as implying any situational displacement, which we know to be the core of the organization of a phobic system.

However, it is clear that the equivalent of a minor school phobia is presented by children who suffer from functional disorders occurring particularly in the morning as it gets closer to the time to leave for school. These disorders usually take the form of abdominal pain and colic, frequently accompanied by diarrhea. These recurrent pains occur in children of families in which maternal phobias contribute to the infantile aspect of the behavior of the child. Here we may observe two facts to which I shall return: (1) the school phobic has a mother who is herself phobic or has suffered phobias in the past; and (2) the child complains of functional disorders which are dealt with therapeutically at some length before there is any mention of phobias.

It must be remembered that phobia is not defined solely by the anxiety that characterizes it; it is often accompanied by a whole series of physical manifestations the presence of which would justify the distinction which is made in French, between *anxiété* and *angoisse*.[1] Phobia transforms simple anxiety into fear—fear of a situation or of a reminder of it. The transition from anxiety to fear evidences the displacement characteristic of phobic elaboration.

From this standpoint, the phobia of the unknown face, which usually occurs during the last three months of the first year of the child's life, can be considered the model infantile phobia. Spitz (1954) described it as eighth-month anxiety: in his view this constitutes the second organizer in the baby's mental life, and it is characteristic of the stage in which the child is able to recognize its mother not only for her value as a functional object, but also as a person. Reference here to the phobia of the unknown face means that the elaboration of the separation anxiety

---

1. Both translate as *anxiety* in English.

has brought about a situational displacement, and the presence of the stranger's face amounts to the disappearance of maternal protection.

There are two points here whose importance must be borne in mind for the discussion to follow.

- The notion of "unknown" is imprecise: for example, the father is familiar to the baby and protects it against the truly unknown stranger. Nevertheless, he is structurally the one who separates the baby from its mother, and Oedipal organization originates in the situation of the presence of the stranger-father (Lebovici and Diatkine 1954).
- Recovery from the phobia of the unknown face occurs spontaneously, first of all as a specific phenomenon: some children achieve autonomy as they go through the various stages of *rapprochement* (Mahler), while others remain tied to their mother's apron strings. In any case, young children all experience fear of solitude and fear of the dark: their nights are crowded with nightmares that in some way help them overcome their separation anxiety. This overcoming is also achieved in children's play, where they can bring about the return of someone who has gone away (S. Freud 1920) and punish them for having disappeared (A. Freud 1936). In this way separation anxiety keeps reappearing all along a path whose end never appears: it follows from the fundamental fear of losing the love object and/or its love, and is elaborated either in situational forms or through fantasies which cause imaginary fears about the wholeness of the body.

Thus we come to the organization of school phobia: the social impairment it entails makes it a significant incapacitating factor and sets it very much apart as a symptom from phobias which are considered normal at the beginning of the latency period and are characteristic of infantile neurosis (Lebovici 1981).

The school phobic child specifically insists on his or her inability to stay in class while giving the impression that it is an unwillingness rather than an inability to do so: the distinction is an invitation to explore the phobia further. The inability to remain in the schoolroom might bring to mind the anxiety suffered by claustrophobics, who talk about suffocating, physical malaises, or terror of being unable to get out of the space into which they feel shut. Although the clinician does not share the actual fears of the claustrophobic, he or she can relate to them through an empathetic understanding. In other words, there is no hesitation in reaching a diagnosis of phobia. Unfortunately, however, the explanations given by the child seem less convincing: "they don't like me; the teacher is too strict," and so on. Or else the child recalls what seems to have been a precipitating event, such as (in a case I followed) hearing the frightening voice of a teacher in a nearby classroom at the school where the child's father was also on the staff and had the reputation of being a very strict teacher. This apparently sudden onset, which is also found in adult phobias, has led to the idea of acute-onset school phobias (Sperling 1967). In any event, neither parents, society, nor many physicians are willing to recognize the school space as potentially phobogenic; they far more readily accept as such the situation of being trapped in a stalled elevator or of being an airplane passenger condemned to a state of passivity.

Agoraphobia is the model panic attack: we know that the person who is listening to the sufferer does not come to identify with the anxiety the latter describes. This is all the more so because the phobic is describing an unfounded anxiety masked by malaise, breathlessness, palpitations, and nausea; in current theories there is a tendency to attribute a causal, or at least reinforcing role to these manifestations. Once the phobia is recognized, it is surprising to find that the sufferer is so easily calmed by the presence of a counter-phobic object, such as a mother's reassuring arm, a baby in a pram, or even the pram without the baby, as was effective in a case I treated.

Agoraphobics are often accused of untruthfulness or lack of sincerity; this suspicion also lies behind the incredulity shown to school phobic children and is the cause of violent or repressive conduct toward them, or even of decisions to give them behavioral treatment. It must be admitted that such mistaken attitudes are inevitable and possibly even to some extent useful: after all, Freud himself recommended insisting that agoraphobic patients should not attend their psychoanalytic sessions with the protection of their counter-phobic object.

In view of these conclusions, though, we should remember several points about phobic conduct with regard to school:

(1) On the one hand, there are mild phobias associated with the specific school situation; these are commonplace components of separation anxiety and possible subclinical forms of expression of childhood neurosis.

(2) On the other hand, there are minor variants of school phobia, among which the classic example is recurrent abdominal pain.

(3) Finally, we have the characteristic school phobias, which, like all forms of childhood neurosis, are usually serious because of the disabling inhibitions they entail. It is hardly surprising that their courses—after remission of the neurotic symptom—can vary greatly; it can include a coercive character neurosis, leading to deeply pathological organization in families founded by former phobic children, or highly delicate mental functioning. Indeed, certain aspects of phobic displacement justify its being considered from the angle of projection; in any event, however, the variety of possible courses shows how valuable the longitudinal study of these cases can be.

The epidemiological study of school phobia illustrates certain features worth underlining (Dugas and Guériot 1977):

- A distinction should be made between samples of children from eight to twelve years old, who are reaching the end of the latency period and are the real school phobics, and samples consisting of adolescents, in whom the phobic symptomatology is more open to further examination. In the latter case it could indicate the onset of schizophrenia, where the phobia would be one of the initial manifestations of morbid rationalization or a melancholic equivalent, or it could also be simple school refusal.
- Contrary to the usual sex ratio in child psychiatric patients, school phobia is found in girls just as frequently as in boys. However, there are reasons to believe that, as in all phobias, it is a more serious problem in boys, as it brings into the clinical picture the element of passivity, which is in principle a feminine trait.

THE SPECIFICITY OF SCHOOL PHOBIA

Clearly, considered as the syndrome whose features and borders we have just outlined, school phobia presents as something quite different from what could be called school refusal. Children who are truant set off for school but do not tell their parents that they are not really going there. They often wander about aimlessly the whole day until it is time to go home, at which point the anticipatory fear of discovery may be assimilated with anxiety. Similarly, the adolescent school refuser's roamings, more or less organized as a runaway situation and often complicated by involvement with groups of dubious character, are a source of anxiety only so far as their consequences are concerned. There may be cases in which a school phobia leads to counter-phobic behavior that can mimic this antisocial attitude, and we have encountered instances of this (Lebovici and Le Nestour 1977).

At any rate, cases such as these have led some authors to reconsider the specificity of school phobias in the framework of school refusal. A number of other arguments are still put forward to justify this clinical compartmentation, and we shall examine them.

The Persistence of Disturbances in the Family Environment

It has often been noted that the mothers of school phobic children are themselves affected by phobias. Berg and his colleagues (Berg 1976; Berg et al. 1976) have shown that school phobic girls frequently become agoraphobic women and that the mothers of school phobic children are often severely phobic. This observation has led to a recommendation of psychotherapy for the mothers of children examined and treated for this type of disturbance.

However, study of the organization of the family system has shown the existence of a rather specific structure in these cases, on which most recent related works agree (Pittman et al. 1968; Dugas and Guériot 1977; Lebovici and Le Nestour 1977). This structure can be defined essentially by the fact that a mother who is neglected and withdrawn herself tries to help her phobic child, which in turn contributes to her having to stay at home. The father is absent but excluded, so that he is forced to resign himself to the reality of the wife–maternal grandmother couple on the one hand and the wife–child couple on the other. He then intervenes in a churlish and clumsy way. In cases in which he has actually disappeared or died—a not uncommon situation—his exclusion is especially ambiguous: he is both revered and spoken of as a villain. A classic case of this family model concerned a boy suffering from a typical and serious school phobia. He was the fifth of six children, all of whom either presented severe phobias or had formerly done so. The older sister closest to his age would not or could not go to school, because she needed constantly to check that her mother was not dead—a true phobia that the mother continued to nurture through her own permanent hypochondria. It would not be unreasonable to speculate that this girl was also preventing her widowed mother from meeting another man. The boy's school phobia began when he witnessed his father's death in a series of dreadful attacks of dyspnea. His father's hat, which in this pious Jewish family should have been handed down to the oldest son, was given to him; he did a drawing of himself wearing the crown of a king succeeding a king who had just died. And yet this king, his father, was described by the mother at some times as a model of virtue, and at others as a gambler and an inveterate cabaret-goer.

This brief case summary shows how maternal phobias—the mother's apparent hypochondria was in fact underpinned by a pervasive system of phobias related to various ailments—were translated into an undermining of the father's virility. This was reinforced by his death, which obviously posed a problem for the boy's process of identification and his resolution of Oedipal conflicts; moreover, it kept an incapacitating phobic system active.

We can see how important it is to highlight these patterns, which are among the factors that maintain homeostasis, in addition to noting those that contribute to the organization of school phobias. However, because such family systems appear to be fairly consistent in these particular cases, they necessarily have to be taken into account as part of any comprehensive treatment plan. Psychoanalysts must learn to assess interpersonal factors affecting the children they examine, just as carefully as they consider disturbances in their mental functioning. In the example above, the patient had been blocked at the pregenital level by maternal activism; speaking of his mother as he crumpled his father's hat in a sacrilegious gesture, he stated "it was the she-tiger who did that." In our view, his case clearly indicates that an interpersonal interpretative elaboration of Oedipal conflicts is essential before school phobia can be understood through an individual analysis.

SCHOOL PHOBIAS AND THEIR ANALYSIS IN LIGHT OF PSYCHOSOCIAL CONSIDERATIONS

Some insist that children considered to be school phobics are simply those who reject school; these theorists stress the value of a psychosocial approach. In their view the so-called school phobic child actually suffers at school; they cite cognitive problems, despite the fact that these patients tend to have upper-level IQs (although, as Dugas and Guériot (1977) indicate, they have some difficulties with the nonverbal parts of the Wechsler test). Some patients dread having a teacher who is not understanding or who is rejecting; others suffer from parental over-ambition, and so on. These considerations are of some interest in that they point to the possible application of cognitive therapies, which could be classified less pretentiously as educational help or psychotherapy-oriented special education.

Still others go so far as to criticize the school system: schools are dreary and ill-equipped to meet children's individual needs (Bolman 1970). As Ivan Ilyich asked, "What are schools for?" This criticism gives rise to the idea that neither school phobia nor school refusal would exist if modern states had not brought in compulsory education; this seems an obvious enough conclusion. In a more serious vein, however, it should be noted that forced attendance can indeed become unbearable in a society in which parents want the few children they have to be successful at any price, and in which one stopgap solution to the problem of adolescent unemployment is to turn schools and universities into human "parking lots."

I am mindful of the fact that some situation must exist in order for anxiety to be displaced and projected onto it; the phobic system produces such projections and the existence of phobias can reasonably lead one to expect the organization of sensitive personalities, as we have already seen. The existence of school phobias cannot be considered proof that the school system itself is actually injurious! Moreover, there can be no doubt that phobic symptomatology varies with different cultures—after all, it was hardly agoraphobia that prevented young women from daring to go out alone in the nineteenth century.

*School Phobia as One of the More Disabling
Forms of Childhood Neurosis*

The school situation appears, then, to provide one of the possible forms that neurotic elaboration of anxiety can take at that stage of life. From this standpoint it can be said that school phobia subverts the latency phase. Because of the massive repression involved in its installation, this phase is the period when instinctual life is contained. Here sublimation and creativity make possible intellectual effort, while the identification process, which also serves as a bulwark against instinctual life, provides an outlet for unconscious conflicts and opens the way to certain accomplishments that satisfy the parental imagos, which are loved, hated, and revered all at once.

Hence, school phobia indicates the failure of repression and leaves open the door for projections of the family situation onto the school milieu, which phenomenon explains the direct and alarming relationship between these pathogenic situations and the ones repeated at school.

School phobia therefore presents all the characteristics of a symptom of childhood neurosis. Is it necessarily and adequately definable in terms of separation anxiety? The answer is yes, if one takes a close look at the importance of the secondary gain: staying at home with the mother, who willingly lets herself be transformed into a counter-phobic object. In order to understand the nature of the conflicts that keep the child bound in the straitjacket of this regressive behavior one must consider Freud's last theories about anxiety (S. Freud 1926). We have seen in passing that at one stage Freud had thought it possible to demonstrate that separation anxiety lay all along the pathway leading from fear of losing the instinctually cathected object, or its love, to the fear of destroying it and thereby being destroyed (or castrated). From such a perspective, anxiety becomes a possible danger signal, and Freud would no doubt agree with a number of theories that would consider apprehension of the anxiety situation as a constituent of a panic attack and its accompanying manifestations (such as breathlessness and palpitations) as exacerbating factors.

It would also be reasonable to say that traumatic outbreaks of anxiety or panic are related to acute phobias, and also alert us to the possible presence of depressive features.

Although it is a serious neurotic symptom, many authors have described school phobia, in terms of the various forms of its evolution, as a crossroads of mental pathology (Dugas and Guériot 1977). Sperling (1967) continues to think it should be included among the childhood phobic neuroses: as my own work shows, I share her opinion. Others prefer to follow a trend to avoid returning to this clinical concept. Yet, there are some minor neurotic symptoms which constitute the core of the developing childhood neurosis and which appear in the course of analytic treatment according to the repetitive model of transference neurosis.

This does not imply that childhood neurosis pursues a silent course until it finally explodes in adulthood as a symptom neurosis or transference neurosis. On the other hand, childhood neurosis organizes character traits established in the calmer latency period; they are the source of repetitive behaviors observed in the transference neurosis during psychoanalytic treatment. The symptoms of childhood neurosis shatter the apparent tranquility of the latency period and are incapacitating: school phobia is a typical example. As it is linked with instinctual life and its regressions, a number of different outcomes are possible if it is not sufficiently untangled by treatment, or if treatment (especially psychoanalysis) is proposed but not followed through. Therefore, we can see that longitudinal and anamnestic studies of these cases show them to be so serious that their evolution places them at the boundary of psychopathological behaviors and on the brink of severe neurosis—in other words, they lie in the borderline area.

These data reinforce information brought to light by the approaches of other disciplines, but it seems that their contribution becomes clearer when a distinction is made between the various other manifestations of school refusal and school phobia itself, which in many cases takes the form of an incapacitating childhood neurosis.

REFERENCES

Berg, I. (1976) School phobia in the children of agoraphobic women. *British Journal of Psychiatry* 128:86–89.
Berg, I., Butler, A., and Hall, G. (1976) The outcome of adolescent school phobia. *British Journal of Psychiatry* 128:81–85.
Bolman, W. H. (1970) Systems theory, psychiatry, and school phobia. *American Journal of Psychiatry* 127:25–31.
Dugas, M., and Guériot, C. (1977) Les phobies scolaires: Etude clinique et psychopathologique. *Psychiatrie de l'Enfant* 20:307–382.
Freud, A. (1936) *Le moi et les mécanismes de défense.* Trans. into French 1964. Paris, Presses Universitaires de France.
Freud, S. (1920) *Au-delà du principe de plaisir.* Tr. fr.. Paris: Payot, 1981, 43–115. *Beyond the Pleasure Principle. Standard Edition, Volume XVIII,* 7–64.
———. (1926) Inhibition, Symptôme, et Angoisse. Trans. into French 1965. Paris, Presses Universitaires de France.
Johnson, A. M., Falstein, E. I., Szurek, S., and Svensen, M. (1941) School phobia. *American Journal of Orthopsychiatry* 11:702–717.
Lebovici, S. (1980) Névrose infantile, névrose de transfert. *Revue Fraçaise de Psychanalyse* 43:783–857.
——— (1981) A propos du traitement des familles. *Psychiatrie de l'Enfant* 24:541–583.
Lebovici, S., and Diatkine, R. (1954) Etude des fantasmes chez l'enfant. *Revue Française de Psychanalyse* 18:108–155.
Lebovici, S., and Le Nestour, A. (1977) A propos des phobies scolaires graves. *Psychiatrie de l'Enfant* 20:383–432.
Mahler, M. (1968) *Psychose Infantile,* Trans. into French 1973. Paris, Payot.
Pittman, F. S., Langsley, D. G., and DeYoung, C. D. (1968) Work and school

phobias: A family approach to treatment. *American Journal of Psychiatry* 124:1535–1541.

Sperling, M. (1967) La phobie de l'école: Classification, dynamique, et traitement. *Revue Française de Psychanalyse* 38:265–286.

Spitz, R. A. (1954) *La première année de la vie de l'enfant.* Trans. into French 1958. Paris, Presses Universitaires de France.

15

Strategies for Research on School Refusal and Related Nonattendance at School

J. GERALD YOUNG

JAMES R. BRASIC

HITEN KISNADWALA

LEN LEVEN

SUMMARY

School refusal is embedded in a group of disorders united by the common characteristic of unauthorized nonattendance at school. The fundamental psychoanalytic and learning theory understanding of these disorders is now being extended by epidemiologic, familial/genetic, and psychopharmacological research. These disorders are especially suited to serve as an example for studies of the shaping of symptoms by family and culture, and of the intrapsychic representation of these influences. Neurobiological research has achieved parallel advances in the specification of brain neuronal systems for the regulation of anxiety as a principal component in vigilance, arousal, and panic. These findings fit well with the results of research on clinical studies of behavior in school refusal and a range of anxiety disorders. Investigation of anxiety, hypervigilance (in internalizing school refusal and anxiety disorders), and hypovigilance (in externalizing truant disorder) may generate clinical measures distinguishing categories of school nonattendance. Such measures would be applicable as diagnostic guides for treatment and as outcome predictors for children at risk. However, a prerequisite to further research is development of an adequate classification system, supported by standardized, operationally defined diagnostic criteria, leading to inclusion in the standard diagnostic systems. Once this is achieved, research can establish for these disorders prevalence rates, cross-cultural influences, natural histories, genetic contributions, specific family interactions, and optimal treatment methods.

SCHOOL NONATTENDANCE: SYMPTOMS AND CLASSIFICATION

Several terms are used to describe disorders in which nonattendance at school is the major symptom: truancy, school phobia, school refusal, separation anxiety, and school dropout. Other terms have included "school avoidance," as an overarching descriptor, or "school withdrawal" or "parental withholding" when permission or encouragement of the parents is associated with absenteeism. In addition, other terms for disorders possibly related to absenteeism might be considered in relation to research on nonattendance at school. For example, "school failure" describes children who attend school in the formal sense, but then fail to participate in a meaningful way; specific developmental disorders are diagnoses that sometimes predispose to or cause nonattendance; "somatic disguise" is a phrase used to describe the predominance of somatic symptoms in some school refusing children (Eisenberg 1958); and "depression" may play a significant role in nonattendance in a subgroup of children (Kolvin et al. 1984).

England and Wales enacted legislation establishing free and compulsory education in 1870 and 1876, thereby simultaneously initiating the need to monitor illegal absence from school. School attendance approximated 65 percent of enrolled students in the early 1870s, but rates in the range of 85–90 percent were achieved by the first few years of this century. An average attendance rate of 89 percent in London in 1970 indicates that there has been no improvement since that time. Thus, the school absentee rate will be more than 10 percent at any one time in England, with an associated great personal, educational, and financial cost (Galloway 1985).

Children fail to attend school for many reasons. The first distinction is between authorized and unauthorized absence from school (table 15.1). Authorized absence from school refers to those children staying home with the permission of their parents and the school administration, most often due to an illness of the child or other family member. The relative frequency of medical absenteeism cited in surveys varies widely, suggesting different views among informants and the possibility that such reasons can disguise other primary motivations for not attend-

Table 15.1 *Proposed Classification of School Nonattendance Disorders*

A. Authorized nonattendance (including for illness)
B. Unauthorized nonattendance
   1. Unauthorized parental withholding
   2. Nonattendance due to the child's realistic fear of dangers in the school setting
   3. Externalizing truant disorder
   4. Internalizing school refusal disorders
      a. School phobia
      b. Separation anxiety
      c. Depressive type
      d. Somatoform type
   5. School dropout
C. Ambiguous school attendance: School failure in a capable student while attending school

ing school. Unauthorized absence from school is due to three major categories of problems: withholding of the child by the parents, truancy, and school refusal.

Parents frequently withhold their child from school, sometimes rationalizing with explanations such as illness (from which the person has long since recovered) or other crisis. Parents have traditionally kept children at home for economic purposes, particularly in agricultural communities, or to care for someone in the house or simply to keep the parents company. Many families do not value formal education for their children, especially after a certain age, in comparison to other activities. Other families judge the quality of a particular school to be poor. Psychiatrists are less attentive to this category of nonattenders, whether because they see it as a social or educational problem, as a family decision into which they have no right to intrude, or because it is apparently accompanied by no conflict or symptoms and is considered a cultural variant.

Psychiatric investigators first classify nonattenders into subgroups of truant or school refusing children. Truant children stay away from school because of their general impulsivity and inability or unwillingness to follow regulations; mandatory school attendance is one of many laws flouted by the child's nonspecific refusal to comply. The second type of nonattendance at school involves children who experience significant conflict and distress about not attending school. Evidence suggests that this is a true categorical distinction, rather than being two groups of children representing a preponderance of symptoms at the poles of a continuous dimension; few children score high on traits related to both categories (Berg et al. 1985a,b). They reflect the more general classes of behavioral symptoms commonly contrasted as impulsive behavior disorder vs. emotional disorder, or externalizing disorder vs. internalizing disorder. These terms clarify the intent of this broad subgrouping of school nonattendance without biasing observations concerning disease status or etiology. Externalizing truant disorder and internalizing school refusal are useful provisional terms for stimulating further research. This approach generates a trial classification for all children failing to attend school, as presented in table 15.1.

Authorized nonattendance. A major disruption to the life of the child or family causes nonattendance, which is agreed to by parents and school administration (serious illness in the child or a parent is the most common cause).

Unauthorized parental withholding. A parental decision to keep the child at home is made according to the parents' needs (such as the economic benefit of a child's working; helping a parent cope with problems due to the parent's own illness, such as substance abuse or agoraphobia; and so on).

Nonattendance due to the child's realistic fear of dangers in the school setting. This is increasingly common in urban schools in poverty areas.

Externalizing truant disorder. The child shows generalized impulsive, defiant, manipulative, noncompliant behavior, and other symptoms of a conduct disorder or delinquency, including nonattendance at school. He or she shows little anxiety.

Internalizing school refusal. The child gives evidence of conflict, anxiety, distress about the symptoms, and symptoms of other emotional disorders.

Children in the school refusal group have been the subject of sustained psychiatric investigation. In contrast, children who have severe, externalizing behavior disorders that include truancy have generated less interest among investigators. This disorder has roots on the border between the medical and legal systems, partially explaining the faltering psychiatric research on truancy. In sum, four criteria have been suggested to differentiate a group of school refusing children from truant children (Berg et al. 1969; Atkinson et al. 1985): 1) severe difficulty in attending school; 2) severe emotional upset; 3) staying at home with the parents' knowledge; and 4) absence of significant antisocial disorders. Another characteristic added by some researchers is that truant children are absent from school more sporadically, while school refusal is characterized by an absence for an unbroken, sometimes quite lengthy, period of time. When referring to school refusal syndromes, clinicians use several terms that have historical roots.

School phobia. This term was initially used to describe the fear of attending school voiced by these children, although it was recognized that reluctance to separate from the mother played a primary role (Johnson et al. 1941). It was not intended to portray the disorder as monosymptomatic, as the presence of hysterical and obsessional features was described in addition to phobic patterns. Additional research characterized school phobic children as obedient and generally well adjusted, and found that they had not disliked school. These features clearly demarcated them from truant children (Hersov 1985).

Separation anxiety. From the outset of research on school phobia, there was a concern that the use of the term phobia removed the focus from its proper field of separation anxiety, and there were soon recommendations to change the name of the disorder (Estes et al. 1956; Bowlby 1973). Investigators agree that clear signs of anxiety or panic are observable when the child leaves home to go to school: anxious about the well-being of a parent at home and events occurring there, he or she may never reach school, returning home in a state of high anxiety. These emotional states may be accompanied or replaced by somatic complaints that are the expressed reason for remaining at home (nausea, abdominal pain, diarrhea). In addition, the intense interactions between the mother and child, noted from the beginning of school phobia research, appeared to be fundamentally expressing separation anxiety dynamics (Hersov 1985). Finally, clinicians began to describe a subgroup of school phobic children who, on questioning, expressed no fear of school, nor of individuals or circumstances at school. Investigators suggested that school phobic children, or a subgroup of these, might be more accurately described as having a separation anxiety disorder, particularly during the younger of the two developmental peak incidences, between five and seven years of age. Separation anxiety disorder is a specific syndrome listed in DSM III R and ICD–9, and one of the possible component symptoms is school refusal; these classifications indicate that this is not the only type of school refusal, as some children fear attending school even when accompanied by their mothers. There is no category directly corresponding to school refusal or school phobia in DSM III R or ICD–9.

School refusal. The terms *school phobia* and *separation anxiety* were applicable only to subgroups of children, and clinicians sought a more general term. The term *school phobia* arose from a psychoanalytic understanding of classic phobic symptom formation, proceeding from the child's externalization of frightening aggressive impulses to displacement of them onto a person or circumstance that was previously neutral. It is then feared and avoided in a phobic pattern. Similar concepts in the language of learning theory and behavior therapy reinforced the use of the term school phobia. However, the absence of manifest fear in some children, and the lack of definitive separation anxiety symptoms in others, suggested the need for a better, theoretically and descriptively neutral term. *School refusal* has been used by many investigators because it is an accurate descriptor applicable to all of these children, avoiding preconceptions about symptoms or causes (Hersov 1985). It is a term for a category that includes all four internalizing disorders, as indicated in table 15.1. These disorders have distinguishing characteristics, in spite of overlapping symptoms. For example, separation anxiety disorder is more common than school phobia, and children with separation anxiety disorder are more likely to be female, prepubertal, and from a lower socioeconomic (SES) family background; moreover, many have another DSM III diagnosis, and their mothers have a higher rate of affective disorders (Last et al. 1987a).

While many children and adolescents defined to be school dropouts are those classically considered to be truant, the increased prevalence of school dropouts in the U.S. cautions that some of these children may be similar to those defined under "school failure" and some may reflect the irrelevance of current educational programs for a sector of society. In addition, some school refusing children may be among this larger group.

Experience with other common, broadly defined disorders suggests the advisability of caution. The study of hyperactivity in the U.S. serves as a good example. Hyperactivity turns out to be not one disorder, but the final common pathway of symptoms from many types of problems suffered by children, largely familial and cultural, but with important genetic, biological, and educational influences. This is analogous to school nonattendance disorders. In addition, some hyperactive children may not be ill, but may instead occupy the upper end of a normal distribution of activity levels. Similarly, although in Japan high school is not compulsory, 95 percent attend and only 3 percent drop out; about half of the absentees were earlier middle-school-age school refusers. Should this be considered a true disorder for these children? Perhaps we should not expect all children to complete all levels of education.

Is there evidence for a neurobiological basis for the distinction between internalizing and externalizing types of school nonattendance? A pragmatic place to begin is the neurobiology of anxiety, which is distinctly more prominent in the internalizing school refusal disorders. Clinical measures of anxiety may be useful in distinguishing not only the internalizing and externalizing categories, but also the types of internalizing school refusal disorders.

BRAIN NEURONAL SYSTEMS REGULATING ANXIETY

*Adaptive and Maladaptive Anxiety
and the Locus Ceruleus*

Environmental dangers elicit an adaptive response causing the animal to escape the source of danger, whether it is a lack of food, another attacking animal, or extremes of weather. An essential component of the capacity to adapt is the evolution of internal alarm systems enabling selective responses to stimuli that become highly significant for survival, either through evolutionary selection or individual experience. This permits anticipation of potential danger through recognition and classification of stimuli. Augmentation of these capacities provides an animal with advantages for escaping threats unharmed, but leaves it vulnerable to miscalculations based on sudden changes in the nature of the most significant environmental threats or associated stimuli. "Sudden" might mean occurring recently within evolutionary time or recently within the life of the individual. Differing requirements for such an alarm system lead to behavioral biases on the part of individual animals, as they are preferentially adapted to certain environments. This adaptation is recognizable by the stimuli that elicit the alarm, as well as by the form and duration of the alarm behavior. Alarm behaviors that are adaptive in one environment may be maladaptive and disordered in another.

The anxiety system is the principal alarm system of man. The filtering of multiple bombarding stimuli occurs through habituation to innocuous stimuli—rather than persistent response to unimportant features of the environment—allowing preparedness when significant stimuli are encountered. Some environmental features retain such a significant valence of danger that habituation fails to occur, reflecting a genetic program for relatively automatic avoidance that is difficult to override (such as fear of fire). Other such chronic avoidance mechanisms, however, whether genetic or (more often) individually determined, can easily become maladaptive (Cloninger 1987).

Abnormalities of internal alarm systems lead to the dysregulation of mood and emotion particularly characteristic of affective and anxiety disorders. Types of anxiety have been examined that aid in categorizing typical responses. A useful contrast is that of acute and chronic anxiety. Acute anticipatory anxiety is the transient anxiety that signals aversive stimuli indicated by specific environmental features. On the other hand, an individual chronically exposed to unpredictable aversive events finds it almost impossible to forecast danger and select behaviors that will achieve safety. There is no reliable warning signal; a state of chronic anxiety ensures. Thus, a threat develops through several mechanisms: the warning signals either do not occur or cannot be recognized reliably by the individual (characteristic of a histrionic personality style); or the warning signals are always present; or the individual retains a vigilant posture even when danger is relatively rare (characteristic of an obsessional personality style). Hypovigilance or hypervigilance then have relative adaptive or maladaptive values depending on the "fit" with current environmental circumstances and the degree to which the individual can modulate these responses (Cloninger 1987).

Alarm systems, and their attendant potential for hypervigilance or hypovigilance, have genetic determinants, are responsive to environmental shaping, and are regulated by specific brain neuronal systems. Molecular mechanisms underlying habituation and long-term sensitization have been characterized. Behavioral concomitants of anxiety are quite familiar. Anxious individuals are in a state of constant sympathetic arousal, with overactive sweat glands, increased skin conductance, elevated resting heart rate and blood pressure, and increased muscle tension. In the face of disturbing stimuli they become more aroused than normal individuals, both subjectively and autonomically, and they habituate less readily to aversive situations. Among neurotransmitter systems implicated in the regulation of these processes, norepinephrine and gamma-amino butyric acid (GABA) have been investigated intensively.

The nucleus locus coeruleus (LC) is the major central noradrenegic nucleus, the source of more than 70 percent of brain norepinephrine. It has been hypothesized that this nucleus increases the "signal-to-noise" ratio of other brain neurons, causing a global modulation of other neuro-transmitter inputs in the context of vigilance, anxiety, fear, or panic (Redmond 1987). The LC neurons fire in parallel with sympathoadrenal activation in response to stress, distinctly discriminated from simple behavioral activation. Stimuli must exceed a threshold in order to achieve sustained activation of the LC, and when stimuli are no longer sufficient to do so, the tonic activation of the LC ceases (Abercrombie and Jacobs 1987a,b). These data point to the LC as a central component in a brain alarm system underlying preparedness. Drugs affecting the LC system, such as opiate antagonists, alprazolam, clonidine, and yohimbine, have significant behavioral effects that fit predictions of their influence on anxiety regulation and parallel their effects on single cell LC studies.

The role of GABA, an inhibitory central nervous system (CNS) neuro-transmitter, has been illuminated by the discovery of brain-specific benzodiazepine receptors structurally associated with GABA receptor sites. Benzodiazepines are among the most potent, most specific anti-anxiety agents; they act by affecting GABA systems. Knowledge accumulating about these and other neuronal systems promises specifically targeted medications for disorders involving anxiety dysregulation and clarification of neurobiological mechanisms mediating the behaviors.

Haloperidol-Induced School and Social "Phobias"

Some children with Tourette's disorder treated with haloperidol develop school refusal characterized by an irrational fear of leaving home. Adults similarly medicated report a dread of going to work, an apparent social phobia or work phobia. Induction of this state replicating the school refusal syndrome is a verification of the specificity of the syndrome, reinforcing optimism that research will yield an understanding of the neurophysiology of related disorders and will guide effective treatment (Mikkelsen et al. 1981).

School nonattendance disorders are differentiated by the role of anxiety, the stimuli eliciting anxiety, and hypervigilance (in internalizing children) or hypovigilance (in externalizing children). It would be beneficial to use clinical measures of anxiety to examine (1) indications of genetic programs determining anxiety stimuli, thresholds, intensity, and responses; and (2) habitual preferences of each group for the management of anxiety.

PSYCHOANALYTIC VIEWS OF SYMPTOM STRUCTURE
AND THE INTERACTIONAL DYNAMICS
OF THE FAMILY IN SCHOOL PHOBIA

Psychoanalytic research anticipated neurobiological models through its extended study of the mediating central role of anxiety in symptom genesis. Freud examined the role of anxiety as a response to danger, and he discussed realistic anxiety and neurotic anxiety. They evolved into concepts of signal anxiety and automatic anxiety, related to acute and chronic anxiety, respectively. He traced the emergence of neurotic or automatic anxiety from childhood helplessness and trauma. Freud specifically described a genetic program for an alarm system as "the congenital preparedness to meet real dangers" which is an "archaic heritage of man" (Freud 1926).

Psychoanalytic views of school refusal center on the role of separation anxiety and the existence of a hostile-dependent relationship between the child and mother. Overdependence on the mother leads to anger toward her when the child experiences her dependent needs. While maternal dependence on the child may not be expressed overtly, it is evident in its replacement of satisfactions usually obtained through adult relationships. The child experiences overprotective restrictions by the mother as both unpleasant and reassuring; he or she is periodically anxious and angry about the suffocating quality of their relationship.

This anger is the focus of the psychoanalytic explication of phobic dynamics. The child's anger becomes increasingly intense and demanding, leading to his or her fear of harming the mother. The anger, projected outward onto others, is also displaced onto a neutral object (school). Alarmed by these emotions, the child prefers staying at home to protect and be nurtured by the mother, as compared to being with school personnel who now are the subject of his or her displaced hostility and dependence. The relative strength of the separation anxiety or phobic elements in an individual case determine whether it is considered primarily to be one disorder or the other.

RESEARCH ON THE INHERITANCE OF SCHOOL
REFUSAL AND RELATED DISORDERS

Is there clinical evidence for the inheritance of internal alarm (anxiety) systems? For data, we look for familial aggregation of anxiety thresholds, intensity, and expression, as well as favored stimuli for anxiety and preferential responses.

Epidemiological Research

Panic disorder is common in the general population, with a six-month prevalence rate of approximately 1 percent and higher rates in women. Rates for agoraphobia are higher than those for panic disorder, and, again, are higher in women. Agoraphobia is often associated with panic attacks (Weissman et al. 1986; Pollard et al. 1987). Fears and phobias are common in childhood. About 2–5 percent of children have simple phobias while 0.4 percent have school phobia (Ferrari 1986). In a community sample of 150 adolescents (14 to 16 years old), 17 percent met criteria for at least one anxiety disorder in a six-month prevalence study (Kashani et al. 1987a). Persons with a history of school phobia or separation anxiety are more likely to develop phobic and panic symptoms at an earlier age when compared to controls (Perugi et al. 1988).

The 150 adolescents in the community study included twenty-six anxious subjects and twelve depressed subjects; nine were both anxious and depressed (Kashani and Orvaschel 1988). Concurrent depression identifies a subtype of school phobia (Kolvin et al. 1984, 1987; Atkinson 1988; Weinberg et al. 1986). In a study of twenty-six school refusers, 69 percent had depression, 62 percent had anxiety disorder, and 50 percent had both depressive and anxiety disorders (Bernstein et al. 1986). However, depression may occur as secondary to many psychiatric disorders and medical illnesses (Winokur et al. 1988).

Conduct disorders and anxiety disorders were the most common psychiatric disorders in the study of fourteen- to sixteen-year-old adolescents (Kashani et al. 1987b). In a sample of fifty-three boys with aggressive conduct disorder, persistence of conduct disorder was associated with various "antisocial or aggressive symptoms, firesetting, early age of onset and family deviance" (Kelso and Stewart 1986) and with hyperactivity and inattention (Stewart and Kelso 1987). Again, these youth appear to be those likely to be truants or school dropouts, but not school refusers.

Substance abuse is not known to play a role in school refusal, but drug and alcohol abuse at the age of sixteen is related to school dropout (Epstein and Tamir 1984).

Children with mild developmental disorders (attention-deficit hyperactivity disorder, specific developmental disorders) are vulnerable to school attendance problems, as their behavioral symptoms and academic deficiencies make school a source of distress. If they are lumped together with school nonattenders, the role of their developmental disability may be overshadowed.

Familial/Genetic Research

Evaluation of first-degree relatives of children with school phobia by the family history method demonstrated higher rates of depressive and anxiety disorders than those in families of children with psychiatric disorders other than school phobia. The parents of school phobia children describe more disturbance in family functioning than parents in a control group; the disturbances were concentrated in the domains of "role performance, communication, affective expression, and control" (Bernstein and Garfinkel 1988). Children with separation anxiety disorder are more likely to be female, prepubertal, and from a lower SES than school phobic children. Mothers of children with separation anxiety disorder are four times more likely to have affective disorders than mothers of children with school phobia (Last et al. 1987a).

There is preliminary evidence for inheritance of panic disorder (Crowe et al. 1987; Judd et al. 1987), and vertical transmission of common fears and phobias (Phillips et al. 1987). There is a large increase in the risk of psychiatric disorders in the relatives of probands with major depression and panic disorder. In one study 58 percent of depressed probands had an additional diagnosis of agoraphobia, panic disorder, or generalized anxiety disorder (Leckman et al. 1983). Major depressive episodes occur often in patients with panic disorder and phobic avoidance (Lesser et al. 1988), but they occur also in patients with other psychiatric disorders and medical illnesses (Winokur et al. 1988). Similarly, in children and adolescents in an anxiety disorders clinic, the majority have multiple diagnoses. Most mothers of children with separation anxiety disorder and/or overanxious disorder experienced an anxiety disorder at the time their child was seen in the clinic (Last et al. 1987b). Mothers of children with overanxious disorder were more likely than other mothers to have had an overanxious disorder themselves as children (Last et al. 1987c). Significantly more adults with panic disorder had separation anxiety in childhood than did controls (Ayuso Gutierrez et al. 1987). There is a strong relation between separation anxiety and panic disorders in female agoraphobics (Gittelman and Klein 1984). A developmental understanding of these disorders is promised by findings of high rates of inhibition to the unfamiliar (a possible precursor to anxiety states) in preschool children of parents with major depression and panic disorder (Rosenbaum et al. 1988).

There is strong evidence of vertical transmission of affective disorders in the families of probands with these disorders, and there is also a high incidence of anxiety disorders in the families (Blehar et al. 1988; Zvolsky 1988). Women are at greater risk for affective disorders (Faraone et al. 1987). The offspring of 133 probands with major depression had twice the risk of major depression compared to offspring of eighty-two normal control subjects group-matched for age and sex. The offspring of depressed subjects also had a higher risk for anxiety disorder or any psychiatric disorder, but not for alcoholism, conduct disorder, or antisocial personality disorder (Merikangas et al., 1988). In general, children of parents with major affective disorder are at significant risk for psychiatric disorder and are considerably impaired (Beardslee et al. 1984; Zerbin-Rudin 1987). Linkage analysis localized a dominant gene for a subtype of bipolar affective disorder to the tip of the short arm of chromosome 11 in an Old Order Amish pedigree (Egeland et al. 1987), but controversies about patterns of inheritance continue.

Examination of familial aggregation of symptoms and provisional subtypes of conduct and antisocial disorders, as well as family interactions, may aid in the understanding of contrasts between school refusal and truant children. Central questions include whether conduct disorder families contain a higher or lower rate of school refusal, and whether a subtype centered on symptoms of truancy exists. Preliminary evidence for familial aggregation of features related to antisocial disorder includes adoption studies (Hutchings and Mednick 1974) and the finding of a higher rate of impulsive disorders possibly related to antisocial syndromes in the pedigrees of psychopaths (Schulsinger 1972; Crowe 1974; Bohman et al. 1982; Cloninger et al. 1982; and Sigvardsson et al. 1982). The natural history of conduct disorder includes a large subgroup who later develop antisocial personality disorder (Loeber 1982).

Available data suggesting familial aggregation of alcohol abuse syndromes (Bohman et al. 1982; Cloninger et al. 1982; Schukit 1982; Sigvardsson et al. 1982) suggest possibilities for research on school refusal and truancy. There are high rates of depression in alcoholic patients and high rates of alcoholism in antisocial disorder patients. There may be at least two major subgroups abusing alcohol, an externalizing (antisocial) subgroup and an internalizing (anxious and depressed) subgroup. If so, would there be differential rates of school refusal and truancy in these alcohol abusing subgroups?

Inheritance biases the style of response of individuals to similar stresses, particularly the motivating role of anxiety. To what degree are these genetically programmed behaviors modifiable by the influences of family and culture?

THE QUESTION OF CULTURAL DIFFERENCES IN THE PREVALENCE AND SUBTYPES OF SCHOOL REFUSAL SYNDROMES

Comparative crosscultural research on the epidemiology of school refusal is rare; the variation in diagnostic definition presents a major roadblock. A study of the prevalence of school refusal and school-related fears in Venezuelan children from three to fourteen years old also compared prevalence figures in ten studies across three other countries (England, Japan, and the U.S.). It concludes that rates of school refusal are similar across the four countries, and apparent crossnational differences reflect diagnostic methods rather than sociocultural characteristics. This runs counter to the expectation that strong cultural influences are operative. The research design of the study adjusted for a lack of consensus definition of school refusal. The cut point for the number of symptoms required for the diagnosis determines the prevalence rate, so the authors used six diagnostic combinations to establish a range of rates. Fear of school is difficult to diagnose reliably; for example, 17.7 percent of the children said they had such fears. Children who fulfilled criteria for fear of attending school from any single informant (child self-report, parent, or teacher rating), together with high absenteeism, constituted 5.4 percent of the sample. However, when the only criterion was the parent report or the child report of fear, plus high absenteeism, the rates dropped to 1.5 percent and 1.2 percent, respectively. When agreement among all informants was required, the rate was 0.4 percent. School refusal rates were higher for younger children, and for children in public and lower SES schools. Their findings suggest stability in the prevalence across cultures, but that school aversion and refusal occur along a continuum on which the rate of a sample will be determined by diagnostic criteria and methods, cut points selected for diagnosis, and the characteristics of the educational systems (Granell de Aldaz et al. 1984).

Research on drug use offers an instructive model for examination of sociocultural influences on truancy and school refusal. The course of heroin use in U.S. soldiers in Vietnam was contrasted to that of heroin abusers in the continental U.S. The expected association with poor educational achievement and criminal behavior, together with a relatively intractable course, occurred in the U.S. group, but not in the Vietnam heroin abusers (Robins 1978). Analagous reasoning proposes that a conduct disordered child might be a truant, sociopathic adolescent in one setting, but a troubled but satisfactory high school student in a different school and/or neighborhood. Similarly, an unhappy eight-year-old boy might become a school refuser in middle school, or an anxious but successful student in another setting.

Within a single culture, subcultures have distinct effects. Among U.S. blacks eighteen to twenty-one years old, 27 percent were school dropouts in 1975, while 17 percent were dropouts in 1985; the graduation rate increased to 71 percent from 61 percent (Tolchin 1988). Nevertheless, The New York Times reported that the number of black men enrolled in higher education has declined during the ten years through 1988 (New York Times 1989); the percentage of black women, on the other hand, has increased (Daniels 1989). For white students the dropout rate decreased from 15 to 14 percent during the period between 1975 and 1985, while the white graduation rate remained at 81 percent. Specific psychopathological behaviors are not necessarily stable; these can be responsive to altered cultural conditions. Crosscultural data support this concept, indicating that children have higher rates of some internalizing symptoms in China (Jin et al. 1987) and Thailand (Weisz et al. 1987), while the rates of some externalizing symptoms may be higher in the U.S.

Many questions surround the relationship of school dropouts to children with school refusal and truancy in the U.S. The problem of defining school dropouts is evident from estimates of its rate. While a single figure is often given—it has been approximated as 25 percent since 1965 (Institute for Educational Leadership 1986; Haggerty 1987) other estimates cover a broad range. One source suggests a 30–50 percent dropout rate in school districts for poor minority children, sometimes greater than 80 percent in inner city schools. Among disadvantaged students who complete secondary education, about half have reading and writing skills insufficient to compete in the job market, apparently examples of "school failure" children who remain in school while obtaining minimal education (Committee for Economic Development 1987). Factors predisposing children to dropping out have a similar influence on the genesis of truancy; these include minority status, poverty, low intelligence, multiple stresses in the home, poor school systems, and poor physical and mental health. They do not play the same predisposing role for school refusal.

Recent estimates suggest that fewer than 50 percent of high school seniors have reading skills sufficient for "even moderately complex tasks" and an astonishing 80 percent have inadequate writing skills. One million students leave public schools without graduating each year (Committee for Economic Development 1987). It does not appear that students make a specific, firm committment to leave school; it is a gradual process, in which truancy plays a crucial role. Related factors include high rates of unemployment among minority inner city teenagers, and the deteriorating quality of educational programs and administrative management in urban schools. For female students, discontinuation of schooling may be hidden under the cloak of school-age pregnancy. School dropouts and truancy conceal school refusal in this type of community. It is deceptive to examine only school refusal in crosscultural epidemiological research.

TREATMENT AND ITS IMPLICATIONS FOR RESEARCH

Treatment for school refusal includes strict behaviorally operant procedures, cognitive therapy (Mansdorf and Lukens 1987), psychodynamic psychotherapy, family therapy, and pharmacotherapy. Despite differences in treatment approach, the outcome is good for treated cases. Investigators agree that rapid treatment and return to school improves outcome. The efficacy of nonpharmacological therapies for school refusal illuminates specific familial and cultural influences on the disorder. Nondrug treatment of internalizing symptoms is successful with school refusal children, but not for school dropouts and truants, verifying a syndromic difference.

Imipramine is useful in the treatment of school phobia. It may exert an antidepressant effect in a disorder considered to be a childhood depressive equivalent (Frommer 1968). However, most consider that imipramine acts by reducing anxiety and preventing panic attacks associated with separation from the parent, making the child accessible to therapy and facilitating return to school (Gittelman-Klein and Klein 1971). A pilot study showed twenty-four of twenty-eight (85 percent) school phobic children returned to school six weeks after beginning imipramine (Rabiner and Klein 1969). A follow-up controlled double-blind study of thirty-five school phobic children (aged six to fourteen years) indicated that 85 percent of the children returned to school in six weeks (Gittelman-Klein and Klein 1973). These findings have theoretical significance because imipramine may act in part by stabilizing rates of release of norepinephrine, ameliorating the hypothesized noradrenergic dysregulation. This would dampen the intensity of anxiety episodes and aid the child's response to other therapies.

A trial of clomipramine failed to benefit school phobic children (Berney et al. 1981). Benzodiazepines have no established role in the treatment of school refusal; nor have they received rigorous therapeutic trials. Sulpiride facilitated the return to school of ten out of sixteen depressive school phobic children (Abe 1975a,b). Treatment combining behavior therapy, psychodynamic psychotherapy, family therapy, and imipramine offers the best outcome for children with school refusal.

Each child meets the demands and nurturance of his or her family and culture with a unique set of strengths and vulnerabilities. Well-designed research on disorders involving school nonattendance carries an optimistic promise for benefitting these children. The next phase of investigation, in a perfect world with full research funding, will be spawned in a fertile bed of research strategies (table 15.2). As Epictetus reminds us in his *Discourses,* "Only the educated are free."

Table 15.2 *Suggestions for Research Strategies on School Refusal and Other School Nonattendance Disorders*

A. DIAGNOSTIC CLASSIFICATION
1. Achieve agreement on a diagnostic classification system for school nonattendance disorders (including school refusal, truancy, dropout, and others) and integrate it into DSM IV and ICD–10. This is the primary research objective, because these are serious disorders with significant morbidity for the individual and society. It has been a regrettable omission in current diagnostic classification systems.
2. Devise standardized operational criteria, including symptoms, duration, and other features.
3. Determine whether classification of school nonattendance disorders should differ for children and adolescents, and at what point adult diagnostic categories should be utilized.

B. EPIDEMIOLOGY AND CROSS-CULTURAL COMPARISONS
1. Conduct cross-cultural epidemiological research examining the prevalence of each of the school nonattendance disorders and possibly of related disorders,
    a. at two or three time points, looking for stability or change; and
    b. in countries selected according to likely cultural and educational influences on these disorders.

(*continued*)

Table 15.2 *(Continued)*

2. Determine the rate of developmental disabilities within each of the school nonattendance disorders.
3. Examine the effects of abrupt sociocultural changes on the prevalence of school nonattendance disorders.

C. NATURAL HISTORY OF SCHOOL NONATTENDANCE DISORDERS
1. Conduct prospective research to identify predictors of symptom manifestation, disease onset, secondary morbidity, and treatment response in school nonattendance disorders.
2. Conduct longitudinal follow-up research to specify outcome and the evolution of the disorders into adult psychiatric disorders or symptom remission and successful adaptation.

D. GENETIC INFLUENCES
1. Carry out additional family aggregation studies, selecting probands from school refusal, separation anxiety, truancy, and school dropout groups. Examine rates of psychiatric and social morbidity in relatives, including truancy, school dropout, school refusal, anxiety disorders, affective disorders, and conduct disorders.
2. Undertake prospective studies of children of parents with a history of school refusal, and/or anxiety disorders, affective disorders, and other disorders possibly associated with school refusal.

E. FAMILY INTERACTIONS
1. Compare blind ratings of videotapes of family interactions in school refusal, truancy, school dropout, and other related disorders.
2. Compare family interactions across cultures.
3. Examine family interactions in response to stresses.

F. PSYCHODYNAMIC INFLUENCES
1. Administer structured psychoanalytic interviews, projective tests, and rating scales to children with each of the school nonattendance disorders.
2. Integrate components examining psychodynamic factors, family interactions, and life stresses in the epidemiological and family aggregation research wherever possible.

(continued)

Table 15.2 *(Continued)*

G. NEUROBIOLOGICAL INDICES

1. Compare neurobiological and clinical indices and treatment response in a group of school phobia subjects to the indices in haloperidol-induced school phobia/social phobia subjects.

2. Monitor clinical sympathetic (noradrenergic) measures in children with school nonattendance disorders:

    a. when leaving their mother vs. arriving at school;

    b. during family interactions;

    c. during intensive psychotherapy;

    d. at the onset of puberty; and

    e. in response to specific drugs.

3. Monitor sympathetic (noradrenergic) measures in children with school nonattendance disorders in order to:

    a. define sympathetic nervous system indices associated with subtypes: separation anxiety, school phobia, truancy, etc.;

    b. differentiate indices associated with chronic and acute anxiety; and

    c. determine the effects of unpredictable dangers and the response to making the dangers predictable.

H. EDUCATION INFLUENCES

Construct a structured characterization of the educational features and influences of the schools of children with school nonattendance disorders.

I. TREATMENT

1. Conduct a rigorous comparison of the effects of drugs from different classes on:

    a. treatment efficacy and side effects;

    b. neurobiological indices that might identify discrete subtypes.

2. Conduct short-term, intensive psychotherapy of school refusal, truant, and dropout children, with other comparison groups, to identify specific preferred defenses, symptom patterns, and typical intrapsychic conflicts.

3. Initiate additional rigorous randomized, double-blind clinical trials to test the efficacy of behavioral treatment approaches, such as systematic desensitization.

REFERENCES

Abe, K. (1975a) Letter: Sulpiride in depressive school phobic children. *Psychopharmacologia* 43:101.

———— (1975b) Sulpiride in school phobia. *Psychiatria clinica* 8:95–98.

Abercrombie, E. D., and Jacobs, B. L. (1987a) Single-unit response of noradrenergic neurons in the locus coeruleus of freely moving cats. (I) Acutely presented stressful and nonstressful stimuli. *The Journal of Neuroscience* 7:2837–2843.

———— (1987b) Single-unit response of noradrenergic neurons in the locus coeruleus of freely moving cats. (II) Adaptation to chronically presented stressful stimuli. *The Journal of Neuroscience,* 7:2844–2848.

Atkinson, L., Quarrington, B., and Cyr, J. J. (1985) School refusal: The heterogeneity of a concept. *American Journal of Orthopsychiatry,* 55:83–101.

Atkinson, L. (1988) Depression in school phobia. *British Journal of Psychiatry* 148:335–336.

Ayuso Gutiérrez, J. L., Alfonso Suárez, S., and Rivera Villaverde, A. (1987) Ansiedad de separacion y trastorno de ataques de angustia ("panic disorder"): Un estudio comparativo. *Actas Luso–Españolas de Neurologia, Psiquiatria, y Ciencas Afines,* 15:359–364.

Beardslee, W. R., Bemporad, J., Keller, M. B., and Klerman, G. L. (1984) Children of parents with major affective disorder: A review. In Chess, S., and Thomas, A., eds., *Annual Progress in Child Psychiatry and Child Development.* New York, Brunner/Mazel, pp. 390–404.

Berg, I., Nichols, K., and Pritchard, C. (1969) School phobia—its classification and relationship to dependency. *Journal of Child Psychology, Psychiatry, and Allied Disciplines* 10:123–141.

Berg, I., Casswell, G., Goodwin, A., Hullin, R., McGuire, R., and Tagg, G. (1985a) Classification of severe school attendance problems. *Psychological Medicine* 15:157–165.

Berg, I., and Jackson, A. (1985b) Teenage school refusers grow up: A follow-up study of 168 subjects ten years on average after inpatient treatment. *British Journal of Psychiatry* 147:366–370.

Berney, T., Kolvin, I., Bhate, S. B., Garside, R. F., Jeans, J., Kay, B., and Scarth, L. (1981) School phobia: A therapeutic trial with clomipramine and short-term outcome. *British Journal of Psychiatry* 138:110–118.

Bernstein, G. A., and Garfinkel, B. D. (1986) School phobia: The overlap of affective and anxiety disorders. *Journal of the American Academy of Child and Adolescent Psychiatry* 25:235–241.

———— (1988) Pedigrees, functioning, and psychopathology in families of school phobic children. *American Journal of Psychiatry* 145:70–74.

Blehar, M. C., Weissman, M. M., Gershon, E. S., and Hirshfeld, R. M. A.

(1988) Family and genetic studies of affective disorders. *Archives of General Psychiatry* 45:289–292.

Bohman, M., Cloninger, C. R., Sigvardsson, S., and Von Knorring, A.-L. (1982) Predisposition to petty criminality in Swedish adoptees. (I) Genetic and environmental heterogeneity. *Archives of General Psychiatry* 39:1233–1241.

Bowlby, J. (1973) *Attachment and Loss. Vol. 2: Separation, Anxiety, and Anger.* London, Hogarth.

Broadwin, I. T. (1932) A contribution to the study of truancy. *American Journal of Orthopsychiatry* 2:253–259.

Cloninger, C. R. (1987) Recent advances in the genetics of anxiety and somatoform disorders. In Meltzer, H. Y., ed., *Psychopharmacology: The Third Generation of Progress.* New York, Raven.

Cloninger, C. R., Sigvardsson, S., Bohman, M., and Von Knorring, A.-L. (1982) Predisposition to petty criminality in Swedish adoptees. (II) Cross-fostering analysis of gene-environment interaction. *Archives of General Psychiatry* 39:1242–1247.

Committee for Economic Development. Research and Policy Committee. (1987) *Children in Need.* New York, Committee for Economic Development.

Crowe, R. R. (1974) An adoption study of antisocial personality. *Archives of General Psychiatry* 31:785–791.

Crowe, R. R., Noyes, R., Jr., Wilson, A. F., Elston, R. C., and Ward, L. J. (1987) A linkage study of panic disorder. *Archives of General Psychiatry* 44:933–937.

Daniels, L. A. (1989) Experts foresee a social gap between sexes among blacks. *The New York Times* 5 February.

Egeland, J. A., Gerhard, D. S., Pauls, D. L., Sussex, J. N., Kidd, K. K., Allen, C. R., Hostetter, A. M. and Housman, D. E. (1987) Bipolar affective disorders linked to DNA markers on chromosome 11. *Nature* 325:783–787.

Eisenberg, L. (1958) School phobia—diagnosis, genesis, and clinical management. *The Pediatric Clinics of North America* 5:645–660.

Epstein, L., and Tamir, A. (1984) Health-related behavior of adolescents: Change over time. *Journal of Adolescent Health Care* 5:91–95.

Estes, H. R., Haylett, C., and Johnson, A. (1956) Separation anxiety. *American Journal of Psychotherapy* 10:682–695.

Faraone, S. V., Lyons, M. J., and Tsuang, M. T. (1987) Sex differences in affective disorder: Genetic transmission. *Genetic Epidemiology* 4:331–343.

Ferrari, M. (1986) Fears and phobias in childhood: Some clinical and developmental considerations. *Child Psychiatry and Human Development* 17:75–87.

Freud, S. (1926) *Inhibitions, symptoms, and anxiety.* In Strachey, J., ed. (1981) *The Standard Edition of the Complete Psychological Works of Sigmund Freud.* Vol. 20:77–174.

Frommer, E. A. (1968) Depressive illness in childhood. In Coppen, A., and Walk, A., eds., *Recent Developments in Affective Disorders. British Journal of Psychiatry* Special Publication Number 2.

Galloway, D. (1985) *Schools and Persistent Absentees*. Oxford, Pergamon.

Gittelman, R., and Klein, D. F. (1984) Relationship between separation anxiety and panic and agoraphobic disorders. *Psychopathology* 17, suppl. 1:56–63.

Gittelman-Klein, R,. and Klein, D. F. (1971) Controlled imipramine treatment for school phobia. *Archives of General Psychiatry* 25:204–207.

———. (1973) School phobia: Diagnostic considerations in the light of imipramine effects. *The Journal of Nervous and Mental Disease* 156:199–215.

Granell de Aldaz, E., Vivas, E., Gelfand, D. M., and Feldman, L. (1984) Estimating the prevalence of school refusal and school-related fears: A Venezuelan sample. *The Journal of Nervous and Mental Disease* 172:722–729.

Haggerty, R. J. (1987) Ensuring a better future for youth and America. *Developmental and Behavioral Pediatrics* 8:341–348.

Hersov, L. (1985) School refusal. In Rutter, M., and Hersov, L., eds., *Child and Adolescent Psychiatry: Modern Approaches*. Oxford, Blackwell Scientific, pp. 382–399.

Hutchings, B., and Mednick, S. A. (1974) Registered criminality in the adoptive and biological parents of registered male criminal adoptees. In Mednick, S. A., Schulsinger, F., Higgins, J., et al., eds., *Genetics, Environment, and Psychopathology*. Amsterdam, North-Holland/Elsevier.

The Institute for Educational leadership. (1986) *School Dropout: Everybody's Problem*. Washington, D.C., The Institute for Educational Leadership.

Jin, X.-M., Pan, H.-Q., He, P.-Q., and Guo, D. (1987) Survey of psychosocial problems of preschool children. *Chinese Medical Journal* 100:911–914.

Johnson, A. M., Falstein, E. I., Szurek, S. A., and Svendsen, M. (1941) School phobia. *American Journal of Orthopsychiatry* 11:702–711.

Judd, F. K., Burrows, G. D., and Hay, D. A. (1987) Panic disorder: Evidence for genetic vulnerability. *Australian and New Zealand Journal of Psychiatry* 21:197–208.

Kashani, J. H., Beck, N. C., Hoeper, E. W., Fallahi, C., Corcoran, C. M., McAllister, J. A., Rosenberg, T. K., and Reid, J. D. (1987a) Psychiatric disorders in a community sample of adolescents. *American Journal of Psychiatry* 144:584–589.

Kashani, J. H., Daniel, A. E., Sulzberger, L. A., Rosenberg, T. K., and Reid, J. C. (1987b) Conduct disordered adolescents from a community sample. *Canadian Journal of Psychiatry* 32:756–760.

Kashani, J. H., and Orvaschel, H. (1988) Anxiety disorders in mid-adolescence: A community sample. *American Journal of Psychiatry* 145:960–964.

Kelso, J., and Stewart, M. (1986) Factors which predict the persistence of aggressive conduct disorder. *Journal of Child Psychology and Psychiatry and Allied Disciplines* 27:77–86.

Kolvin, I., Berney, T. P., and Bhate, S. (1984) Classification and diagnosis of depression in school phobia. *British Journal of Psychiatry* 145:347–357.

———. (1987) Depression in school phobia. *British Journal of Psychiatry* 150:268–270.

Last, C. G., Francis, G., Hersen, M., Kazdin, A. E., and Strauss, C. C. (1987a) Separation anxiety and school phobia: A comparison using *DSM III* criteria. *American Journal of Psychiatry* 144:653–657.

Last, C. G., Hersen, M., Kazdin, A. E., Francis, G., and Grubb, H. J. (1987b) Psychiatric illness in the mothers of anxious children. *American Journal of Psychiatry* 144:1580–1583.

Last, C. G., Phillips, J. E., and Statfield, A. (1987c) Childhood anxiety disorders in mothers and their children. *Child Psychiatry and Human Development* 18:103–112.

Leckman, J. F., Weissman, M. M., Merikangas, K. R., Pauls, D. L., and Prusoff, B. A. (1983) Panic disorder and major depression: Increased risk of depression, alcoholism, panic, and phobic disorders in families of depressed probands with panic disorder. *Archives of General Psychiatry* 40:1055–1060.

Lesser, I. M., Rubin, R. T., Pecknold, J. C., Rifkin, A., Swinson, R. P., Lydiard, R. B., Burrows, G. D., Noyes, R., Jr., and Dupont, R. L., Jr. (1988) Secondary depression in panic disorder and agoraphobia. (I) Frequency, severity, and response to treatment. *Archives of General Psychiatry* 45:437–443.

Loeber, R. (1982) The stability of antisocial and delinquent child behavior: A review. *Child Development* 53:1431–1446.

Mansdorf, I. J., and Lukens, E. (1987) Cognitive-behavioral psychotherapy for separation anxious children exhibiting school phobia. *Journal of the American Academy of Child and Adolescent Psychiatry* 26:222–225.

Merikangas, K. R., Weissman, M. M., Prusoff, B. A., and John, K. (1988) Assortative mating and affective disorders: Psychopathology in offspring. *Psychiatry* 51:48–57.

Mikkelsen, E. J., Detlor, J., and Cohen, D. J. (1981) School avoidance and social phobia triggered by haloperidol in patients with Tourette's disorder. *American Journal of Psychiatry* 138:1572–1576.

New York Times. (1989) Fewer black men on U.S. campuses: But study finds 10-year gain for minorities generally. *The New York Times* 17 January.

Perugi, G., Deltito, J., Soriani, A., Musetti, L., Petracca, A., Nisita, C., Marcemmani, I., and Cassono, G. B. (1988) Relationships between panic disorder and separation anxiety with school phobia. *Comprehensive Psychiatry* 29:98–107.

Phillips, K., Fulker, D. W., and Rose, R. J. (1987) Path analysis of seven fear factors in adult twin and sibling pairs and their parents. *Genetic Epidemiology* 4:345–355.

Pollard, C. A., and Henderson, J. G. (1987) Prevalence of agoraphobia: Some confirmatory data. *Psychological Reports* 60:1305.

Rabiner, C. J., and Klein, D. (1969) Imipramine treatment of school phobia. *Comprehensive Psychiatry* 10:387–390.

Redmond, D. E., Jr. (1987) Studies of the nucleus locus coeruleus in monkeys and hypotheses for neuropsychopharmcology. In Meltzer, H. Y., ed., *Psychopharmacology: The Third Generation of Progress.* New York, Raven.

Robins, L. N. (1978) The interaction of setting and predisposition in explaining novel behavior: Drug initiations before, in, and after Vietnam. In Kandel, D. B., ed., *Longitudinal Research on Drug Use.* Washington, D.C., Hemispheric Publishing.

Rosenbaum, J. F., Biederman, J., Gersten, M., Hirshfeld, D. R., Meminger, S. R., Herman, J. B., Kagan. J., Reznick, J. S., and Smidman, N. (1988) Behavioral inhibition in children of parents with panic disorder and agoraphobia: A controlled study. *Archives of General Psychiatry* 45:463–470.

Schuckit, M. A. (1982) A study of young men with alcoholic close relatives. *American Journal of Psychiatry* 139:791.

Schulsinger, F. (1972) Psychopathy: Heredity and environment. *International Journal of Mental Health* 1:190–206.

Sigvardsson, S., Cloninger, C. R., Bohman, M., and Von Knorring, A.-L. (1982) Predisposition to petty criminality in Swedish adoptees. (III) Sex differences and validation of male typology. *Archives of General Psychiatry* 39:1248–1253.

Stewart, M., and Kelso, J. (1987) A two-year follow-up of a boy with aggressive conduct disorder. *Psychopathology* 20:296–304.

Tolchin, M. (1988) Dropout rate off for black pupils: Significant decline reported in period from 1975–1985. *The New York Times* 11 May.

Weinberg, W., Emslie, G., and Wilkes, C. (1986) Depression in school phobia. *British Journal of Psychiatry* 148:335.

Weissman, M. M., Leaf, P. J., Blazer, D. G., Boyd, J. H., and Florio, L. (1986) Panic disorder: Clinical characteristics, epidemiology, and treatment. *Psychopharmacology Bulletin* 22:787–791.

Weisz, J. R., Suwanlert, S., Chaiyasit, W., Weiss, B., Achenbach, T. M., and Walter, B. A. (1987) Epidemiology of behavioral and emotional problems among Thai and American children: Parent reports for ages 6 to 11. *Journal of the American Academy of Child and Adolescent Psychiatry* 26:890–897.

Winokur, G., Black, D. W., and Nasrallah, A. (1988) Depressions secondary to other psychiatric disorders and medical illnesses. *American Journal of Psychiatry* 145:233–237.

Zerbin-Rudin, E. (1987) Psychiatric genetics and psychiatric nosology. *Journal of Psychiatric Research* 21:377–383.

Zvolský, P. (1988) Některé otázky a novinky genetického výzkumu primárních afektivních poruch. *Časopis Lěkaru Českych* 127:104–107.

INDEX

Abe, K., 63, 215
Adolescence, 182–83
Adulthood, outcome of treatment in, 33–34
Agoraphobia, 191; school phobia and, 33–34; separation anxiety and, 30–31
Alcoholism, 211
Anger, 208
Antidepressant medication, 28–29, 135, 214–15
Anxiety system, 205–07
Attainment, school attendance and, 114–15
Attendance of school in Brazil, 154–55
Attention in classroom, 149–50

Behavioral approach to treatment, 27
Behavioral problem-solving techniques, 119–20
Benzodiazepines, 214–15
Berg, I., 20, 22, 23, 29, 31, 32, 33, 34, 116, 124, 142, 193, 202, 203
Berney, T., 29, 214
Bernstein, F. A., 18, 22
Bernstein, G. A., 124, 209, 210
Blagg, N. R., 20, 22, 23, 110, 118, 120
Bowlby, J., 17, 22, 203
Brazil: attendance of school, 154–55; school competency, 157; sociocultural influences, 154–57
Britain: educational system, 112–13, 117–18; Education Welfare Service, 116–17; legal sanctions, 116–17; mandatory schooling, 16
Broadwin, I. T., 17–18, 22, 23, 110
Bullying in Japan, 66, 161

Cain, B., 29, 32
Case history, 135–39
Cathexis: of language, 176–77; of teacher, 175–76
Causes: of school phobia, 125–27; of school refusal, 66–67, 95–97
Celia, S., 5, 12
Chazan, M., 19, 22
Chevènement, Jean-Pierre, 59–60
Chiland, C., 5, 9, 12–13, 166–67
Childhood neurosis, 195–97
Clinical cases, 75–79
Clinical picture, 67–71
Clomipramine, 29, 214
Cloninger, C. R., 206, 211
Committee for Economic Development, 7, 10, 213
Competitive examinations in Japan, 51–53
Conduct disorders, 209
Coolidge, J. C., 18, 24, 32
Cooper, M., 20, 23
Cram schools in Japan, 51–52
Cross-cultural research, 11–14, 212–14
Crowe, R. R., 210, 211
Cultural influences: in nonattendance at school, 4; on psychopathology, 10–11

Davidson, S., 18, 24, 32
Day-care programs, 8–9
Delinquency, 115
Denmark, 145–51
Developmental disorders, 209
Diatkine, R., 9, 13, 190
Disadvantaged children, 5, 160–62, 168–70
Dugas, M., 192, 193, 194, 196
Dyslexia, 166

Early return to school, 27
Educational system: in Britain, 112–13, 117–18; in France, 46, 162–64; in Japan, 45–60
Egosyntonic refusal, 183
Eisenberg, L., 21, 22, 24, 27, 93, 123, 200
Elite education in Japan, 56–57
Epidemiological research, 209
Estes, H. R., 24, 26, 203
Etiology. See Causes
Eysenck, H. J., 23, 25, 27

Failure in school in France, 12–13
Familial research, 210–11
Family cooperation in therapy, 130–31
Family dynamics, 93–94, 100–102, 126–27, 130, 208
Family structure, 102–05, 193–94
Family therapy, 98–105, 135
Family violence in Japan, 21
Fantasy, 148–49, 179–80
Father-child relationship, 103–04
Feminization of poverty in United States, 7
Fielding, D., 29, 32
Flakierska, N., 19, 34
Fogelman, K., 17, 20, 114
France: day-care programs, 8–9; disadvantaged children, 160–62, 168–70; educational system, 46, 162–64; failure in school, 12–13;

nursery schools, 164–65, 174–78; primary schools, 165–67, 178–82; secondary schools, 167–68; social stratification in, 168–69
Freud, S., 190, 191, 196, 208
Frommer, E. A., 28, 214
Fukuzawa, Yukichi, 46, 57
Furukawa, H., 24, 63

Galloway, D., 110–12, 113, 114, 116, 117, 200
Garfinkel, B. D., 18, 22, 124, 210
Genetic-familial studies, 31–32
Germany, school phobia treatment in, 123–43
Gillberg, C., 19, 34
Gittelman, R., 124, 210
Gittelman-Klein, R., 25, 28, 30, 214
Glaser, K., 27, 124
Granell de Aldaz, E., 125, 212
Guériot, C., 192, 193, 194, 196

Haloperidol-induced phobias, 207
Heath, A., 20, 22, 23
Hersov, L. A., 11, 17, 18, 20, 22, 24, 27, 28, 29, 30, 32, 110, 115, 118, 153, 203, 204
Hirohito, emperor of Japan, 47
Hishiyama, Y., 24, 63
Honjo, S., 21, 24, 65
Hospitalization. See Inpatient treatment
Hsia, H., 23, 26
Hyperactivity, 204

Imipramine, 28–29, 214
Imperial Rescript on Education (Japan), 47–48
Inamura, H., 100–101, 161
Incidence of school refusal, 19; in Japan, 63–65, 88–90
Individual therapy, 35
Infantile phobia, 189–90
Inheritance of school refusal, 208–11

Inpatient treatment, 29–30, 32–33, 68–69, 131–33, 139–43

Japan: bullying, 66, 161; causes of school refusal, 66–67, 95–97; competitive examinations, 51–53; cram schools, 51–52; educational system, 45–60; elite education, 56–57; family violence, 21; Imperial Rescript on Education, 47–48; Japanese Education Association, 57–59; liberalization ideology, 55–56; nationalism, 59–60; Provisional Educational Reform Commission, 53–55; school populations, 51
Japanese Education Association, 57–59
Jensen, R., 3, 13, 150
Johnson, A. M., 17, 18, 22, 24, 26, 91, 93, 110, 123, 203
Jung, C. G., 18
Junior Eysenck Personality Questionnaire, 23

Kahn, J. H., 19, 110
Kennedy, W. A., 27, 28, 32
Klein, D. F., 25, 28, 30, 124, 210, 214
Klein, E., 18, 23, 27, 119
Koizumi, E., 12, 67
Kolvin, I., 18, 124, 200, 209
Koyama, Kenichi, 56–57

Landsdown, R., 5, 12
Language: cathexis of, 176–77; reading and, 180–82
Last, C. G., 22, 25, 204, 210
Learning theory, 27–28, 119–20
Lebovici, S., 13, 190, 193
Legal sanctions in Britain, 116–17
Leventhal, T., 23, 25
Lindstrom, M., 19, 34
Locus coeruleus, 206–07

Long-term studies in Japan, 63–65
Lukens, E., 27, 28, 214

Mandatory schooling, 16
Mansdorf, I. J., 27, 28, 214
Maternal phobias, 193–94
Mattejat, F., 13, 142
Mediating factors in school refusal, 10–11
Medication, 28–29, 135, 214–15
Millar, T. P., 17, 18
MIT Commission on Industrial Productivity, 9–10
Mother-child relationship, 24–26, 96, 101–02. See also Separation anxiety
Multifaceted approach in treatment, 79–84

Nakane, A., 12, 63
Nakasone, Y., 49, 54–55
Nationalism in Japan, 59–60
Neurosis. See Childhood neurosis
Nonattendance at school: in Britain, 12, 109–18; classification of nonattenders, 110–12, 200–205; counteractive measures, 116–18; cultural influences, 4; in disadvantaged children, 5, 160–62, 168–70; explanations of, 115–16; factors associated with, 113–15; in Japan, 90–93; syndromes of, 3–4
Nursery schools in France, 164–65, 174–78
Nurstein, J. P., 19, 33, 110

Ohtaka, K., 65–66
Outpatient treatment, 133

Parent-child relationship, 84–85, 95–96, 103–05
Petersen, R., 146, 150
Phobias: infantile phobia, 189–90; maternal phobias, 193–94. See also School phobia

Pittman, F. S., 33, 193
Plowden Report (1967), 115
Poverty among children in United States, 6–7
Preadolescence, 182–83
Primary schools in France, 165–67, 178–82
Provisional Educational Reform Commission (Japan), 53–55
Psychopathology: cultural influences on, 10–11; socioeconomic influences on, 7–8
Psychosocial considerations in school phobia, 194–95

Rachman, S., 25, 27
Reading, language and, 180–82
Reading difficulties, 165–67
Rejection of schooling, forms of, 182–83
Remschmidt, H., 13, 143
Responsiveness to schooling, 179–80
Reynolds, D., 20, 111, 115
Richardson, K., 17, 114
Rodriguez, A., 27, 32
Ross, A. O., 23, 27
Ruopp, R. R., 8, 9
Rutter, M., 5, 19, 25, 114, 115, 124

School competency in Brazil, 157
School factors in school refusal, 23–24
School failure, 12–13, 160–62, 168–70
School fatigue, 146–47; diagnostic criteria for, 147–48; role of fantasy, 148–49
School phobia: causes of, 125–27; characteristics of children with, 124–25; as childhood neurosis, 195–97; haloperidol-induced, 207; organization of, 190–92; psychosocial considerations, 194–95; school refusal and, 187–88; specif-icity of, 192–94; as term, 18, 22–23, 203
School refusal: clinical picture in, 20–22; cross-cultural research of, 11–12, 212–14; diagnostic labels, 22–23; differential diagnosis, 21–26; epidemiological research of, 209; familial research of, 210–11; incidence of, 19, 63–65, 88–90; inheritance of, 208–11; long-term studies of, 63–65; mediating factors in, 10–11; origin of concept, 17–18; precipitating factors, 21; school factors, 23–24; school phobia and, 187–88; as term, 204; transcultural perspectives on, 11–14, 212–14; truancy distinguished from, 20
Secondary dynamics, 128–29
Secondary schools in France, 167–68
Separation anxiety, 93–94, 188, 190, 196, 203–04; agoraphobia and, 30–31; school phobia and, 123–24; school refusal and, 24–26, 63. See also Mother-child relationship
Sex difference, 63–65, 192
Shaffer, D., 124, 129
Sills, M., 23, 25
Skynner, R., 28, 119
Smith, S. L., 19, 22, 24, 25
Social policy for children in United States, 6–8
Social stratification in France, 168–69
Sociocultural influences in Brazil, 154–57
Socioeconomic influences on psychopathology, 7–8
Somatic symptoms, 21–22, 126, 138, 203
Sperling, M., 23, 119, 191, 196
Substance abuse, 209, 211
Sulpiride, 215

Suttenfield, Y., 17, 18, 23
Sweden, 165
Symptom formation, 93–94, 99–100

Takagi, R., 62–63, 99–10
Talbot, M., 18, 26, 27
Teacher, cathexis of, 175–76
Tennent, T. G., 20, 115
Therapeutic contract, 133–35
Tourette's disorder, 207
Transcultural perspectives, 11–14, 212–14
Travers, J., 8, 9
Treatment, 119–20; adulthood outcome, 33–34; use of antidepressant medication, 28–29, 135, 214–15; beginning therapy, 131–33; behavioral approach, 27; use of benzodiazepines, 214–15; use of clomipramine, 29, 214; early return to school, 27; family cooperation, 130–31; family therapy, 98–105, 135; use of imipramine, 28–29, 214; individual therapy, 35; inpatient treatment, 29–30, 32–33, 131–33, 139–43; integrative approach, 127–28; learning theory in, 27–28; use of medication, 28–29, 135, 214–15; outcome of treatment, 32–34; outpatient treatment, 133; preparation for, 129–31; recommendations for, 84–86; research strategies and, 214–17; use of sulpiride, 215; therapeutic contract, 133–35; theraputic plan, 80–81; use of tricyclics, 28–29
Treseder, J., 27, 28
Tricyclics, 28–29
Truancy, school refusal distinguished from, 20
Tyerman, M. J., 17, 20, 115
Types of school refusal, 93–94, 100–102

United Kingdom. *See* Britain
United States: day-care programs, 8–9; feminization of poverty, 7; mandatory schooling, 16; poverty among children, 6–7; social policy for children, 6–8
Unknown face, phobia of, 189–90

Wakabayashi, S., 21, 63, 65, 92
Waldfogel, S., 22, 23, 24
Waldron, S., 24, 25, 29, 33, 124
Warren, W., 17, 18, 29, 33
Weiss, M., 29, 32
Weissman, M. M., 31, 209
Winokur, G., 209, 210

Yates, A. J., 25, 27
Young, K. T., 8, 14
Yule, W., 27, 28, 119–20